Social work

Making a difference

Viviene Cree and
Steve Myers

First published in Great Britain in 2008 by

The Policy Press
University of Bristol
Fourth Floor
Beacon House
Queen's Road
Bristol BS8 1QU
UK

Tel +44 (0)117 331 4054
Fax +44 (0)117 331 4093
e-mail tpp-info@bristol.ac.uk
www.policypress.org.uk

British Library Cataloguing in Publication Data
A catalogue record for this book is available from the British Library.

Library of Congress Cataloging-in-Publication Data
A catalog record for this book has been requested.

ISBN 978 1 86134 778 7 paperback
ISBN 978 1 86134 779 4 hardcover

The Policy Press works to counter discrimination on grounds of gender, race, disability, age and sexuality.

Cover design by The Policy Press.
Front cover: image kindly supplied by www.JohnBirdsall.co.uk
Printed and bound in Great Britain by Henry Ling Ltd, Dorchester.

Contents

Acknowledgements

We would like to express our sincere thanks to the following people who contributed their experience and insights to this book in many ways:

- Rachel Balen
- Jim Campbell
- Gary Clapton
- Ann Davis
- Marianne Hughes
- Marie Irwin
- Niall Kearney
- Jill Manthorpe
- Janice McGhee
- Fergus McNeill
- Arlon Pullar
- Dina Sidhva
- Vicky Thompson
- Susan Wallace

SOCIAL WORK IN PRACTICE series

Series editors: **Viviene Cree**, University of Edinburgh and **Steve Myers**, University of Salford

"This new series combines all the elements needed for a sound basis in 21st century UK social work. Readers will gain a leading edge on the critical features of contemporary practice. It provides thoughtful and challenging reading for all, whether beginning students or experienced practitioners." **Jan Fook**, Professor in Social Work Studies, University of Southampton

This important series sets new standards in introducing social workers to the ideas, values and knowledge base necessary for professional practice. Reflecting the current curricula of the new social work degree and post-qualifying programmes and structured around the National Occupational Standards, these core texts are designed for students undertaking professional training at all levels as well as fulfilling the needs of qualified staff seeking to update their skills or move into new areas of practice.

Titles in the series:

Social work: Making a difference by Viviene Cree and Steve Myers
Social work and multi-agency working: Making a difference edited by Kate Morris
Youth justice in practice: Making a difference by Bill Whyte
Social work and people with learning difficulties: Making a difference by Susan Hunter
Radical social work in the 21st century: Making a difference by Iain Ferguson and Rona Woodward

Making a difference

1

Introduction

This book, as the title suggests, is about social work and how social workers can make a difference in the lives of individuals and communities. The term 'making a difference' has become something of a cliché in recent years. A quick check through any internet search engine will introduce a whole host of sites which promote making a difference, whether this is in volunteering, management, health services, community action or government. Our focus in this book is not simply to explore how social work and social workers can make a difference. After all, by its very nature, social work intervention is bound to make a difference, of one kind or another. Instead, we are suggesting a strategy for engaging in social work practice which we believe will make a *positive* difference in the lives of individuals and communities.

The book sets out to provide an introductory text for students and educators involved in qualifying degree programmes in social work. It describes the context in which social work currently takes place in the UK, using the National Occupational Standards for Social Work as its organising framework (see www.topssengland.net). In each chapter, students are introduced to one of the standards as it affects an area of social work practice. Using an enquiry-based approach, key legislation and social policy, social work models and methods, values and underpinning theories are then explored as they relate to each scenario. What distinguishes this book from other beginners' practice guides is the critical, reflexive approach that is adopted throughout. Moreover, in each example, service user, carer and practitioner knowledge and experience play a vital part in the construction of good practice. To this end, others have read and commented on chapters in draft stage, and contributed to the overall product.

What is social work?

Our target audience for the book is, as stated, social work students and their educators. This does not imply that we see social work as a single entity. An examination of social work's history demonstrates that social work has always been 'up for grabs'; its task and direction by no means self-evident (Cree, 1995, p 153). In recent years, social work has undergone massive organisational and institutional change, as specialist teams in departments of health and education and (in criminal justice social work in Scotland) community justice departments,have replaced generic local authority social work departments. As structures have shifted, so job titles have changed. Social work posts are now described in narrow terms such as 'qualified social worker: children and families', and, in one current advertisement, 'qualified social worker: referral and assessment'. Job titles are not the only things that have changed. Social work practice today frequently takes place in multidisciplinary, or multi-agency, contexts. Because of this, social work's ideas and practices are becoming diffused, and what was social work knowledge is becoming more available to other professionals. At the same time, activities that were, in the past, social work functions (such as comprehensive assessments) are being carried out, more and more, by members of other professional groups, such as health visitors and nurses. The end result is that social work as a profession is becoming fragmented, paradoxically at the very time it has been strengthened through professional accreditation and registration.[1] (Social work's regulatory framework is discussed more fully in Chapter Eight.)

It is important to acknowledge at this point that local government agencies are not the only, or indeed the largest, employer of social workers in the UK. Social work services are delivered by a host of agencies in the voluntary and independent sectors and, since 1997, the New Labour government has sought to expand the use of these agencies as an alternative to state services (Jones, 2006). In these settings, social work practice is often quite different to that in statutory agencies. This is illustrated acutely in the 'My Typical Week' accounts of 13 social workers in Cree (2003), where Bob Holman's narrative of neighbourhood social work is a world removed from Penny Thompson's description of social services management.

In reviewing social work as a profession, Payne (2006, p 12) argues that it is best understood as a three-way discourse: social work practice, ideas, organisation and policy all demonstrate the coming-together of three views of social work characterised as follows:

- *Therapeutic views*: social work is understood to be about 'seeking the best possible well-being for individuals, groups and communities, by promoting and facilitating growth and self-fulfilment' (2006, p 12).
- *Transformational views*: it is argued that social work must 'develop cooperation and mutual support in society so that the most oppressed and disadvantaged people can gain power over their own lives' (2006, p 13).
- *Social order views*: social work is seen as 'an aspect of welfare services to individuals in societies. It meets individuals' needs and improves services

of which it is a part, so that social work and the services can operate more effectively' (2006, p 14).

Payne suggests that each view says something about the activities and purpose of social work in welfare provision in society; moreover, each view criticises or seeks to modify the others. But the different perspectives all share some affinities, including a commitment to change and development. Payne (2006, p 21) concludes that social work's claim, unique among similar professions, is 'to combine in a professional role both social transformation and also individual improvement through interpersonal relationships'.

Payne's categorisation of social work resonates with the findings of three government reports on social work, conducted in Scotland, Wales and England in 2005, and with the outcomes of a review held in Northern Ireland in 2006. In Scotland, *Changing Lives: The 21st Century Review of Social Work in Scotland* (Scottish Executive, 2006) highlights the lack of time available for social workers to develop therapeutic relationships with clients, yet social workers themselves valued relationship-building highly. The report describes social service departments as 'risk-aversive' in their decision making, and social workers as 'overly-driven by processes' rather than outcomes. A similar evaluation in England, conducted by the Commission for Social Care Inspection, published its first report in December 2005, entitled *The State of Social Care in England 2004–05* (CSCI, 2005). This review stresses the positive difference that social care can make, but suggests that people want, most of all, independence, choice and control in their lives, and to be treated with dignity. It was followed up in 2007 with a public consultation on the roles and tasks of social work, with the aim of defining 'a profession with service users at its heart, capable of meeting the challenges of 21st century society'.[2] Wales has carried out its own review of social work: *Social work in Wales: A Profession to Value* (ADSS, 2005). This asserts that pay is not the driver in encouraging practitioners to remain in social work, but the culture of the organisation is; this is therefore where improvement needs to take place. The 'more of the same isn't good enough' message from the Scottish report is mirrored in the recent review of public administration in Northern Ireland, which anticipates a major overhaul of the way the workforce engages with other professionals and with service users (NISCC, 2006).

Cree and Davis's (2007) study provides further insight into social work as it is practised in the UK today. Here social work practitioners, carers and service users (the 'voices from the inside' of the book's subtitle) all bear witness to the reality that social work 'is fundamentally about being alongside people in their lives' and that good social work must have an organisational context that allows it to thrive (Cree and Davis, 2007, p 158). The respondents show that social work practice, even at its most difficult, can make a positive difference in the lives of individuals and families. In summarising their findings, the authors offer the following characteristics of good social work. It:

- is responsive;
- is about building relationships;
- is person-centred;
- is about support that is both emotional and practical;
- is holistic;
- is about balancing rights, risk and protection;
- is knowledgeable and evidence-based;
- is future-orientated;
- is there for the long term.

The themes echo the international definition of social work, adopted as the Key Purpose of Social Work within the National Occupational Standards in Social Work:

> Social work is a profession which promotes social change, problem solving in human relationships and the empowerment and liberation of people to enhance well-being. Utilising theories of human behaviour and social systems, social work intervenes at the points where people interact with their environments. Principles of human rights and social justice are fundamental to social work. (Topss UK Partnership/Skills for Care, 2002, p 4)[3]

These ideas are continued and reinforced in the Quality Assurance Agency (QAA) Benchmark for Social Work, which provides the academic standards for the degree in social work in the UK. They will be familiar and relevant to social work as it is taught and practised across the globe, recognising that there are commonalities in how we go about making a difference, no matter where we are located. The standards were published in 2000 and are subject to periodic review.

> 2.4 Social work is a moral activity that requires practitioners to make and implement difficult decisions about human situations that involve the potential for benefit or harm. Social work honours degree programmes, therefore, involve the study, application of and reflection upon ethical principles. Although social work values have been expressed at different times in a variety of ways, at their core they involve showing respect for persons, honouring the diverse and distinctive organisations and communities that make up contemporary society and combating processes that lead to discrimination, marginalisation and social exclusion. This means that honours undergraduates must learn to:

- recognise and work with the powerful links between intra-personal and inter-personal factors and the wider social, legal, economic, political and cultural context of people's lives;
- understand the impact of injustice, social inequalities and oppressive social relations;
- challenge constructively individual, institutional and structural discrimination;
- practise in ways that maximise safety and effectiveness in situations of uncertainty and incomplete information;
- help people to gain, regain or maintain control of their own affairs, insofar as this is compatible with their own or others' safety, well-being and rights.[4]

These clear statements about the purpose of social work reflect the complexities of the task, and the QAA also identifies how social workers should be prepared by social work educational programmes to achieve these demands:

> 2.5 The expectation that social workers will be able to act effectively in such complex circumstances requires that honours degree programmes in social work should be designed to help students learn to become accountable, reflective and self-critical. This involves learning to:
>
> - think critically about the complex social, economic, political and cultural contexts in which social work practice is located;
> - work in a transparent and responsible way, balancing autonomy with complex, multiple and sometimes contradictory accountabilities (for example, to different service users, employing agencies, professional bodies and the wider society);
> - exercise authority within complex frameworks of accountability and ethical and legal boundaries; and
> - acquire and apply the habits of critical reflection, self-evaluation and consultation, and make appropriate use of research in the evaluation of practice outcomes.[5]

It is our intention that this book will be a useful resource in helping social work students to achieve the learning outcomes above, in order to become effective, confident and knowledgeable professional social workers.

National Occupational Standards

National Occupational Standards have been devised for a large number of occupations and professional groups. The National Occupational Standards for Social Work offer a set of descriptions of the functions of social workers. They aim to provide a benchmark of 'best practice' in social work competence across the UK and they form the basis for the new social work degree introduced in 2003 in England and in 2004 in the rest of the UK. The standards were developed from a detailed analysis of what social workers do, through consultation with employers and practitioners and they include service users' own statements of their expectations of social workers. The statutory Codes of Practice for Social Care (Social Service) Employers and Employees have also been incorporated into the National Occupational Standards. They are for all kinds of social workers, statutory or independent sector-based, working for health, education or social services (and for justice agencies in Scotland), regardless of who their service users are.

There are differences in the way that the standards are used in different parts of the UK. In England, Wales and Northern Ireland, the standards are described as key roles, with units and elements within each key role. The key roles are as follows:

(1) prepare for, and work with, individuals, families, carers, groups and communities to assess their needs and circumstances;
(2) plan, carry out, review and evaluate social work practice with individuals, families, carers, groups, communities and other professionals;
(3) support individuals to represent their needs, views and circumstances;
(4) manage risk to individuals, families, carers, groups, communities, self and colleagues;
(5) manage and be accountable, with supervision and support, for your own social work practice within your organisation;
(6) demonstrate professional competence in social work practice.

Scotland presents the standards within the context of an overarching framework for standards in social work education (SISWE), and identifies 'learning focuses' for each key role (see www.scotland.gov.uk). Beyond this, underpinning knowledge and transferable skills are identified for each learning focus. The key roles are set down in a slightly different order from the rest of the UK, with the introduction of the word 'assess' in the key role on risk. For simplicity, we will use the order and language of the England, Wales and Northern Ireland standards in this book.

An enquiry-based approach

The approach that we are modelling in this book is known as 'enquiry and action learning' (EAL) or 'problem-based learning' (PBL). This approach has been adopted in a number of social work courses in the UK since the early 1980s. Using this model, students work in small groups on a 'case study' that derives from social work practice. Their task is to find out as much as they can about this particular scenario: identifying resources that might be useful, setting learning objectives, breaking down the work into manageable tasks and coming to a decision about an appropriate course of action (see Cree and Davidson, 2000).

The EAL or PBL approach makes a number of basic assumptions. The first is that people learn through experience (see Kolb, 1984), and that in doing so they build on their own prior experiences of learning. As Miller and Boud (1996, p 9) claim, 'Learning can only occur if the experience of the learner is engaged at some level.' The implication is that in order to promote learning, we must find ways of encouraging students to learn through concrete situations, and set up the conditions that allow them to draw on their past knowledge and experience. The second proposition is that there are many different kinds of knowledge to which learners have access. These can be described as:

- conceptual knowledge (knowing *that* – that is, facts, theories and propositions);
- procedural knowledge (knowing *how* – that is, skills);
- strategic knowledge (knowing *what to do when*);
- personal knowledge (knowing *about* their own values and belief systems);
- professional knowledge (knowing *about* social work values and codes of practice).

This suggests that the artificial division between knowledge, skills and values that is so prevalent in social work literature is unhelpful: skills and values are better understood as kinds of knowledge, since both are based on specific theoretical ideas and ways of thinking about the world. Moreover (and this leads to a third proposition in PBL), there is no hierarchy of knowledge implicit in this approach. Personal knowledge (gained from our own experience and background) is a source of knowledge in the same way that academic learning is. Both must therefore be reflected on and interrogated as potential sources for decision making and action.

Our approach has been to build knowledge in each chapter from the starting point of a vignette or scenario. We have avoided use of the word 'case', because this has too many potentially negative resonances with 'casework' in the 1950s and 1960s, and with medical practice today. We have also chosen not to use the word 'problem', because we do not want to suggest that the individual, family or group at the centre of each chapter might be construed as the 'problem'. All the scenarios are drawn from practice, but they are not direct representations of real people: any similarity with a real person or family is accidental. In devising the vignettes, we have tried not to repeat stereotypical representations of those who use and provide services. We hope, instead, that the pictures that we present of service users, carers, practitioners and managers reflect the complexities of people's lives, and their strengths, as well as the areas with which they are seeking and receiving support. Our decision to share chapters with others at the draft stage has allowed us to keep this under constant review.

Critical reflexivity

We have stated that the book adopts a critical reflexive approach. This requires some explanation. The first important point to make is that the word 'critical' is not being used in its everyday sense. 'Critical' (from the Greek 'krino' meaning to choose, decide or judge) is most commonly used in the sense of being disparaging, disapproving or judgemental about someone or something. But in the context of critical thinking, critical sociology, critical reflexivity in social research and critical practice, it is used quite differently. We will unpack each in turn before coming up with our own definition.

The concept of *critical thinking* derives from educational psychology. It is premised on the belief that students should be taught critical thinking skills, which are defined as questioning, analysing, assessing and reaching conclusions based on evidence. Although proponents argue that these skills are generalisable (that is, they can be used whatever the context), it is also suggested that students need to reflect on the specific context within which they are located, both personal and institutional (see McPeck, 1990).

Critical sociology emerged in the 1960s and 1970s as a development from within Marxist theory. It is argued that social class and the capitalist economic system are insufficient explanations for oppression and inequality in society. Instead, other structural factors, including gender and 'race', need to be taken into account. Drawing on insights from the interpretive paradigm, critical sociologists furthermore propose that analysis should take account of interactions between people, not just issues of structure (see Cree, 2000).

The notion of *critical reflexivity* has had a major influence on social research in recent years. It assumes, along with all writing on reflexivity, that researchers must interrogate themselves within their research; they must look to see how they are impacting on the research process, from the identification of a research idea at the beginning to the dissemination of findings at the end. Critical reflexivity takes this interrogation one step further, by inviting researchers to locate themselves in terms of their gender, ethnicity, age and so on, thus enabling an examination of power (see Finlay, 2003). The concept of critical reflexivity has also been applied to practice, enabling practitioners to consider how the knowledge they bring to working with people has been developed. Understanding how knowledge is used and generated in practice is also a key element of reflexivity (Taylor and White, 2000), allowing for relations of power to be illuminated in a helpful way.

The idea of *critical practice* is developing increasing prominence in social work, as a way of confronting the difficulties of working in situations that are ever-changing, complex and contradictory. As Payne et al (2002, p 2) state, 'Critical practice gives us a way of organising our thinking and action to respond to uncertainty and risk.' They argue that critical thinking leads to critical action, which in turn forms critical practice. They suggest that there are various stages to this:

- examining language (what are our undisclosed assumptions?);
- exploring agenda setting (who is setting the agenda?);
- considering the content of judgements (what is the basis for our beliefs and assessments?); and
- questioning ideology (what are its underpinning assumptions and implications?).

Pulling this together, Issett (2000, pp 129-30) in turn offers a useful model for the critical professional, who:

- recognises that professional knowledge is imperfect and can always be improved;
- realises that technical expertise is necessary but that there are not formulaic answers to complex questions – what Schon (1983, 1987) has called 'indeterminate zones of practice';
- operates within an integrated personal/professional/political value-base, which uses an analysis of power relations and commitment to anti-oppressive practice, that seeks to understand and change the social and political context affecting practice;
- 'builds a cycle of critical reflection to maximise the capacity for critical thought, and produces a sense of professional freedom and a connection with rather than a distance from clients' (Pietroni, 1995, p 43);
- needs a safe supportive environment in which to honestly reflect and practise;
- listens and learns from ways of reflecting in different cultures and groups.

To reiterate, in adopting a critically reflexive approach in this book, we are not being negative. Instead, we are saying something about how we see society and individuals within it. More specifically, we are making it clear that we believe that knowledge is structured by existing sets of social relations and that these sets of social relations are oppressive in nature, whether rooted in differences of class, gender, sexuality, 'race', ethnicity, age or disability. We are also acknowledging our own part in this process. As individuals and as social work professionals (and social work academics), we are each implicated as oppressors and the oppressed, based on our own situations and biographies. Nevertheless, we believe that by recognising this, we have the opportunity to do something about it. This is not to suggest that inequalities disappear simply because we draw attention to them. Rather, it is to stress that a more open engagement with issues of power is necessary in order to open up the possibilities of negotiation and transformation. A critically reflexive approach also encourages the valuing of different discourses, including those of people who use social work services. While there has arguably been a revolution in recent years in the acceptance of the importance of service user involvement, we support Beresford and Croft's (2004) assertion that practitioners still need to give this a much higher priority.

Structure of the book

Each chapter (with the exception of Chapter Two) focuses on a National Occupational Standard and is built around a detailed vignette or scenario. The vignettes are set in different parts of the UK, and encourage examination of different legislative and policy contexts and different aspects of social work practice. The spread of chapters is as follows. Chapter Three explores the first standard and is set in a children and families centre in South Yorkshire. Chapter Four examines the second standard and is located in an adult services team (disability) in Wales. Chapter Five considers the third standard and takes place in an adult services team (older people) in a village in England. Chapter Six examines the fourth standard and is set in a youth offending team in the North East of England. Chapter Seven explores the fifth standard and is located in a general hospital in Northern Ireland. Chapter Eight considers the sixth standard and takes place in a criminal justice social work centre in a city in Scotland.

The chapters start with a scenario, then go on to explore the issues that this raises in relation to the Occupational Standard and its units, beginning with the legal and social policy context in which the scenario is located. We have not attempted to cover every unit within the standards; we believe this would have made for a rather dull, and overly mechanistic, book. Instead, we have developed what we see as the key learning from each of the standards, with the intention of covering as much essential information about social work as we can when the book is taken as a whole. We have looked at different models and methods, values and underpinning knowledge in distinct chapters, in order to cover as wide a range of material as possible. This is inevitably something of an artefact. It does not suggest that these are the only models and methods that we could have chosen, or that they are exclusive to one setting or another. On the contrary, most (especially those parts which relate to social work values) could have appeared in every chapter. We hope, however, that by using this approach, we have been able to give a flavour of different approaches and ideas across the board.

It should be stated that at times we have struggled to make a separation between models and methods, values and underpinning knowledge. This is because all social work models and methods have a basis in theory of one kind or another, whether this is medical, psychological, sociological, political, philosophical or any other theory. Likewise, social work models, methods and theories all demonstrate one or more sets of values; that is, they are rooted in ways of thinking about the individual and society, and about the place of social work within society. In consequence, there is a large measure of overlap between the themes that have been explored. Table 1.1 sets this out in diagrammatic form.

We have not separated out research evidence as if it were something separate from social work methods and models and underpinning knowledge. Instead, research findings are drawn on at various points throughout each chapter, reflecting our view that research evidence should be integrated in all social work practice. Likewise, skills have not been treated as detached from methods/models or theories. They are explored within social work models and methods and knowledge, because skills are best understood as the application of knowledge (see Eraut, 1994). We have also included a section entitled 'Other forms of knowledge' in each chapter, a device to ensure that service user perspectives are maintained within the practice described.

Chapter Two stands in contrast to the other chapters. It examines social work history, drawing on three separate strands of social work's past. Social work history is also explored in all the other chapters, reflecting the importance it is given in the National Occupational Standards where all six standards and 21 units cite 'historical perspectives of social work and social welfare' as fundamental to knowledge and understanding of the context of social work practice.

How to approach this book

This is not a book that we expect people to read from start to finish. Instead, it is a book to be picked up and explored as a resource in a specific situation.

TABLE 1.1: Themes within the book

Chapter	Models and methods	Values	Underpinning knowledge
Three	Strengths perspective Systems approach Community social work	Anti-oppressive practice Cultural competence	Child development and attachment Sociology of childhood Mental health
Four	Crisis intervention Person-centred approach	Anti-disablist practice Identities	Models of disability Caring
Five	Advocacy Task-centred approach	User empowerment Anti-ageism	Dementia Structural perspective
Six	Risk assessment Solution-focused practice	Respect Justice	Sociology of risk Postmodernism
Seven	Interprofessional collaboration Supervision	Mind-body-spirit approach Inequalities in health	Loss and bereavement Coping Sociology of health and illness
Eight	Offence-focused work Motivational interviewing	Relationship Feminism	Cognitive-behavioural theory Labelling theory

Readers who would like to find out about specific theories or models should refer to Table 1.1 or the Index for guidance as to where to locate a subject. Beyond this, we hope that readers will get to know the scenarios and begin to develop an understanding of the approach being used. This is, finally, our aim: that we demonstrate a way of thinking, knowing and acting as a critically reflexive practitioner.

Notes

[1] The 2000 Care Standards Act and the 2001 Regulation of Care (Scotland) Act required that all qualified social workers should be registered. Social workers were invited to register from April 2003, then from 2005 the title of 'social worker' was protected for the first time, so that only those with

an 'entitling qualification' (set at degree level) can call themselves social workers.

[2] See www.gscc.org.uk/News+and+evnts/Consultations (accessed 18 May 2007).

[3] This definition was agreed in 2000 by the International Association of Schools of Social Work and later adopted by the European Association of Schools of Social Work. It has been incorporated as the Key Purpose of Social Work within the National Occupational Standards in Social Work (Topss UK Partnership/Skills for Care, 2002).

[4] See www.qaa.ac.uk/academicinfrastructure/benchmark/honours/default.asp

[5] *Ibid.*

Useful websites

- www.basw.co.uk
- www.carecommission.com
- www.dh.gov.uk
- www.scotland.gov.uk
- www.sssc.uk.com
- www.ukstandards.org

2 Making a difference: lessons from history

Introduction

This chapter is different from the following ones in two ways. Unlike the other chapters, the focus is not on a single vignette: that is, on the story of one social work agency, or one service user group. Instead, we have drawn on a number of different narratives of social work history because we believe that each tells us something special about social work, and that, taken together, they provide a good understanding of the complexities at the heart of social work. The chapter is also different in that there is no National Occupational Standard or unit that relates solely to social work history. Nevertheless, whether we are making assessments, carrying out interventions or evaluating our practice, the critically reflexive practitioner needs to know about the historical context in which they are working. History helps us not only to see where we have been, but to make better sense of where we are now and the direction in which we are travelling. A historical perspective also helps us to practise sensitively and ethically. The opening words of the novel, *The Go-between* (Hartley, 1953, p 1) describe this well: 'The past is a foreign country. They do things differently there.' This reminds us that in reviewing stories from the past, just as in working with others from different cultural, ethnic or social class backgrounds to ourselves, we should seek not to judge only on the basis of our own experience. Rather, we must be open to the experiences of others from their own standpoints. So to lessons from social work history.

Newtown, 1820

Imagine a city on a cold winter's day in 1820. This could be any city in the UK – let's call it Newtown. What do you see, hear and, above all, smell?

You see a city that has undergone incredible expansion in the last 100 years. What was a small market town of 5,000 people has grown to be a sprawling city of over 80,000 men, women and children, all living on top of one another and competing for space in the narrow city streets. Buildings have been thrown up quickly, with little attention to planning or safety;

evidence of industry is everywhere, from the breweries in the city centre to the mills and mines on the edge of town. You hear the din of the city streets: vendors yelling their wares, cattle being driven to market, music playing in the distance, children crying. You also hear the noise of industry: the clanking of machines, the blaring of factory sirens, the banging and shouts from the docks. You smell the overpowering stench of sewage flowing down the city streets, the rivers and streams polluted with waste, unwashed bodies, perfumes and spices from distant lands, smoke belching from chimneys. This is a city that has none of the social welfare systems which we take for granted in the 21st century. There is no health service free at the point of delivery for citizens, no universal education for children and no legislation regarding building control and sanitation. There is no system of social security and no public housing.

This does not, of course, suggest that no one was concerned at this time about the adverse effects of urbanisation and industrialisation, or that there were no agencies seeking to address the vast and growing social and economic needs of the population. On the contrary, there was widespread public concern about the state of the nation; politicians, philanthropists, clergymen and journalists all railed against the evils of the day. Reverend Thomas Chalmers demonstrates this in a sermon written in 1817. He is writing about Glasgow, but this could have been any city in the UK:

> … on looking at the mighty mass of a city population, I state my apprehension, that if something be not done to bring this enormous physical strength under the control of Christian and humanised principle, the day may yet come, when it may lift against the authorities of the land its brawny vigour, and discharge upon them all the turbulence of its rude and volcanic energy.[1]

The story of the history of social work is the story of the development of initiatives – statutory and voluntary – that sought to respond to the new conditions in which people found themselves – and to the crisis of industrialisation.

Stories from social work history

Social work emerged as a response to the social problems created by industrialisation and urbanisation. The late 18th and 19th centuries saw the creation of a vast number of statutory (public) schemes for sanitation, education, hospitals and clinics, policing and prisons, juvenile correction, workhouses and mental asylums. New laws governing working conditions and the treatment of children were introduced, at the same time as new mechanisms for recording population change (Cree, 2007). On the voluntary front, there was an explosion in philanthropic activity, from visiting societies to charities dedicated to treating every conceivable social ill. We will now look in more detail at the development of three such initiatives: workhouses, friendly visiting societies and rescue organisations.

Workhouses

Workhouses occupy a dark space in the public imagination. They are envisaged as places of cruelty and degradation; of hunger and separation; of illness and death. Older people throughout the 20th century preferred to die alone at home in poverty rather than be taken into local authority care, or into what they saw as 'the workhouse'. Charles Dickens' novel, *Oliver Twist*, was, for generations of readers, the authentic picture of life in the workhouse. But why were these prisons for the poor and older people built in the first place? What functions did they serve? What vestiges, if any, remain today in the social institutions and practices of 21st-century social work?

Origins

To understand where workhouses came from, we need to look much further back in history to the breakdown of mediaeval systems of care and patronage. In mediaeval times, care for those who were unable to look after themselves (that is, people who were too old to work, disabled people, orphans, the sick and so on) was seen as largely a problem for the individual and their families. Beyond this, landlords gave some support (financial and practical) to their tenants in times of short-term need. Voluntary collections were distributed by churches to those in need, while monasteries provided residential and hospital care (almshouses) for some sick and older people.

This is not, however, to imply that life was comfortable in this rural idyll. On the contrary, for most people life was extremely hard, punctuated by bad harvests, wars and famine. A particularly devastating plague in the 1340s (known as the 'Black Death') is estimated to have wiped out 75 million people worldwide, including 70% of the population of England (Lehfeldt, 2005). The Black Death led to severe labour shortages across the country, driving up wages and encouraging vast numbers of dislocated people to move around in search of work. Several Acts were passed from this time on in an attempt to control population movement (what we would today call 'economic migrants') and keep a lid on wage inflation. For example, in 1388, the Statute of Cambridge was passed, restricting the movements of all labourers and beggars. Each county ('Hundred') was made responsible for relieving its own 'impotent poor', that is, those who, because of age or infirmity, were incapable of work. Servants wishing to move out of their own area needed a letter of authority from the 'good man of the Hundred' (the local Justice of the Peace), or risked being put in the stocks.[2] This legislation, which has been described as the first English Poor Law, sought to draw a line between those who *could* not work (because of age or disability), and those who *would* not work (portrayed as idle beggars and vagabonds). It also confirmed the belief that help should only be available to needy people who belonged to the neighbourhood; all others were to be banished. Although at the time, the statute was not enforced and so had little impact, subsequent legislation continued to distinguish between those unemployed people who were in need of care and those who were in need of punishment (also called 'sturdy beggars').

The decline of the monasteries and their subsequent dissolution in 1536 further exacerbated social and economic problems by, quite literally, throwing sick and old people out onto the street. In 1601, the Elizabethan Poor Law Act (England & Wales) restated the principle of the paramountcy of family duty in welfare:

> It should be the duty of the father, grandfather, mother, grandmother, husband or child of a poor, old, blind, lame or impotent person, or other poor person, not able to work, if possessed of sufficient means, to relieve and maintain that person.

The 1601 Act authorised parishes to raise income through a tax on property to pay for help for those who had no family support. It also determined what help should be provided:

- the 'impotent poor' (the aged, chronically sick, blind and mentally ill people who needed residential care) were to be accommodated in voluntary almshouses;
- the 'able-bodied poor' were to be set to work in a workhouse (they were felt to be able to work but were lazy);
- the 'able-bodied poor' who absconded or 'persistent idlers' who refused work were to be punished in a 'house of correction' (Fraser, 2003).

An essential distinction is being made here, between those who were poor through no fault of their own (they were to receive care from voluntary agencies), and those who were to blame for their poverty (they were to receive statutory care). On a parallel track, Scottish parishes were permitted by a Poor Law Act of 1579 to raise taxes through rates to pay for poor relief. However, few did so, and in most areas, assistance remained in the hands of the Church (through the Kirk Session) or the estate. Scotland differed from the rest of the UK in another key respect. While England, Wales and Ireland built workhouses to set the able-bodied poor to work, Scotland preferred to build poorhouses for those who were unable to work, believing that there should be no statutory relief for the unemployed; the workhouses that were built (usually in the larger towns and cities) were run, not by parish authorities, but by charitable trusts (Levitt, 1988). In the years that followed, workhouses and poorhouses sprang up in an uneven way across the UK. At the same time, localised income maintenance schemes (like the Speenhamland system) emerged from time to time to 'top up' low wages and so relieve extreme hardship.

The Poor Law Amendment Act of 1834 (England & Wales) (also known as 'the New Poor Law') demonstrates that by the 19th century, poverty and unemployment were still major problems for society. Not only this, industrialisation and urbanisation were actually increasing demands for poor relief, as more people left the countryside in search of work, and those left behind had no one to turn to for help. The Poor Law Amendment Act stated that there should be no poor relief for the able-bodied unemployed outside the workhouse. It divided the poor into two groups:

- the 'deserving poor' (for example, older, sick or disabled people, orphans and widows) who were to receive financial and practical support (often home-based) from charitable or voluntary organisations;
- the 'undeserving poor' (for example, able-bodied unemployed men, single mothers, prostitutes) who were forced to turn to the state, and thus to the workhouse (Mooney, 1998).

This legislation, for the first time, created a new administration process to oversee its implementation, organised around Poor Law unions with a central board. Following this, a major building programme turned rhetoric into reality, as workhouses were built in towns and cities across England, Wales and, after an 1838 Act, in Ireland. Scotland passed its own Poor Law Act in 1845, in large part because after the Disruption in the Church of Scotland in 1843 (when 40% of ministers left to form the new Free Church of Scotland), there were simply not enough Kirk Session members to manage poor relief across Scotland. Poor relief gradually became passed to parish authorities, but still with the proviso that the able-bodied poor should not be given assistance.

Functions

Workhouses were deliberately harsh places; the 'workhouse test' was the central means of finding out just how needy an individual was. In other words, the workhouse was, by its very existence, a deterrent; only the desperate would be willing to enter its doors. The Reverend James R. McCulloch explained this in a sermon in 1828:

> The real use of a workhouse is to be an asylum for the able-bodied poor.... But it should be such an asylum as will not be resorted to except by those who have no other resource.... The able-bodied tenant of a workhouse should be made to feel that his situation is decidedly less comfortable than that of the industrious labourer who supports himself.[3]

Once admitted to the workhouse, men, women and children were separated, and all who were fit enough were set to work, usually without pay (in return for their board and lodgings), on hard physical tasks such as breaking stones and picking apart old ropes ('oakum'). The lucky ones were given jobs inside the workhouse: cooking, cleaning, laundry work and nursing sick and elderly inmates who were accommodated in 'infirmary' buildings. By the middle of the 19th century, those entering workhouses were increasingly, as in Scottish poorhouses, the old, the sick, unmarried mothers, those with alcohol problems and people with mental health problems. By the beginning of the 20th century, the Poor Law's days were numbered. On 1 April 1930, the Boards of Guardians in England and Wales were abolished and their responsibilities passed to local authorities. Some workhouses were sold or knocked down; others, however, became residential homes for older people, and their memory passed on well into the 20th century.

Legacy

The legacy of workhouses, and of the Poor Law, can be seen throughout social work and social policy in the UK today. Three key principles remain:

- that the family should be the main provider of care;
- that poor people should be deterred from seeking help;
- that public assistance should be set at a level below that of a minimum wage.

But there are other, perhaps less explicit, messages that are just as influential in social work practice today, although we might wish to distance ourselves from them. For example, there is a fundamental notion that there are 'deserving' and 'undeserving' people, and that it is social work's task, on behalf of society, to make these distinctions. Many contemporary social work assessments are premised on meeting the eligibility criteria for available resources, that is, deciding who deserves (needs) the services. There is also the idea that help should only be available to those who are local. Refugees and asylum seekers today experience the same kind of discrimination and oppression as those who travelled much shorter distances in search of work in the past. There is also, finally, the belief that voluntary and statutory measures of care should function side by side, with statutory authorities carrying the major responsibility for containing and controlling – punishing? – those who are not deemed to be worthy of voluntary care.

Friendly visiting societies

The story of friendly visiting societies seems to offer a much more positive slant on social work history than that of workhouses; the very name 'friendly visiting' suggests something that we are likely to find more comfortable, more acceptable to our view of ourselves as a good, caring profession. In considering this in more detail, we will examine the story of one friendly visiting society, the Edinburgh-based Indigent Old Women's Society, placing it in its wider context.

Origins

In 1797, a small group of middle-class women met in an Edinburgh drawing room to discuss what to do about the problem of their older domestic servants who were too old and too infirm to work. The women decided to form a visiting society, the 'Senior Female Society for Indigent Old Women' (later changed to the simpler Indigent Old Women's Society). In establishing the society, they each contributed a sum of money which would then be distributed in the form of a monthly pension to older women in need; they also held fundraising events (such as door-to-door collections and public sermons) to set the society on a firm financial footing.

Functions

The Indigent Old Women's Society provides a fairly typical example of a friendly visiting society; societies like this flourished throughout the 18th and 19th centuries in towns and cities across the UK. There would probably have been up to 50 visiting societies operating in Newtown by 1820, some connected with the many different branches of Churches, and others not. The Indigent Old Women's Society continued on this basis for over 200 years. Although it merged with other visiting societies over the years, and increasingly relied on grants from statutory authorities as well as voluntary bodies, its activities continued much as before. A cadre of middle-class women (and latterly a few husbands) undertook monthly visits to poor, older women in Edinburgh, where they, in the tradition of friendly visiting, shared narratives of their families and lives. They also handed over a small sum of cash, and distributed Christmas gifts and special allowances for fuel and sometimes food or clothing.

The period 1780 to 1850 has been called 'an age of societies' (Davidoff and Hall, 1992, p 416): at this time, everything from soup kitchens, to chambers of commerce to arts societies were established in towns and cities across the UK. Most of these enterprises were run by middle-class men, who used the societies to foster their emerging power base in the cities. But visiting societies and housing associations also offered particular opportunities for the wives and daughters of the middle classes. These women learned to speak at meetings, make new friends and administer their voluntary organisations. They were able to move independently, in areas of the towns and cities from which they had hitherto been excluded. Florence Nightingale expressed this eloquently when she wrote: 'Charity work, free from chaperons and prying relatives represented deliverance from the stitch-stitch-church-stitch routine of female existence. It was adventure.'[4] The one-to-one relationship that was established between the visitor and visited was seen as a reciprocal, although not equal, one: the visitor felt able to share the benefits of her greater knowledge and education (and social class) with the poor person. The social work historian Philip Seed (1973, p 37) argues that visiting was part of a social mission to understand and to influence the social environment through personal intervention, in the spirit of 'not money, but yourselves'.

The growth in societies was not, however, without its critics. One commentator of the day, Henry Fawcett, writing in 1871, complained that: 'One chief cause of poverty is that too much is done for those who make no proper effort to help themselves and thus improvidence in its various forms is encouraged.'[5] From the late 1860s onwards, branches of the new Charity Organisation Society (COS) became established in major cities, with the primary aim of coordinating (and controlling) voluntary effort. The system that the COS attempted to put in place was that any person in need should apply first to the COS. Their case would be assessed by a trained caseworker, who would recommend either help from a specified local voluntary society (if they were deemed to be 'deserving' of help, such as an older or sick person without family support) or referral to the Poor Law (if they were seen to be an 'undeserving' case, that is, long-term unemployed, an alcoholic or a prostitute). It was intended that no one would receive help except by going through this formal procedure. The introduction of casework and the written recording of assessments and decisions are functions that have resonance in social work today. Record-keeping was designed to assist in reducing fraud and multiple claims, ensuring that the resources were not abused and only the 'right' people received the appropriate assistance.

In practice, the COS never managed to exert the control it needed or wished over the voluntary societies or their service users. Needy people continued to apply direct to societies for help, and the COS was never able to attract enough visitors to carry out the necessary home visits and checks on claimants. Most crucially, the COS was never able to sustain the distinction between 'deserving' and 'undeserving' poor; there were simply too many people in need, and too many overlaps between the two groups (Mooney, 1998). As a national organisation, the COS collapsed within 20 years, although local societies did continue to act as clearing houses for voluntary initiatives. For its part, the Indigent Old Women's Society functioned as a friendly visiting society until December 2002, when its assets and 'clients' were transferred to another voluntary society.

The failure of the COS can be seen as a cause for celebration or for commiseration, depending on your point of view. The fact that it failed to rationalise charitable effort was, in part, an illustration of the vitality and independent spirit of voluntary agencies like the Indigent Old Women's Society. The members of this and other societies did not want to be managed by another agency; they wanted to carry out their own assessments and to conduct their own affairs without interference, even if this meant some people receiving help from more than one agency. The demise of the COS also, however, demonstrates both the scale of the social and economic problems being experienced by citizens and the increasing dominance of public (statutory) systems for poor relief. The same is true for the closure of the Indigent Old Women's Society. This society had begun at a time when there was no notion of a state pension or public housing. Gradually over the years, the real value of the pension that was distributed by the society's visitors declined, just as statutory measures of social assistance improved.

Legacy

The legacy of friendly visiting societies, like the legacy of workhouses, is complex and contradictory. It is clear that, at their core, the two systems depended on one another: just as the workhouse was there to control and punish the 'undeserving' poor, so the friendly visiting society (in common with housing associations and the settlement movement) existed to support the 'deserving' poor. They were, in the end, two sides of one coin.

But there is another important consideration here. The two systems were not, as might at first be thought, separable into systems of 'control' (the workhouses) and systems of 'care' (the friendly visiting societies). Instead, care and control operated together in both settings. While the workhouse provided food, shelter and medical care to those with nothing, so the friendly visiting society operated strict rules about behaviour that was, and was not, permitted, by the older people in receipt of its care. So, for example, if an older woman was found with alcohol (or to have a man living with her) she would be removed from the society's list. This suggests that any categorisation of a voluntary agency as 'care' (and so, implicitly, 'good') and a statutory agency as 'control' (hence 'bad') is not sustainable. Social work is always about care *and* control; we care for others through control, and an analysis of social work history shows that this has been the case at all times.

There is one final aspect of the legacy of friendly visiting societies which merits attention: that is, the motivation of the visitors. We have already commented that the middle-class women who visited the poor did so for both humanitarian and selfish reasons. They felt genuine concern for older women less fortunate than themselves and were prepared to share a little of their wealth because of this. But many also believed that charity was essential to earn their place in heaven (Fraser, 2003). Moreover, beliefs about class and gender played a large part in determining the women's motivation. They brought to their voluntary work specific (middle-class) ideas about class and gender, family and work, age and sexuality. They believed that their own, bourgeois, culture and beliefs were superior to those of working-class people; their goal was to make the working classes more like themselves; more 'middle class'. They also believed that men and women had different 'natural' qualities and abilities, and that, as women, they had a special contribution to make to the management of poorhouses and workhouses, school boards and prisons, as well as to the daily household management of poor families and the care of sick and older people. Social workers today are unlikely to express their motivations in terms of heaven or the 'here-after'; professional social work has secularised its language and its activities (Cree, 1996). Nevertheless, there remains a tension, at times, between the class and gender backgrounds of the 'helpers' and the 'helped'. There are still far more women in social work, particularly at the level of main grade workers, and more women are applying to social work courses (Perry and Cree, 2003); meanwhile, those using services remain, fundamentally, the poor (Jones, 2002). And social workers still fail, at times, to comprehend and work with those whose values are different from their own.

Rescue organisations

The third sphere of social work history that we will examine concerns the activities of rescue and campaigning organisations. Alongside the growth of the more conservative visiting societies in the 18th and 19th centuries, a host of new, more politicised organisations sprang up, dedicated to everything from rescuing children, women and animals to campaigning on subjects as diverse as slavery, sexuality, factory conditions, voting rights and prostitution. We will take a closer look at one such organisation, the National Society for the Prevention of Cruelty to Children (NSPCC).

Origins

The first Society for the Prevention of Cruelty to Children was founded in New York in 1874. The society was established as a direct outcome of one particularly distressing case. A friendly visitor had gone to see a dying woman in the Hell's Kitchen district of New York. Here she had heard a child's screams, and, unable to find anyone who was prepared to intervene, she approached the Society for the Prevention of Cruelty to Animals to ask for help. Officials from this society removed the child, eight-year-old Mary Ellen Wilson, arrested her mother, and brought a case before the Supreme Court on the grounds that a 'little animal' of the human race had been harmed. The case was successful, and a new society was formed. Following a visit to the New York society by a Liverpool banker in 1881, a Liverpool society was formed in 1883, soon joined by other similar societies across the UK. The various English branches came together to form the NSPCC in 1889, with the stated aims of protecting children from cruelty, supporting vulnerable families, campaigning for changes to the law and raising awareness about abuse. The same year, 1889, marked the passing of the Prevention of Cruelty to, and Protection of, Children Act, sometimes known as the 'Children's Charter'. This Act, for the first time, made it lawful to intervene in relations between parents and children, by giving police the power to obtain a warrant to enter the home of any child thought to be in danger and to arrest anyone found to be ill-treating a child. The Act also restricted the employment of children and made begging by children unlawful.

Although there were no child protection societies before the 1880s, orphanages (then called 'foundling hospitals') for the care of abandoned, illegitimate and bereaved children had existed across the UK for many years; a small number had been founded as early as the 1500s. Children had also been routinely accommodated in workhouses in England and Wales, when their parents or parent had been admitted to the institution. Some children spent their entire childhood in workhouses, only leaving at 15 years of age. The practice of raising children in workhouses was later replaced by the use of children's homes, also called 'cottage' homes. In Scotland, poorhouses rarely held on to children for long; the preference had always been to 'board out' children with foster parents, often in rural parts of the country, or to send them to specialised children's homes run by charitable organisations. What this brief account illustrates is that concern for children was not a new phenomenon. What *was* new, however, was that the focus of the Societies for the Prevention of Cruelty to Children was, for the first time, children who were still in the care of their parents. This therefore represented a major challenge to patriarchal values and to society as a whole.

Functions

Over the years that followed, the NSPCC and other child protection societies went about their daily business of investigating reports of child abuse and neglect and raising funds to pay the salary of their inspectors, colloquially known as 'the cruelty men', or 'the cruel men' (Ferguson, 2004). A Circular from 1909, reported by Clapton (2008: forthcoming), tells us something about the preoccupations of the inspectors. This states that the following points about the family should be specially noted:

- state of their health, conditions of their clothing, beds and bedding, their personal cleanliness – state of vermin present and where;
- the appearance and condition of the health – cleanliness, furniture, fire and food;
- the character of the parents or guardians and the earnings of the family.

Inspectors used a classic 'carrot and stick' approach: they gave advice, and sometimes material help, but if the condition of the children did not improve, they had no compunction in removing them from their parents or reporting their parents for prosecution, and sometimes both. This mirrors perfectly the care and control mix that we have already identified as central to the workings of both workhouses and friendly visiting societies, and fundamental to the practice of social work today.

But developments in child protection were not located only in the voluntary sector. Just as voluntary societies expanded, so events gathered momentum in the public arena. A mass of legislation was passed at the beginning of the 20th century governing all spheres of children's lives, including education, employment, health, living conditions, entertainment and crime. The roots of this legislation can be found in two, related, public anxieties: fear about crime and concern about the physical condition of the poor. Fear of crime was fuelled by the idea that a 'criminal class' was passing on its criminal habits to the next generation, hence the necessity of separating children from criminal parents. Concern about the health of the poor was accentuated after it was discovered that 70% of recruits to the Boer War between 1899 and 1902 had to be rejected because of poor heath (Jones, 2002). By the middle of the 20th century, a new Children Act passed in 1948 set up childcare departments in local authorities across the UK and created the new social work role of 'childcare officer'. This legislation, Munro (2007) suggests, should be seen as part of the post-Second World War creation of a welfare state; it embodied the notion that the state should positively intervene to support families and children. However, there was never sufficient funding to make this a reality. For example, the one part-time Children's Officer appointed in 1948 to the city of Dundee in Scotland was also responsible for burials and cemeteries! Section 1 of the 1963 Children and Young Person's Act broadened the preventive remit of local authorities, by authorising them to 'make available such advice, guidance and assistance as may promote the welfare of children by diminishing the need to receive children into or keep them in care ...'. Again, lack of adequate resources made this little more than an aspiration. The 1970 Local Authority Social Services Act and the 1968 Social Work (Scotland) Act heralded a different approach. Local authorities were required 'to prevent abuse and neglect', and the new social services departments (and social work departments in Scotland) had, for the first time, resources at their disposal to make this a possibility. Subsequent legislation has confirmed the notion that child protection (investigation, prosecution and prevention) is primarily a matter for the state, not the voluntary sector. In consequence, the scope and purpose of the NSPCC and other child protection societies in the UK have changed considerably. Today, the voluntary sector's role is focused on campaigning, on education and on providing support for families and children in need.

Legacy

What is striking in reviewing this history is that it was a *voluntary* body, not the statutory police force, that held the task of investigating child cruelty and bringing about prosecutions; what went on in families and behind closed doors was not considered a concern of government. The legislation, and the child protection agencies, thus represented a compromise between those who wanted greater involvement of the state, and those who held the liberal position that 'a man's home is his castle'; nobody had the right to enter without his permission.[6] This point has been made earlier by Cree (1995) in an examination of historical attitudes towards sexuality and morality. While campaigning organisations fought for changes in the law and in private behaviour in relation to sexual conduct, they nevertheless preferred to keep the control of prostitution and immorality a matter for voluntary agencies, not the state.

The shift towards greater acceptance of the notion that the state has a right and, indeed a duty, to intervene in the lives of citizens is one that we can see increasingly over the last 100 years or so. Today we expect statutory authorities (police, teachers, health visitors, doctors, social workers) to intervene in cases of neglect or harm to children and vulnerable adults, just as we expect the authorities (police or procurator fiscal) to prosecute such cases. In situations where they are deemed to have acted not quickly enough or without sufficient force, statutory agencies are held up for public blame (see, for example, the long list of child abuse and adult abuse scandals that have plagued social work from the death of Maria Colwell in 1974 to the death of Victoria Climbié in 2000). But notwithstanding widespread acceptance of a duty on the part of the state to intervene, there is still a line beyond which it cannot cross. The UK has never gone so far as to abolish all physical chastisement of children by their parents; despite pressure from European law and from UK pressure groups and children's rights organisations, successive governments have continued to uphold the right of parents to 'fairly' punish their children.[7]

There is one, final legacy of the child protection societies that must be acknowledged. In concluding his history of the Royal Scottish Society for the Prevention of Cruelty to Children, Clapton (2008: forthcoming) argues that 'the cruelty men' could be both a force for good and a force that was resented. He poses the question: 'How close is this description to a characterisation of social work with children and families in the 21st century?' This is a critical question that all social workers must ask themselves as they intervene in the lives of individuals, families and communities.

Conclusion

This chapter began with the picture of Newtown: a growing industrial city in the early stages of the development of industrial capitalism. Newtown is a very different place today. The industries on which it flourished have all but gone; the dockyards have been transformed into single-person flats for the young and upwardly mobile; the city centre is a place for shopping and entertainment, not for living. Some children are now at school until 18 years of age, and a welfare state guarantees a minimum level of care and protection for most citizens. But what has remained?

Newtown, in common with Poor Law times, is still a society that seeks to exclude and discriminate against those who are seen to not belong. Refugees and asylum seekers are not locked up in workhouses, but are held in detention centres and sometimes in prisons. Children are still separated from their parents; families are still forcibly evicted and transported to lands from which they have fled. A recent Joseph Rowntree report argues that children of refugees and asylum seekers remain among the most vulnerable in society (Hirsch, 2006). Children who commit crimes can be excluded from the community at an increasing rate, either into prisons (Secure Training Centres, Detention and Training Centres) or other provision (Muncie, 2004;

www.nacro.org). Homeless people can be given Anti-Social Behaviour Orders and excluded from localities, and imprisoned if they do not comply (www.asboconcern.org.uk). Furthermore, there is evidence of changing patterns of poverty over the last 40 years or so, with increasing polarisation between rich and poor. Dorling et al (2007) point out that the very rich and the very poor now live in very different areas, and in parts of some cities over half of all households are 'breadline poor' (Dorling et al, 2007). The exclusion of people may be different in form than in previous years, but it still occurs to the detriment of a large part of the population.

The family remains the main provider of care: whether in the community or in residential institutions, there is still a fundamental acceptance that care should be provided by family members. Successive research studies have shown that this 'burden of caring' often falls on women – on wives, daughters and mothers, in spite of changes in women's employment (Featherstone, 2004). Yet studies have also shown that caring operates in the space of a relationship; it is usually reciprocal, and those who give and receive care do so willingly (www.carersuk.org). They just wish that the state could provide more back-up, more respite, so that they could continue to care for longer.

Social work is still characterised by care and control. As all three examples have shown, social work continues to seek to mould the behaviour and standards of the poor and disenfranchised while helping and supporting them; social work, along with all the other 'psy' professions (Foucault, 1977; Rose, 1985), is fundamentally in the business of managing populations and policing families. We do so, hopefully, in a respectful, empowering way, but this is nevertheless what we are paid to do on behalf of society. Whether we are working in the statutory or the voluntary sector, the reality is the same.

Finally, social work and social workers remain a force for good but, at the same time, a force that can rightfully bring huge resentment from individuals, families and communities. It is important to recognise that not all that has been done in the name of social work over the last 100 years or so has been positive to those who have experienced it. All the agencies that we have described had conservative, punitive aspects to them, just as all sought to 'do good' in their own terms. This seems a good point to move on to the main substance of our book, that is, how social work can make a difference in the lives of people in the UK today.

Notes

[1] From a sermon by Reverend Thomas Chalmers, quoted in Brown (1997) *Religion and Society in Scotland since 1701*, Edinburgh: Edinburgh University Press, p 95.

[2] See http://users.ox.ac.uk/~peter/workhouse/index.html
[3] From a sermon by Reverend James R. McCulloch, printed in the *Edinburgh Review, XLVII* (1828, pp 303-29), quoted in Fraser (2003).
[4] Quoted in Prochaska (1980, p 11).
[5] Speech reprinted in Fawcett (1975, p 33).
[6] This is an old saying, which reflects basic concepts in English common law. See Morris (1977, 1988).
[7] The physical chastisement of children by their parents is permissible under section 58 of the 2004 Children Act. This was reconsidered and confirmed by government in August 2007, to much fury from the professional association, the British Association of Social Workers (see report in BASW's magazine *Social Work*, September 2007).

Key questions

(1) Why is a historical perspective important for social work?
(2) What does it mean to suggest that statutory and voluntary solutions went hand in hand in the 19th century?
(3) Who are the 'undeserving' and 'deserving' poor, historically and in the present day?

Further reading and resources

- Cree, V.E. (2007) 'Social work and society', in M. Davies (ed) *Blackwell Companion to Social Work* (3rd edition), Oxford: Blackwell, pp 289-302.
- Fraser, D. (2003) *The Evolution of the British Welfare State: A History of Social Policy since the Industrial Revolution* (3rd edition), Basingstoke: Palgrave Macmillan.
- Lewis, G. (1998) *Forming Nation, Framing Welfare*, London: Routledge.
- http://users.ox.ac.uk/~peter/workhouse/index.html

3

Making a difference in preparation and assessment

Introduction

The focus of this chapter is on preparing for, and working with, individuals, families, carers, groups and communities to assess their needs and circumstances, that is, Key Role 1 of the National Occupational Standards. This is subdivided into three units.

(1) Prepare for social work contact and involvement.
(2) Work with individuals, families, carers, groups and communities to help them make informed decisions.
(3) Assess needs and options to recommend a course of action.

Vignette: social work with children and families

Sally Main is a social worker based at a Family Centre in Coaltown, a predominantly white, former mining community in South Yorkshire in England. Since the closure of the pit in the mid-1980s, the area has been characterised by high levels of poverty, unemployment and ill-health. Sally is a white woman in her mid-forties. She has just received a letter of referral from a local health visitor, Karen Smith.

Karen has written to say that she is concerned about two-year-old Jamila Khan and her mother Naz, and would like an assessment to be carried out to see what help is needed and to explore what options might be available. Karen reports that Jamila lives with her parents, Naz and Jamal, in a small flat above the convenience store which is managed by the family. Karen describes Jamila as small for her age and 'a tearful, clingy child, who seems to spend all day in her pushchair behind the counter of the shop'. Jamila's mother, Naz, seems flat and rather detached; Karen thinks she may be depressed, and has recommended that she make an appointment to see her GP.

Discussion

The scenario is, on the face of it, a familiar one for Coaltown Family Centre. Here is a young mother who seems to be isolated and depressed and a young child who is fretful and not meeting her developmental milestones physically. This is an Asian family, suggesting that there may be additional factors to be considered, such as cultural differences and language difficulties (if one or both parents does not have sufficient grasp of English). We do not yet know anything about the social and economic context within which the Khan family is living, but it is reasonable to suspect that they may be experiencing poverty, with few resources to draw on, materially or personally. As an Asian family living in a white community, it seems likely that they will have experienced social isolation, and possibly outright racism. If Sally is going to make a difference in working with this family, she will have to take into consideration individual, family, cultural and structural perspectives.

The referral itself raises a number of interesting issues. Karen Smith, the health visitor, has passed on the task of carrying out the assessment to the Family Centre, rather than conducting this herself, although, under the Common Assessment Framework for Children and Young People (CAF),[1] she would have been entitled to do so. There may be a number of reasons for this. The local authority children's department may have decided that Social Work should take the lead role in all CAF assessments. Alternatively, Karen Smith may have made a professional judgement that the Family Centre is best placed to undertake the full assessment that she feels is needed in this situation. Then again, Karen may be a relatively new worker who has not yet had training in use of the CAF. Whichever is the case, Sally Main is an experienced social worker who is highly capable of conducting this assessment.

Preparing for social work contact and involvement

In preparing for social work contact and involvement, Sally will need to find out as much as she can in advance of her first meeting with Jamila and her parents. This will entail checking agency records to see if there is any history of involvement with the family. (Lord Laming's [2003] inquiry into the death of eight-year-old Victoria Climbié in 2000 highlighted the importance of social workers reading case files.) She will also need to check whether a Common Assessment on Jamila already exists. If one has already been carried out by another agency, this will become Sally's starting point in the new assessment. Sally will wish to telephone or speak in person to the referrer, Karen Smith, to find out if she has any additional information that she wishes to share. This will be important in clarifying, even at this early stage, whether Karen believes that Jamila is likely to need to be considered a child in need under Section 17 of the 1989 Children Act, or, more seriously, a child in need of protection under Section 47 of the 1989 Children Act (see 'Legal and social policy context' below). Problems in communication between professionals have been identified as a key factor in fatal child abuse cases (Reder and Duncan, 2003), so Sally will need to prepare well for her conversations with others. Sally may wish to contact the family's GP for a background report, but she will only be able to do this with the Khans' agreement, unless there are identified child protection concerns, in which case she will inform the parents that she is intending to speak with the GP. Lastly, Sally will need to find out from the Khans in advance of their first meeting whether an interpreter will be needed. This may be done by asking the question directly in the appointment letter that Sally sends to Mr and Mrs Khan.

Once she has gathered all the background information that is available, Sally will need to complete the Pre-assessment Checklist to help her decide whether an assessment under the CAF is suitable in this instance, and if so, whether additional services may be required. The checklist asks if the child appears to be:

- healthy;
- safe from harm;
- having a positive impact on others;
- free from the negative impact of poverty.

The health visitor's letter of referral does not, one way or another, answer any of these questions. Instead, the referral raises questions about all of them, perhaps with the exception of the 'safe from harm' question (but even here it is not really known at this stage whether Jamila is at risk of harm). Sally Main must keep an open mind about Jamila. The health visitor may have seen Naz and Jamila only once or twice, and then in the context of a busy clinic, where Naz may have felt under scrutiny, and hence unconfident in her handling of Jamila. The health visitor may not have met Jamal at all, so the part he plays in the family may be unknown at this stage. Sally must adopt a position of 'healthy scepticism' (Laming, 2003) in her approach to this family. She must be mindful of the concerns that have been raised and not minimise the risks, but at the same time be prepared to independently assess the situation. It is evident that, in this scenario, a Common Assessment will be helpful in clarifying the strengths and needs, and, at the same time, in identifying the services that may be required.

Legal and social policy context

In order to work effectively, Sally needs to know about the legislative and social policy framework that underpins children's services today. However, if she is really going to make a difference, she also needs to understand that intervention by statutory authorities is always subject to contestation, negotiation and change; moreover, intervention is never neutral, in either its purpose or its effects.

Historical background

Chapter Two has already demonstrated that up until the 19th century, there was a view that the state should not intervene in the lives of families. This mirrored the 'laissez-faire' approach to economic affairs, which held that government intervention could achieve little positive good and should be reserved to ensure the elimination of abuses that hinder the free market. As John Stuart Mill wrote in 1859, 'Letting alone should be the general practice, every departure from it unless required by some great good is a certain evil' (Mill, [1859] 1992, p 33).

Towards the end of the 19th century, we can see a growing acceptance of the idea that the state could, and should, intervene to safeguard the lives of citizens. The 20th century witnessed a strengthening of statutory involvement across all spheres of life. Early Liberal reforms were succeeded by the creation of the welfare state at the end of the Second World War, promising support 'from the cradle to the grave'. But ambivalence remained about the place of social work within this. While health and education became universal services, social work remained a residual service, targeted at those who fell through the welfare net. Legislation in 1970 (in England and Wales) and in 1968 (in Scotland) heralded a new approach, bringing provisions for children, older people, disabled people, those with mental health problems, those with learning disabilities and offenders into a comprehensive service. Local authority social services were to be open to all; 'a single door' on which anyone might knock. In practice, however, services remained targeted at the poor (Jones, 2002).

Governmental policy over the last 30 years or so has demonstrated continuing ambivalence towards the place of social work. The rhetoric from both Conservative and Labour governments has focused on the idea of the advantages of 'rolling back' the state. It is argued that the state's role is primarily to set targets and quality control, not to provide services; services are better provided, it is argued, by a mixed economy of private and public sectors. Citizens, for their part, are expected to be independent and to work for their living; in return, government will provide financial support towards childcare, and help in old age if their savings are not enough (Jordan, 2006). But in spite of the rhetoric of reduced state involvement, what we have actually seen, in recent years, has been increasing involvement of the state in family life. Families are 'policed' and regulated today in a way that would have been unthinkable 100 years ago, by a host of 'social' professionals: health visitors, teachers, psychologists and, of course, social workers (Parton et al, 1997). Justification for this increased intervention can be found in a series of high-profile inquiries into the deaths of children, beginning with the Colwell Report (DHSS, 1974) into Maria Colwell's death, and repeated again, more recently, in the Laming Inquiry (2003) into Victoria Climbié's death. What these inquiries have in common is that the child who died in each instance was known to social services; child protection measures had failed to prevent the abuse and deaths of these children. Social services have also been criticised for acting too precipitately, and for taking protection too far, as illustrated in two key inquiries into the sexual abuse of children in Cleveland (Butler-Sloss, 1988) and in Orkney (Clyde, 1992).

Current legislative and policy framework in relation to children

Recent legislation and policy guidance illustrate current understandings about the balance between the state and the family. The stated aim of the Children Act of 1989 (and similar legislation passed in Scotland in 1995[2]) was to encourage an approach to child welfare based on negotiation; parents and children were to be involved in agreed plans as far as possible. The Act also promoted the delivery of family support at an early stage, in order to reduce the need for more coercive interventions later. Munro (2007, p 21) points out that in this process, the notion of 'prevention' was broadened so that it was no longer simply about preventing a child coming into care; instead, prevention was to include the provision of services to 'promote the care and upbringing of children in their families'.[3] The Act made a key distinction between children 'in need' (see section 17) and children 'in need of protection' (who were to be dealt with under section 47). In a review of the evidence from a number of research studies concerned with child protection, the Department of Health's *Messages from Research* (DH, 1995) highlighted, with regret, that the aspirations at the heart of the Children Act had not been met. Widespread fear of overlooking a child at risk had led to a lowering of the threshold for child abuse investigations; increasing numbers of investigations were being carried out, yet in most instances, no further action was taken. *Messages from Research* argued again for a refocusing of energies away from child protection towards children 'in need', and stressed the importance of a positive working relationship between the family (parents and children) and the local authority.

Following the publication of *Messages from Research*, the Children's Fund was launched in November 2000 with the aim of tackling disadvantage among children and young people by identifying children and young people at risk of social exclusion at an early stage, and making sure that they receive the help and support they need to achieve their potential. Soon after, in 2003, the UK government published the Green Paper *Every Child Matters* (DH, 2003) alongside its response to Lord Laming's (2003) report. The Green Paper built on existing plans to strengthen preventative services by focusing on four key themes:

- increasing the focus on supporting families and carers;
- ensuring that necessary intervention takes place *before* children reach crisis point and protecting children from falling through the net;
- addressing the underlying problems of weak accountability and poor integration;
- ensuring that the people working with children are valued, rewarded and trained.

Every Child Matters was followed by the 2004 Children Act, which created a Children's Commissioner in England.[4] It also prescribed information-sharing systems to encourage professional collaboration, with the aim that professionals might identify children in need of support at an early point in their lives and provide help for them (Munro, 2007). The programme, *Every Child Matters: Change for Children*, was subsequently published in November 2004 (DH, 2004) with the objective that *every* child, whatever their background or circumstances, should have the support they need to:

- be healthy;
- stay safe;
- enjoy and achieve;
- make a positive contribution;
- achieve economic well-being.

In order to achieve this, a mandate was placed on organisations involved in providing services to children (from hospitals and schools, to police and voluntary groups) that they cooperate through Children's Trusts to 'share information and work together, to protect children and young people from harm and help them achieve what they want in life'. The focus on multi-agency cooperation led to the development of Directors of Children's Services within each local authority, placing education and children's social services under one organisational hierarchy, with the intention of providing 'joined-up' approaches to children's needs.[5] The implications of merging children's social work and education services have yet to be seen.

The programme also states that children and young people will have more say about issues that affect them as individuals and collectively, reflecting the spirit of the United Nations Convention on the Rights of the Child (UNCRC), which was adopted by the United Nations General Assembly on 20 November 1989 and ratified by the UK on 16 December 1991.

There is little doubt that, in Munro's (2007, p 28) words, the scope of children's services has been 'dramatically widened' by the 2004 Children Act and its subsequent programmes; as protection has come to mean protection of children from failing to achieve their 'potential', so the problem of child protection has become 'framed as a problem of social exclusion' (Penna, 2005, p 157). Today, *all* children in England and Wales have come under heightened scrutiny through the creation of new electronic databases, and it seems likely that early intervention will draw *more* children (and more families) under statutory surveillance and control 'for their own good'.

Other relevant legislation

The question of how far statutory agencies can go in intervening in the lives of citizens is central to the 1998 Human Rights Act, which came into force in the UK on 2 October 2000 and brings the European Convention on Human Rights into domestic law. This legislation makes it unlawful for public authorities to act in a way that is incompatible with one or more of the Convention rights; most crucially for social work in this situation, Article 8 sets out a right to respect to private and public life and prohibits any arbitrary interference with this right by the state. The European Court of Human Rights has acknowledged that a decision to remove a child from their parents' care must be based on sufficient and relevant reasons; it must be a measure of last resort, and should be 'no more than is necessary to protect the interests of the child concerned' (Calder and Hackett, 2003, p 25). How far the 2004 Children Act directly contradicts this legislation remains a disputed question.

Our vignette also raises questions in relation to the law, and ethnicity and race relations. The 1976 Race Relations Act states that it is unlawful to discriminate against anyone on grounds of race, colour, nationality (including citizenship), or ethnic or national origin. The Act applies to the fields of employment, planning, housing, the exercise of public functions (both by public authorities and also private bodies exercising public functions), the provision of goods, facilities and services, and education. It makes it unlawful for a public authority, in carrying out any of its functions, to do anything that constitutes discrimination. In 2000, the Act was amended to give public authorities a new statutory duty to promote race equality, thus aiming to help public authorities to provide fair and accessible services, and to improve equal opportunities in employment.[6]

Discussion

We introduced this section by suggesting that statutory intervention in family life is always contested; it is never neutral. Because of this, Sally Main must take a step back now, to consider some of the complex and contradictory aspects of the new legislation, and her role within it. As a statutory social worker, she has obligations under the legislation that she must fulfil. However, as an ethical and critical practitioner, she must seek not to do harm; her intervention must be targeted and timely. In order to achieve this, her practice must be grounded in social work values, and in a good understanding of anti-discriminatory, and culturally competent, practice.

From policy to practice: working with individuals and families and assessing need

Sally Main's task is to carry out a Common Assessment on Jamila Khan and her parents, with a view to making a recommendation for further (or no further) action. Her initial enquiries have led her to believe that this seems more likely to be a situation of a child 'in need' (section 17 of the 1989 Children Act) as opposed to a child 'in need of protection' (section 47 of the same Act).[7] Thorpe and Bilson (1998) offer a useful way of distinguishing between the two:

Section 17

(1) The parents are having difficulties and support is required to help look after the children.
(2) An assessment is needed to clarify the type of support required and which agency is most appropriate to deliver this support.
(3) The moral character of the parents is given as a reason for concern over care of the children.
(4) General concerns are expressed about care of the children but no direct allegation of harm is made.

Section 47

(1) Information has been offered that clearly indicates that a child has been harmed or injured, or an adult has behaved in a way that would normally cause harm or injury, and an investigation is needed to clarify this information.

(2) It is necessary to clarify whether the alleged actions were deliberately intended to cause harm or injury or were the consequence of an accident or excessive discipline.
(3) It is necessary to investigate if allegations have been received from a number of different sources.
(4) It is necessary to determine if reports are required from other professionals in health, education and criminal justice who have first-hand evidence of the alleged harm or injury.

We have said that Jamila Khan is more likely to be considered under section 17 than section 47. Beyond this, Sally is determined that the assessment process should be as positive an experience as possible for all the family members. The CAF guidance notes (April 2006) suggest that assessment should be:

- child-/young person-centred
- not discriminatory
- collaborative
- continuous
- progressive
- transparent
- consensual
- current
- sufficient and formative
- sound.

With this in mind, Sally now sets out to meet Mr and Mrs Khan and Jamila. She identifies three models that she sees as relevant to her practice: a strengths perspective, a systems approach and a community development approach.

Models and methods

Strengths perspective

The strengths perspective is a relatively new arrival to UK social work, but is already well established in many areas of practice, including child protection and mental health social work (Healy, 2005). It is popular with social workers and with service users because it suggests a positive, optimistic view of practice by focusing on the capabilities and potentialities of service users; service users are encouraged to express their hopes for the future, rather than seeking to remedy problems from the past or even the present.

Healy (2005) notes that the strengths perspective originally came from mental health practice in North America in the 1990s, as part of a backlash against the predominant psychosocial ideas that saw people in terms of needs, pathology, deficits and problems. She locates the intellectual and practice inspirations for this approach in a number of places: in research on social labelling and stigma; in the concept of resilience; and in ego psychology. She notes that this perspective is not the same as a problem-solving approach, which tends to stress the need for a *worker* to help a service user identify realistic goals and work towards them. The strengths perspective uses service users' hopes and dreams as the way forward, even if they seem to the worker to be unrealistic. (Note the connections with a solution-focused approach, discussed more fully in Chapter Six.)

Healy (2005, pp 157-8) identifies the following key assumptions of the strengths perspectives, paraphrased here:

- All people have strengths, capacities and resources.
- People usually demonstrate resilience, rather than pathology, in the face of adverse life events; 'all human organisms have an inclination for healing' (Saleebey, 2002, p 10).
- Service users have the capacity to determine what is best for them.
- Social workers tend to focus on perceptions of clients' problems and deficits while ignoring their strengths and resources.
- Collaborative partnerships between workers and service users reflect and build service users' capacities.

In working from a strengths perspective, Sally Main will first, as already identified, seek to approach the family with an open, yet aware, mind. This means that she will not automatically assume that Jamila is unhappy or unloved; that Mrs Khan is depressed; or that Mr Khan is unconcerned or too busy to care for his wife and child. She will approach Mr and Mrs Khan openly, and seek to convey this positive attitude in her encounters with them. Second, in carrying out her assessment, she will seek to find out from the Khans what they see as working in their situation. In other words, where do they see their strengths and resources? What can be built on? Third, she will wish to explore with them what they want (what are their hopes and dreams?) and to consider what her role might be in working with them to achieve this. Finally, Sally will wish to encourage Naz, Jamal and Jamila to make use of possible sources of support in their community, as a way of building their strengths for the future.

Systems approach

Social work has drawn on systems approaches since its very beginnings, seeking to place individuals and families in the context of their communities and of society as a whole. Healy (2005) usefully identifies three distinct phases of systems approaches. The first wave, prominent in the 1960s and 1970s, drew on general systems theory to explain clients' needs, situations and the purpose of social work practice. The social worker's task was envisaged as being to intervene to restore balance to the (disordered) client system. In the second wave, demonstrated from the 1990s onwards, eco-systems perspectives took over from a general systems approach, and the focus of attention became the transactions that occur within and across the person and their environment. The third wave of systems theory, which has emerged in recent years, is more concerned with complex systems and chaos theories. It is recognised that relationships are not linear, as previous versions of systems theory seemed to suggest. Not only this; in addition events may snowball, or repeat themselves. If order is to be found, it is only at the very deep level; when outcomes are successful, this will be as a result of the interaction between a host of complex factors.

An example of practice that is influenced by a systems or *ecological* approach is the *Framework for the Assessment of Children in Need and their Families* (DH, 2000a). This sets out three dimensions to be considered in an assessment of a child: the child's developmental needs, the adults' parenting capacity and the family and environmental factors. These are set out diagrammatically in Figure 3.1.

FIGURE 3.1

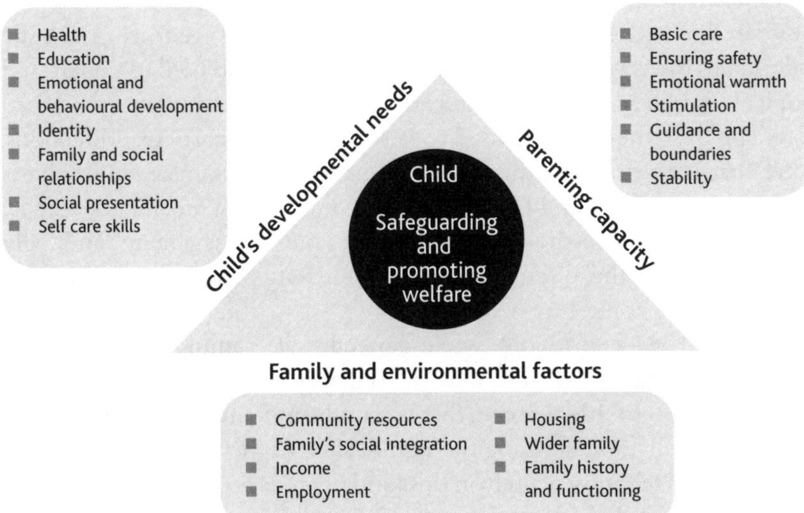

Using this framework, Sally's assessment will place Jamila firmly in the context of her family, her community and wider society. Sally will, first, conduct her own assessment of Jamila, using observation (see Fawcett, 1996) as well as the information provided by her parents and other adults. In doing so, she will draw on her knowledge of child development theory, as well as her practice experience gained from working with children over many years. Second, she will assess Naz and Jamal's capacity to parent Jamila, taking into account Naz's possible mental health and social needs, as well as Jamal's role in the family. Finally, she will wish to find out whether there are any other family members or friends who may be available to help: who may be able to spend time with Naz; to accompany her to a local women's group; to relieve her at times from working in the shop; to look after and entertain Jamila. She will also need to give attention to wider environmental factors, including the impact of housing, employment, neighbourhood and racism on this family. It seems likely that with more material resources, the Khans' situation might be improved, so Sally will need to have a good grounding in relevant welfare benefits. If Naz and Jamal are struggling to make ends meet and raise themselves out of poverty, there is little opportunity for fun, relaxation and time away from the daily grind. Research evidence from studies over many years has consistently demonstrated the connections between poverty and stress in parenting (see Ghate and Hazel, 2002).

Research suggests that parents have generally found the assessment framework helpful, and have felt more involved in the process of assessment (Millar and Corby, 2006). However, there have been warnings that the assessment framework may be informed by guidance (Horwath, 2001), including checklists and factors (DH, Cox and Bentovim, 2000) that are value-laden and based on evidence that does not acknowledge the normative assumptions behind it (Garrett, 2003). The guidance will need to be considered reflexively by Sally (Taylor and White, 2000), ensuring that she understands the ways in which knowledge is created and used to understand people. This will allow her to think about how the questions she is advised to ask and the issues she is advised to raise may lead in particular directions, rather than ensuring that they are relevant to the particular family she is working with. Milner and O'Byrne (2002) discuss how specific theoretical perspectives influence the process and outcome of assessments, and Sally will be aware of the often competing knowledges that make claims to understanding people.

Calder and Hackett (2003), while generally welcoming the assessment framework, criticise the fact that it conflates community and societal considerations into one domain, that is, 'family and environmental factors', hence potentially downplaying the significance of the wider sociopolitical context. This is felt most acutely in this kind of scenario where racism, social isolation and fear of racist attacks are all likely to have a major impact on this family's functioning in the neighbourhood. This leads us into a consideration of the value of a community development approach.

Community development approach

In their fourth edition of a popular social work textbook, Coulshed and Orme (2006, p 264) acknowledge that debates about the relationship between social work and community work have been a common feature of social work literature. Some have argued that community work is a distinct form of practice and that social workers do not 'do' community work (Coulshed and Orme, 2006, p 264). Others recognise the importance of community approaches as a key part of social work. We tend to the latter view, believing that since communities can be a major source of support for individuals and families (as well, of course, as places of exclusion and isolation), community social work approaches should be an essential part of social work practice.

Community social work is described well in a review of the roles and tasks of social work that was published in the early 1980s. Twenty-five years on, the language that we might use today is likely to be rather different but the sentiments are nevertheless the same. The Barclay Report (1982) defined community social work as:

> Formal social work which, starting from the problems affecting an individual or group and the responsibilities and resources of social services departments and voluntary organisations, seeks to tap into, support, enable and underpin the local networks of formal and informal relationships which constitute our basic definition of community, and also the strengths of a client's communities of interest. (Barclay, 1982, p xvii)

This suggests a different way of thinking about social work to an approach that is based only at the level of individuals and families. Fundamentally, it is an approach that forefronts the 'social' in social work. It reminds us that local networks and relationships play a crucial part in people's lives. The task of social work therefore becomes one of supporting individuals in their communities: hence connecting individuals to the networks that exist, and where these are lacking, contributing to the creation of new associations. The report of the 21st Century Social Work Review in Scotland states that 'Social work services don't have all the answers':

> Tomorrow's solutions will involve professionals, services and agencies from across the public, private and voluntary sectors in a concerted and joined-up effort, building new capacity in individuals, families and communities

> and focusing on preventing problems before they damage people's life chances irreparably. (Scottish Executive, 2006, p 7)

This places social work services firmly in the context of other services, both universal (for example, health and education) and more localised (whether playgroups or food cooperatives). Social workers working in statutory settings do not have to become quasi-community workers. But they need to adopt a mindset which sees people in the context of their lives, not as atomised individuals or 'clients'. Writing from New Zealand, Munford and Walsh-Tapiata (2005, p 98) describe community development as 'a process and a way of perceiving the world'. They see it as a central means of working with indigenous people: valuing their cultures and practices and working collectively to bring about social change. An evaluation of family support services in England suggests that successful services are likely to be based in communities and offer preventative support before parents' difficulties get too severe (Statham, 2000). This is very much what Sally, as a qualified social worker working in a Family Centre, hopes for in her work with the Khan family.

Values

Anti-oppressive practice

Anti-oppressive practice places emphasis on the impact of wider structural issues, including social class, 'race' and ethnicity, gender and sexual orientation, age and disability. It is argued that the existence of oppression is not an accident; instead, it is built into society, and is a means of maintaining the (unequal) status quo within society. Anti-oppressive practice has been the main expression of critical ideas since the late 1980s. One of its major exponents, Lena Dominelli (2002a, p 6), defines anti-oppressive practice as:

> A form of social work practice which addresses social divisions and structural inequalities in the work that is done with 'clients' (users) or workers.... Anti-oppressive practice embodies a person-centred philosophy, an egalitarian value-system concerned with reducing the deleterious effects of structural inequalities upon people's lives; a methodology focusing on process and outcome; and a way of structuring social relationships between individuals that aims to empower service users by reducing the negative effects of hierarchy in their immediate interaction and the work they do.

Anti-oppressive practice is relevant in all situations and with all service user groups, not just in work with minority ethnic individuals and families. Although different kinds of oppression exist, they tend to occur at the same time, so that, for example, an older person who is experiencing oppression based on age may also experience oppression based on gender or disability. This does not suggest that there is a hierarchy of oppression – that one is more serious than another. Instead, it suggests that many service users experience multiple forms of oppression, operating at the personal, the cultural and the social level. Thompson (1997) has been influential in anti-oppressive practice theorising and in taking forward the PCS (Personal, Cultural, Social) model of conceptualising structural oppression. This can be a useful starting point for thinking about how structural forces may influence people's lives. The broader social structures of 'race', class, gender and so on influence how culture, communities and families work, which in turn has an impact on the personal lived experience. These categories provide a framework for recognising the importance of wider issues and may assist in avoiding the pathologising of individuals.

Turning to our scenario, Sally must take into account issues to do with 'race' and ethnicity, social class, age and gender in her work with the Khan family. This means that, from the outset, she will have to think reflexively about her own age, ethnicity and class, and how these may influence the assessment. As a white woman in her forties, she inevitably carries some power, based on her more mature years and her ethnicity, although this may be complicated, for example, by her position as a woman in a sexist society. But just as importantly, as a social worker, she brings power related to her professional status. Sally's analysis must also be firmly rooted in her understanding of the nature of oppression. So she will seek to find out if Naz's reluctance to leave the shop is to do with fear of racist attacks; furthermore, she will want to ascertain to what extent poverty is having an impact on choices and opportunities available to family members.

Gender must also be considered. Much of what is written about parenting assumes that it is the mother who will take the role of primary carer for children in a family. Although this seems to be the situation in the Khan family, it will be important that Sally does not make assumptions without first checking this out for herself. Recent research has shown that fathers are often excluded from discussions about children and parenting and so-called 'family centres' and 'parents' groups' are frequently women-only environments, which can make men feel unwelcome (see Featherstone, 2003). Sally must also avoid viewing the Khan family as 'total' victims of structural oppression, as this may reduce professional expectations of their capabilities and inhibit service user agency, creating a situation of dependency on expert judgement (Healy, 2005).

Sally will want to keep these issues at the top of her agenda as she sets out to conduct an anti-oppressive assessment with the Khan family. She will start by explaining to Mr and Mrs Khan what an assessment is, and why it has been requested. She will then seek to involve them at every stage as her assessment progresses, and to identify, with them, ways forward that would allow them to achieve their desired quality of life.

Cultural competence

The notion of 'cultural competence' has been gaining in prominence within social work and social work education in recent years. This seems to carry with it the promise that if only students can be taught certain 'facts' about different cultures, they will be able to act appropriately. Our scenario demonstrates that knowledge about cultural difference is not enough to ensure good practice; on the contrary, it might even be harmful, by leading practitioners to make stereotypical assumptions based on their (inevitably limited) knowledge. Ideas about how 'Asian' families work will tend to deny the differences within this category and reduce individual choice and agency. A contemporary analysis suggests that much more is needed to achieve cultural competence. Husain (2006) argues that becoming culturally competent necessitates working on three interrelated and interdependent components: cultural knowledge, cultural awareness and cultural sensitivity. She adds that this commitment must be demonstrated at all levels to be effective, including the organisation's policy framework, service administration, and manager and practitioner training. O'Hagan (2001, p 235) makes a similar observation. He suggests that. first and foremost, workers must 'approach culturally different people with openness and respect – a willingness to learn. Self-awareness is the most important component in the knowledge base of culturally competent practice.'

Sally Main will wish to work with the family in ways that show sensitivity and respect, so that Naz and Jamal do not feel undermined or disempowered. Taking this further, she will seek to identify ways of empowering Naz, and involving her in the life of the Family Centre might be one step towards achieving this. There is an assumption, of course, that the Family Centre already has a culturally appropriate group (likely to be women only), which Naz can access. Although legislation may place on public agencies an imperative to promote race equality, the reality is that many services still operate on the basis of 'treating everyone the same'; in other words, they function as white services, with little attention to difference and diversity. It may therefore be that one of the major outcomes of this case is that Sally works with others in the community (including the Khan family) to develop local resources for Asian families.

Underpinning knowledge

Child development theories

Child development theories assume that there are sequential steps through which all children can be expected to progress, and that these are demonstrated in physical, cognitive, social, emotional and moral growth. These stages are often linked to children's ages, although Daniel at al (1999) point out that the sequencing of developmental milestones is more consistent than the actual age at which they are attained and there can be considerable variation between different children at the same age. Child development theorists assume that it is possible to make a distinction between normal healthy behaviour for a particular stage of development and those aspects of behaviour that might be an indication of unmet developmental needs. For further details of two frequently used theories, see Erikson's (1959) eight stages of psychosocial development and Piaget's (1952) stages of child development.

Fawcett (1996) brings a word of caution about developmental theories. She argues that psychological research on children's ages and stages has primarily been carried out by middle-class, white men, and that the objects of their research have been predominantly middle-class mothers and their small families. She reminds us that for many children the world over, this bears little resemblance to their lifestyles. Not only this, she suggests that much of what we know about childhood is based on our own, very particular, biographical and cultural experiences, and we should therefore be wary of making assumptions about others. Nevertheless, Fawcett believes that some kind of guide to milestones or steps in general development is helpful.

As already stated, the *Framework for the Assessment of Children in Need and their Families* (DH, 2000a) asks a set of key questions related to the child's developmental needs:

(1) *Health*: including growth, development, physical and mental well-being;
(2) *Education*: covers all areas of the child's cognitive development from birth onwards; including opportunities for pay and interaction with adults and children;
(3) *Emotional and behavioural development*: is concerned with the child's responsiveness to others, and with attachments, temperament and self-control.
(4) *Identity*: focuses on the child's growing sense as a separate and valued being; feelings of belonging and acceptedness;

(5) *Family and social relationships*: covers the development of empathy and the capacity to place oneself in someone else's shoes; relationships with parents/caregivers and peers;
(6) *Social presentation*: concerns growing understanding of own appearance and behaviour; age/gender appropriateness; cleanliness, personal hygiene and so on;
(7) *Self-care skills*: focuses on acquisition of skills for increasing independence.

Using this framework, there may be concerns about Jamila on a number of counts:

- *Health*: she is small for her age, and is reported to be spending hours in a confined space where she cannot run about and where there is little scope for physical challenge and development. If her mother Naz (with whom she spends most time) is not talking with her enough, there may be a delay in her acquisition of language. Jamila may also have some (as yet unidentified) disability that is affecting her capacity to relate to others, such as a hearing or sight impairment. This will need to be checked out by the health visitor.
- *Education*: Jamila may not be getting sufficient opportunity for play and stimulation. If Naz has little English, there may also be difficulties in Jamila getting enough exposure to the language that she will need once she goes to school.
- *Emotional and behavioural development*: the health visitor has said that Jamila is a 'clingy, demanding' child. Daniel et al (1999) stress that there is a strong association between maternal depression and behavioural difficulties in young children. In addition, Weir (2002) indicates that severe postnatal depression carries particular risks for babies and young children and several child fatalities have occurred in these cases.
- *Identity*: this links with an earlier point. If Naz does not feel good about herself, it seems reasonable to assume that she may be communicating this to her daughter.
- *Family and social relationships*: again, the lack of contact with others may be seen as a cause of Jamila's behaviour.

Attachment theory

Attachment theory, with its origins in the work of John Bowlby (1969), provides one of the fundamental principles on which social work practice is based. Howe (2003) argues that most children, even in situations of abuse and neglect, develop a selective attachment relationship to their main carer.

Childcare practitioners must therefore examine the quality and character of that attachment; understanding parent–child relationships provides the key to understanding children's behaviour, mental states and developmental processes (Howe, 2003, p 375). Howe offers a brief review of the main theoretical features of modern attachment, paraphrased here as follows:

- The baby arrives with a number of automatic behavioural systems already in place; the attachment system is activated when the young child feels anxious, frightened, distressed or confused. Children are also born prosocial: there is a universal human need for attachment.
- The combination of attachment behaviour and prosocial behaviour results in infants forming a clear-cut attachment to a primary attachment figure and possibly a number of other secondary attachments by about seven months of age. With the attachment bond comes an affectional relationship, which leads to psychological and social understanding.
- Children who find themselves in caregiving relationships that are broadly sensitive, loving, consistent and responsive develop secure attachments. Where these are not present, children may develop one of a number of problematic attachments, including insecure attachments, avoidant attachments, ambivalent attachments and disorganised or controlling attachments. The majority of children brought to the attention of childcare agencies show insecure attachment (Howe, 2003, p 385).

It seems reasonable to assume that if Naz is depressed (as has been suggested), Jamila may be presenting insecure attachment. However, Sally will have to be careful not to jump to hasty conclusions. There are major differences between individuals as to what constitutes 'normal' and 'acceptable' self-presentation and behaviour for adults and children; what is more, there are differences within groups. Dwivedi (2002) points out that Western culture's emphasis on independence, nuclear family life, and direct and clear communication is at marked variance to the value placed on dependability, extended family life and indirect communication in Eastern culture. This has an impact on behaviour and also, of course, on how that behaviour is perceived by others. But, Dwivedi continues, 'in real life there are enormous variations'; as some traditional practices change and die out, others are adopted in their place. He writes (2002, p 59):

> Due to global communication and influences of other cultures and their media, it is now becoming hard for the cultural transmission of traditional values to take place smoothly whether in the east or the west, even within societies where those values actually originated.

This suggests that Sally will have to adopt an open approach to the issue of attachment, while acknowledging that identification of this as an area of concern may provide a helpful way forward in working with Naz and Jamila in the future.[8]

Sociology of childhood

Sociology has influenced greatly our understandings of children and childhood. Although classical sociology had little interest in children (Cree, 2000), from the mid-1980s onwards, there has been an explosion of sociological research into, and writing about, children and childhood. Sociologists have been keen to find out why it is that as children become an increasingly scarce commodity in the developed world (as the birthrate falls), so their childhoods have become increasingly regulated and controlled. Ferguson (2004, p 131) argues that the child has become 'the focal point of a re-enchantment of private relationships and intimacy'. This creates incredible pressure on children and childhood. On the one hand, children are more protected now than ever before. Their childhoods are increasingly 'curricularised' (Ennew 1994), as they move from one controlled setting to another, from playgroup to school to university, from dancing class to piano lesson to youth club. At the same time, there is a furore when something goes wrong and a child is harmed; with so much control in place, how could a child have slipped through the net? Sociologists point out that this outcry of public sentiment is in marked contrast to the developed world's lack of concern for the plight of millions of children who live (and die) in poverty in the developing world.

This is significant for our scenario. While Coaltown Family Centre may prove to be a helpful resource for Jamila Khan and her parents, it is possible that the family's situation would be better served without social work intervention, and instead by them getting support from their local mosque or Asian self-help project, that is, through a community development approach. This might allow Jamila to grow up to have a more positive self-definition as an Asian woman; at the same time, Naz might get more strength from the support of women in a similar situation to herself. This suggests that part of Sally Main's assessment should be about what resources are available beyond the Family Centre; in doing this, she needs to make a realistic appraisal of the potentially positive and negative impact of social work involvement.

Mental health

Psychology and sociology have both influenced theory and practice in the field of mental health social work. The psychologist Anthony Clare (1989) offers a useful breakdown of approaches:

- *Organic and biological approaches* emphasise genetic and physiological factors leading to preferences on the part of practitioners for physical treatments such as drugs, electroconvulsive therapy and psychosurgery.
- *Psychotherapeutic approaches* are based on the belief in the power of the helping relationship between the practitioner and the client.
- *Sociotherapeutic approaches* emphasise the social functioning and social capacities and skills of the patient or service user.
- *Service user approaches* argue that self-advocacy and self-help are more appropriate than professionally led work with people with mental health problems.

It is widely recognised that there is a gender component to mental health. Women are overrepresented in particular types of mental health problems, especially depression, as noted by feminist writers (see Prior, 1999). This may, of course, be in part related to men's greater reluctance to seek help. There are also special issues for black and minority ethnic people in relation to mental health. The Commission for Racial Equality notes that, in many instances, racial stereotyping prevents people from minority ethnic communities from receiving the recognition and treatment to which they are entitled. Moreover, the social and economic disadvantages facing minority ethnic communities in Britain, compounded by discrimination, racial hostility and insensitivity, have had, and continue to have, serious consequences for their health (www.cre.gov.uk).

Returning to our vignette, there are indications that Naz Khan may be experiencing depression. This may be related to physical, possibly hormonal, changes in the postpartum period and may also be social in origin. It seems likely that a GP opinion will be helpful in this instance. Sally will have to keep in mind both possibilities as she takes forward her work with this family.

Other forms of knowledge

In recent years it has been increasingly acknowledged that service users have struggled to have their feelings, wishes and needs heard in social work practices. In their interviews with those using children and families' social work services, Cree and Davis (2007) draw attention to the ways in which social workers' actions can totally disempower parents, leaving them feeling devastated. For example, a social service department's refusal to give Jason a loan to pay for his housing arrears led to him and his children being taken into care (thus costing the authorities substantially more money). Julie's story was a much more positive one, in which she felt valued and supported by her social worker, in spite of her drug problems. These, and other accounts of the impact of social work intervention, stress the importance of being transparent and being clear, while building good, trusting relationships with those who use services. (Relationship is explored in more detail in Chapter Eight.)

Conclusion

The focus of this chapter has been preparation and assessment in the context of social work with children and families. We have identified that there is a key distinction to be made between children in need and children in need of protection. Although the outcome in terms of intervention is likely to be very different, the process of assessment is the same (unless an early assessment has ruled out the necessity for further investigation). The underpinning thread throughout all the current legislation and programmes across the UK is that 'it's everyone's job to make sure I'm alright' (Scottish Executive, 2002). This is an optimistic message for social work and for those accessing social work services. It holds within it the possibility of people working together to support families who are excluded and marginalised; it suggests that, as a society, we share responsibility for caring for each other, and for society's children. The principles hold true for all service users, not only for families with children, and we explore these in further chapters. But there are risks for individuals and for society as a whole, in the increasing amount of surveillance and control that has accompanied these developments. We have suggested that, in order to work ethically and professionally, it is vital that, as social workers, we critically reflect on our role, and on the place of social work more generally. In this way, we hope that we can make a difference in this area of practice.

Notes

[1] See www.everychildmatters.gov.uk/deliveringservices/caf

[2] 1995 Children (Scotland) Act.

[3] The 1989 Children Act echoes the broad proposal contained in the Social Work (Scotland) Act of 1968, which states that it shall be the duty of local authorities to 'promote social welfare'.

[4] The first Children's Commissioner for England was appointed in March 2005, following similar appointments in Wales in 2001, and in Scotland and Northern Ireland in 2003.
[5] Since 1 January 2008 all local authorities in England have appointed Directors of Children's Services (www.everychildmatters.gov.uk).
[6] See www.opsi.gov.uk/acts/acts2000
[7] Social workers with specific child protection concerns also make use of the framework in the Department of Health *Orange Book* (DH, 1988) as an addition to the CAF. See Holland (1999) for a review of assessment frameworks.
[8] For a critical perspective on child development theories, see Taylor (2004).

Key questions

(1) How has the state's involvement in family life changed over the years?
(2) What does it mean to suggest that early intervention may draw more children under statutory surveillance and control?
(3) Whose job is it to protect children?

Further reading and resources

- Department of Health (2000) *Framework for the Assessment of Children in Need and their Families*, London: The Stationery Office.
- Dwivedi, K.N. (ed) (2002) *Meeting the Needs of Ethnic Minority Children* (2nd edition), London: Jessica Kingsley.
- Munro, E. (2007) *Child Protection*, London: Sage Publications.
- www.everychildmatters.gov.uk

4

Making a difference in intervention

Introduction

The focus of this chapter is Key Role 2 of the National Occupational Standards: that is, to plan, carry out, review and evaluate social work practice with individuals, families, carers, groups, communities and other professionals. This is subdivided into six units:

(4) Respond to crisis situations.
(5) Interact with individuals, families, carers, groups and communities to achieve change and development and to improve life opportunities.
(6) Prepare, produce, implement and evaluate plans with individuals, families, carers, groups, communities and professional colleagues.
(7) Support the development of networks to meet assessed needs and planned outcomes.
(8) Work with groups to promote individual growth, development and independence.
(9) Address behaviour that presents a risk to individuals, families, carers, groups and communities.

Vignette: social work in an Adult Services team

Magda Kaczynski is a white social worker based in an Adult Services team in a city in Wales. Originally from Poland, she studied an MA in Social Work in England three years ago and has been working in her current post since graduating. She has a 'hidden' disability of dyslexia for which she receives appropriate support from her employers.[1]

Susan is 45 years old and was diagnosed four years ago with multiple sclerosis (MS). She lives with her partner Dave (aged 47) in a suburb of the city, where they own their home. Dave works as an area manager for a company and his job takes him travelling around the country on a regular basis. Susan had worked in a bank since leaving school but is now unable to work. She and Dave have been married for 27 years. They have three children: John who is 26 and lives nearby with his partner and their two children aged four years and 18 months; Julie who is 24 and at university in London; and Hugh who is 17 and lives at home.

Hugh has been providing significant care for Susan since her diagnosis, which is of primary progressive MS, a type of MS that affects between 10% and 15% of those people with MS and often appears later in life (www.mssociety.org.uk/). Susan has symptoms which include motor coordination difficulties, acute periods of pain, muscular spasms and occasional difficulties in swallowing. She experiences mood swings when she sometimes feels depressed about her situation, particularly the contrast with her previous independence and her current reliance on intimate care by her family.

All the family members have been managing their situation well and have developed approaches that have responded to Susan's changing circumstances. Recently, Hugh decided to move to London to take up a job offer and to live with his sister. His parents support this, recognising that Hugh has to develop his career and life as his siblings are doing. This has created anxiety and concern about how Susan is going to be cared for and everyone is desperately trying to seek assistance in maintaining Susan at home. Susan has said that she wants the best for her children and will move into residential care if this is the only option.

Discussion

Families and individuals often find that their strengths and coping strategies are thrown into disarray by changing circumstances or events. The vignette reflects the ways in which disability can impact on people's preferred lifestyle, recognising that lives are dynamic and both the specific impairment and the social and environmental situation have interacted to generate a crisis for all concerned. Magda is faced with the task of assisting the family members to identify and achieve their goals, within the context of her role as a care manager of services. This raises questions about how she will engage with the family, working with Susan in the context of the family structure and support and providing services that are helpful in maintaining a lifestyle that they choose. She will need to consider how she will understand and make sense of Susan's disability in order to be respectful, promoting dignity and working *with*, rather than *for*, the family. This will be undertaken in the context of her knowledge of the services that may be available locally and the restrictions that may be placed on access to these.

Magda has experience of the structures and services available to support disabled people and had always wanted to work in this area. She is committed to providing the best service possible and needs to take into account the ways in which images and perceptions of disability can be problematic for professionals, the public and disabled people and their families. The progressive nature of MS will have to be taken into account, not just in planning but in acknowledging the emotional impact this may have on people. Magda knows that services for disabled people can be located in different organisations, with health, social care, self-help groups and financial support often scattered and difficult to negotiate, with a multitude of assessment protocols and criteria. She has to maintain an overview of these and assist in coordinating effective provision.

The specifics of the condition are new to Magda, who sensibly researches what is known about MS in order to share this with the family. She has found the website of the Multiple Sclerosis Society helpful, as this is a service user's perspective that allows her to gain some information about the condition and how others have experienced and managed this (www.mssociety.org.uk). Such information may be helpful in discussions Magda will have with Susan and her family, although they may well have accessed this and other sources themselves, and, given that they have lived with Susan's illness for the last four years, they are likely to be more knowledgeable than Magda is.[2] Of course, such information is helpful in a broad sense but Magda has to remember that the individual experience of MS varies and she needs to avoid making assumptions based on such knowledge. Detailed knowledge of a particular condition or impairment is not necessary, and Magda would be more interested in taking a value position about promoting independence in the community and exploring the local effects of MS for Susan and her family.

Magda's experience of her own disability has influenced her understanding of processes that claim to be helpful but can have limitations, as her assessment for her dyslexia produced a document that made general recommendations but had little relevance to the specifics of her learning needs. This was important for Magda, who recognised that there can be similarities between disabled service users and social workers and that she needs to incorporate this into her practice without assuming that her experience is the same as that of the service user. Recognising similarities can avoid constructing a professional–service user divide where the social worker is making decisions *for* people.

Legal and social policy context

A number of areas of legislation and social policy are pertinent to the situation in which Susan and her family find themselves, including legislation in relation to community care and, more specifically, disability legislation. First, however, we place this in its historical context.

Historical background

Concern about people with physical disabilities has a social and legislative context that can be traced back to the development of the welfare state in the UK in the 1940s, although Borsay (2005) identifies that there have been references within state policy since the Middle Ages. The 1946 National Health Service Act and the 1947 National Assistance Act, which provided the bedrock of the welfare state, both referred to providing for the needs of disabled people including financial, health and social care, establishing the role of the state in having a responsibility for the well-being of disabled citizens. Oliver and Sapey (2006) comprehensively chart the development of legislation that impacted on disabled people, identifying that the 1970 Chronically Sick and Disabled Persons Act codified much of the social welfare provision in this area and placed specific duties on local authorities, including (under section 1):

(a) the duty to inform themselves of the number and needs of handicapped persons in their areas; and
(b) the duty to publicise available services.

Section 2 of the Act outlined the services that should be provided following the above assessment of needs, which included practical assistance in the home; recreational facilities, both in the home and outside; travel facilities, either free or subsidised; social work support to families; adaptations to the home and special equipment including telephones; holiday arrangements; and meals (Oliver and Sapey, 2006, p 146).

Current legislative and policy framework

Despite subsequent changes, amendments and new legislation, the Chronically Sick and Disabled Persons Act provided a framework that still influences the organisation of services for disabled people. At the time of its introduction it was seen as providing recognition of the particular needs of disabled people in society and in allocating resources to ensure the participation of disabled people in civic life (Topliss and Gould, 1981). However, there were emerging criticisms of the Act that raised questions about the way in which disability was conceptualised; the role of the state and social work; and the resourcing of the requirements. Surveying the needs of disabled people does not always lead to comprehensive service provision, as resources are often dependent on financial and economic circumstances. The vagaries of local government funding affect the availability of such services. Linked to this is the variation in local government priorities, where crude spending on services has not been nationally consistent, so that different local authorities have provided different levels or elements of service. Where you lived often determined the type of service you received, with local authorities questioning the meaning and scope of the term 'duty' to provide services, often interpreting this in a limited fashion.

A further consequence of the wording of the Act was that the provision of services was dependent on assessing the general and specific needs of disabled people. If the local authority delayed or limited its assessments then ipso facto it was unaware of such needs and did not have to implement its duty to provide services. This latter point was recognised and addressed to a certain extent by the 1986 Disabled Persons (Services, Consultation and Representation) Act, section 4 of which established a duty on local authorities to assess the needs of a disabled person when asked to do so.

As early as 1981, Shearer (1981) raised questions about the way in which the Chronically Sick and Disabled Persons Act reinforced notions of dependency, by placing decision making in the hands of professionals and by providing goods and services for people rather than allowing them some autonomy or choice. This paternalistic approach was criticised as compromising the potential independence of disabled people and has been the subject of much concern by disabled people themselves. The 1990 National Health Service (NHS) and Community Care Act was intended to address some of these problems, particularly the lack of coordination between services, through introducing mandatory collaboration between health and social care provision. It also focused on a needs-led assessment, rather than one that was geared to responding to services that were available under section 2 of the Chronically Sick and Disabled Persons Act (Middleton, 1992). However, Oliver and Sapey (2006, p 148) identified that the NHS and Community Care Act was also designed to manage and restrict the financial costs of such care, leading to the situation where the NHS and local authorities 'institutionalised their boundaries and made assessment a far more instrumental process', which was contrary to the stated aims of the Act.

The NHS and Community Care Act also introduced significant changes to working practices for social workers, who had been the main providers of community care up to this point. Implemented in 1993, the Act established a care management approach to community care with the intention of providing 'joined-up' services, particularly with regard to health and social care provision. Social workers became assessors and coordinators of practical community support packages, a role that was also undertaken by other professionals or by newly created positions. (The Act is also discussed in the context of social work with older people in Chapter Five.) There have been many criticisms of the new system, not least that the value of a qualified social worker may seem superfluous if the tasks can be done by anyone. Concerns about the de-professionalising and managerially led aspects of the reforms have been raised (for example, Cowen, 1999), with suspicions that the new ways of working had at their heart a drive to limit resources in a world of budget constraints.

Lloyd (2002) argues that social work has demonstrated that it can make a significant contribution within care management, particularly where there is complexity. Based on principles of empowerment and participation, social work intervention was appreciated by service users, and evaluations of service highlighted elements of good practice. Lloyd identified these as including keeping the service user central; maintaining a holistic approach; and having an inclusive notion of quality. Keeping the service user central is aided through ensuring that any assessments are focused on the needs of the person, rather than within the context of available services and resources. If workers are consciously or unconsciously matching emerging need with organisational resources, then there is a danger that the specific needs of the individual will be lost or manipulated into these structures: a service-led rather than needs-led assessment. Paradoxically a service-led assessment may create a package of care that is more expensive than the one that is preferred by the service user, who may not require the formal provision on offer and may prefer to enhance their existing social/informal networks.

Taking an empowering approach can also be productive in itself, as many service users report that their self-worth is enhanced through active participation, an outcome that is valuable for quality of life but often difficult to measure (Priestly, 2000). Social work can also bring perspectives of holism to working with people, recognising that individuals are located within systems and structures that are intertwined and that to focus only on one aspect (that is, the individual, the family or the social environment) will not reflect the *wholeness* of the person's experience. Lloyd also raises the need to value different evaluation methodologies to ensure that the complexities of outcomes are understood. The bureaucratisation of care management may lead to an over-reliance on limited quantitative measurements, whereas qualitative approaches may well provide understanding of processes that are difficult to quantify through numerical calculation. Using a range of evaluative methods to assess interventions is helpful in promoting good practices.

Subsequent legislation has made some inroads into this situation, recognising that disabled people should have the right to decision making about their needs and circumstances. The 1996 Community Care (Direct Payments) Act gave local authorities the power to give disabled people money to purchase the services they require, which was made mandatory by the 2001 Health and Social Care Act. Since implementation of this Act in 2004, all local authorities must make this provision available, although the assessment of need (and calculation of financial support) remains with the authority. This changed the relationship between disabled people and social workers/care managers from monitoring and policing to one of supporting people to make informed choices about their services.

Research into the implementation of Direct Payments has found that there have been some barriers to the effective operation of the new scheme. The Joseph Rowntree Foundation commissioned a study in the North East of England (Hasler and Stewart, 2004) and found that there were four key elements that had to be addressed to ensure that the scheme was meeting its objectives:

- First, the culture and communication channels of the local authority had to change to accommodate the new expectations, as previous practices could inhibit full implementation.
- Second, there needed to be a commitment to valuing and consulting with service users, as their involvement was central to the success of the scheme.
- Third, the financial structures of the local authority needed to change to ensure that such payments were properly managed and delivered effectively.
- Fourth, the scheme was hindered by a lack of existing networks among staff and service users to share the introduction of a new way of working.

Overall, the benefits of Direct Payments were seen to be substantial, and the key message was one of the centrality of user involvement in planning, implementing, managing and reviewing the system.

The 1995 Disability Discrimination Act was another key legislative initiative that illustrated the increasing recognition of the rights of disabled people, although it has been severely criticised as being inadequate and ineffective. Gooding (1996) discussed the ways in which the Act made positive statements about eliminating discrimination, yet was constructed in such a way that it was inevitable that there would be confusion about definitions of discrimination, significant exemptions from the headline provisions and a concern with the costs of introducing equality. For example, although there were provisions to enforce access to services, there were exemptions for small businesses, and the Act did not create an effective structure to enforce the provisions. The establishment of the Disability Rights Commission assisted in the extension of some of the original provisions, including requiring organisations not to treat disabled people less favourably than non-disabled people, and to make reasonable adjustments in the provision of services to enable access by disabled people. These provisions directly affect the delivery of social work and social care services.

The 2005 Disability Discrimination Act amended the 1995 Act to insert the disability equality duty, known as the general duty. The duty is aimed at tackling systemic discrimination, and ensuring that public authorities build disability equality into everything that they do, and came into force in December 2006. Section 49A of the Act says that public authorities must, when carrying out their functions, have due regard to the need to:

- promote equality of opportunity between disabled people and other people;
- eliminate discrimination that is unlawful under the Act;
- eliminate harassment of disabled people that is related to their disability;
- promote positive attitudes towards disabled people;
- encourage participation by disabled people in public life;
- take steps to meet disabled people's needs, even if this requires more favourable treatment.[3]

The provisions of the Disability Discrimination Act were extended in December 2005 to ensure that certain conditions were recognised from the point of diagnosis, rather than when the symptoms became problematic. These conditions included HIV, cancer and MS, and allowed for planning for the future, rather than just responding to problems as they arose, as well as providing protection under the Act.

The 1998 Human Rights Act is also relevant to the circumstances of disabled people in a general way, providing further protection to ensure that civil, legal and political rights are maintained for all citizens. Disabled people can use this legislation to challenge unfair treatment and the Act provides a basic framework that social workers and services can use to assess the compliance of their practices with human rights.

The 1995 Carers (Recognition and Services) Act acknowledged that those who provide care for vulnerable people have a key role in maintaining their quality of life in the community, often avoiding the use of expensive state resources. Further to this, it was recognised that such caring was disproportionately undertaken by women and there were few services in place to support people. The Act provided for assessment of their needs and for the provision of welfare for them, and is a helpful legal framework to gain resources for what can be a difficult and demanding role. The Act has not been without its critics, in particular with regard to the way in which it can reinforce the dependency of disabled people on carers and view them as a burden to be managed (Oliver and Sapey, 2006, p 116). If used in a way that takes an individual approach to disability, it may continue to exclude disabled people from mainstream social activities. Caring for vulnerable people is complex, and not all carers are helpful all the time to disabled people. Abuse is not unheard of and ensuring that carers are recognised and supported needs to be undertaken without losing focus on the need of the disabled person to be as independent as possible.

Discussion

This overview demonstrates that there has been significant progress in recent years with regard to people with disabilities and their carers. There is little doubt that much of this movement has been prompted by demographic and economic changes and the activism of disabled people and their allies, rather than by honourable intentions. Because of improvements in medicine and in life expectancy, not only are people living longer, but also more people are living with disabilities and illness. At the same time, changes in employment and career expectations mean that there are fewer people available to provide daily, informal caring for family members who need it (see Cree, 2000). We saw in Chapter Two that the basis of community care has *always* been care by family members. In our vignette, Susan's partner and children want to care for her as long as possible, but she does not want to become a 'burden' to them. This is a familiar theme in community care social work, and one which we will pick up later in this chapter.

From policy to practice: planning and carrying out interventions

Returning to our vignette, Magda is aware of the legal and policy context of services for disabled people, including their rights and the role of the social worker in care management. In planning for intervention, she will draw on guidance and research to ensure that she is working with Susan and her family to inform them of the range of legal protection and the duties of the welfare services to meet her needs. This avoids 'information disability' (Davis and Woodward, 1981), where disabled people are unaware of what is available due to the complexities and different (and often obscure) locations of relevant information on issues of disability. Magda will plan to share with Susan the best ways to access information to enable her to make informed decisions. Being clear about her role will also bring clarity to the relationship and avoid confusion. Commentators such as Nichols (2003) maintain that social care professionals do not need specialist counselling skills to provide emotional support for disabled people; this is more appropriately provided as part of a care routine, blended into the overall care plan. This gives people the opportunity to identify, express and progress the normal emotional processes evoked by the situation.

Good assessment is the key to this and Magda may endeavour to take an 'exchange' model of assessment (Smale and Tuson, 1993) that recognises the strengths of the person and provides an approach that encourages the service user to articulate their needs, thus reducing the potential of imposing a service-led assessment. Smale et al (1994, p 68) argue that the exchange model is the desirable one within social care, stating that 'Routine, service-led "assessments" are the antithesis of an empowering approach to assessment and care management.' Fruin, who undertook a study for the Social Services Inspectorate, found that for people with physical disabilities, 'Many assessments were partial with an emphasis on deficiencies, lacking an holistic approach to the person being assessed' (2000, p 4). Establishing what Susan wants is central to effective assessment and Magda will need to hear her perspectives and those of her family, perhaps acting as a facilitator to clarify their concerns, hopes and ideas. We saw in Chapter Three how a strengths-based approach (Healy, 2005) can be helpful in generating constructive change and Magda may find this a helpful model for the family.

This chapter, however, focuses not on assessment but on intervention. Two models will be helpful in this situation: crisis intervention and a person-centred approach.

Models and methods

Crisis intervention

Social workers are often faced with people who are deemed to be in crisis, where their usual coping mechanisms are thrown into disarray due to events that they are unable to accommodate or cope with. Intervening in a crisis situation is common, but it is important to remember that, as Trevithick (2005, p 266) says, 'crisis intervention is often confused with crisis work'. Crisis intervention is a specific approach that is based on a theoretical understanding of people and not simply working with people who are experiencing extreme and sudden difficulties. Key writers in the field of crisis intervention have been Caplan (1964), Lindeman (1965) and Rapoport (1967), and in this model crisis is described as when people have their psychological balance, equilibrium or 'homeostatis' upset, with their usual coping mechanisms and strategies failing to enable them to adjust to the new circumstances. Crises are seen as inevitable, where something occurs that changes the expectations people had of their lives, such as illness or unemployment.

An assumption in crisis intervention theory is that when faced with a crisis people generally adjust to a state of psychological equilibrium, dealing with everyday events that may upset their balance through various techniques either that they have learned or that are biologically driven. It can be visualised through the image of rocking a boat, where a wave may upset the state of the boat and it may list, but its natural buoyancy will roll it back and then it will eventually go back to an even keel. It may be a bumpy ride but the boat seeks to gain some equilibrium despite the knocks it may take. The mind can be viewed in this way, taking emotional knocks but finding a way to regain its balance most of the time. When something happens that is unexpected (a large wave) or cumulative in its effects (a series of waves that do not allow for rebalancing), the mind 'capsizes' into a crisis state.

Based on the empirical work of Lindeman, the theory maintains that any state of disequilibrium usually lasts no longer than six weeks, and Trevithick (2005, p 267) identifies that there are three factors that need to be taken into account in regaining equilibrium: people's internal strengths and weaknesses (ego strength); the nature of the problem faced; and the quality of help provided. The theory is influenced by psychoanalytic approaches, particularly ego psychology, and requires considerable skill and training in order to provide the rigour required. Practitioners need to be familiar with the concepts of ego states, Freudian personality development, transference and countertransference and the techniques for understanding and supporting someone who may be in ego crisis (Kanel, 2003). Such work can be very difficult for the service user, as it can question their current ways of managing feelings and raise anxieties and fears from the past. Indeed, the service user needs to be robust enough to undertake this work, although it has the potential to support the service user to strengthen and further develop their coping skills and general functioning.

Magda may be faced with Susan and the family expressing the 'symptoms' of a crisis. Their usual coping strategies are failing to deal with the current situation, where a new event has created disequilibrium. However, this opens up opportunities to learn new and more robust psychological coping strategies and Magda could discuss with the family the potential for building their resilience. The theory requires swift intervention to take advantage of the potential for change during the period of emotional crisis so Magda will have to plan for this. She will be faced with people who are struggling to make sense of a situation and will have to ensure that the information she gives is clear and understood, as well as providing the space for the family to discuss the complex practical and emotional issues. The family may feel confused and not process information in the way that they normally do, as well as feeling paralysed and helpless with no way out of the situation (Beckett, 2006). There may be a temptation to make quick decisions in response to the crisis and Magda will need to be aware that people may change their views as they work through the problems. This can be exhausting for Magda as well, who will need to be supported in dealing with the strong emotions that arise.

A person-centred approach

A person-centred approach is based on the work of Rogers (1951, 1961, 1980) and is humanistic, with a strong belief that people know what the problem is and how best to deal with it, provided they have a relationship that offers the climate in which to grow. This emphasis on growth requires two main conditions, the first being the right conditions for growth and the second the conditions for a successful process in which to achieve change.

Rogers' ideas stemmed from a distrust of the conventional psychoanalytic approach that tended to pathologise people, and he had a more optimistic view of people, which accepted that they had a 'constructive directional flow' or 'constructive tendency' (Rogers, 1980) to make progress in achieving growth and in becoming self-actualised (Kirschenbaum and Henderson,1989). Person-centred counselling claims to release this directional flow with the person, allowing them to find their own way through problems and to develop their potential. It is premised on notions of relationships, where people develop a sense of self through interactions with others, becoming truly human through caring for ourselves and for others. In this theory, 'we do not begin to exist until we have related' (Milner and O'Byrne, 2004, p 121), thus the therapeutic relationship is the vehicle for promoting growth and change. Rogers was clear that if there is a constructive relationship then people will grow.

Person-centred counselling provides a relationship of respect and care, often described as a shared journey, where possibilities are explored and diagnostic categories are set aside so that people's defences and rigid emotional states become less pronounced, providing the opportunities for considering change. Problems come from difficulties in two areas: *conditions of worth* and *incongruence*. Conditions of worth are constructed when someone external sets expectations against which the person is judged. These conditions affect how the person values themselves, and can lead to high expectations that create difficulties when they cannot be achieved. Rogerian theory posits that people need to be valued for simply being themselves in order to have a true sense of their worth. This is described as *unconditional worth*, accepting ourselves for who we are rather than against the expectations of others. If unconditional worth is not present, then we may compromise our true self in order to respond to external expectations, leading to conflict between the self and the conditions of worth, what Rogers described as incongruence. Self-esteem is lowered as parts of the self (feelings and their expression) are denied in order to accommodate these external expectations. This can lead to a loss of the self, a lack of confidence in accepting and saying what we really want, trying to please others over our own needs and being led by the views and wishes of other people.

The person-centred social worker will support, accept and validate the feelings of the person, challenging times when they fall into self-criticism or avoid taking responsibility. If people have been subjected to persistent undermining of their self-worth (often in childhood) then they may internalise this and act in ways that confirm this external image of themselves. Such actions need to be questioned, as Rogers believed that if such negativity could be removed then people would be free to find their own way forward. Susan may have been subjected to external views of herself that are damaging, reducing her sense of self-worth through images of disability and illness that she has internalised. This will impair her abilities to make true decisions and to express her true feelings, perhaps leading her to going along with decisions for the benefit of others rather than herself. Magda will need to be aware of the potential for this and that Susan may be hiding her true wishes and needs.

Trevithick (2005, p 269) outlines three 'facilitative conditions' that the worker will need to create to enable a service user like Susan to work towards actualising her potential: unconditional positive regard, congruence and empathy. Unconditional positive regard is where the social worker accepts and values the person as they are. Taking a non-judgemental stance and demonstrating warmth, concern, care and respect are important skills in a person-centred approach, even when the person may express views that are problematic or repugnant to the social worker. Such acceptance is a prerequisite of growth and is enhanced by the congruence of the social worker; that is, being open about the social worker's feelings and attitudes, underpinned by being genuine and not hiding behind a professional role. Magda thus needs to engage with Susan as another person, rather than as a distant expert.

Empathy includes experiencing the service user's world as if it were their own, 'entering the private perceptual world of the other and becoming thoroughly at home in it' (Rogers, 1975, p 2), but without becoming enmeshed in the feelings. There is a balancing act to be made in demonstrating that the social worker has truly understood the other's feelings while maintaining the distance to be helpful in providing the conditions for growth. This empathy needs to be communicated through reflective questions about the person's feelings, checking out that the social worker has understood what the person is experiencing, as well as by facial and bodily expressions.

Milner and O'Byrne (2004, pp 126-7) summarise what is required to sustain a positive relationship to enable a service user like Susan to achieve growth:

- Be trustworthy, reliable, consistent, 'dependably real', open to be what you deeply are.
- Communicate unambiguously, be aware of feelings and able to accept and express them, listen to what is going on inside of Susan, be transparently real; no feeling relevant to the relationship should be hidden.
- Experience positive caring, warmth, liking, respectful feelings and attitudes towards Susan.
- Be strong enough to be a separate person from the other, respect your own needs as well as Susan's, so as not to become downcast when Susan is depressed.
- Permit Susan separateness. Do not induce conformity to your own views, but interact with Susan without interfering with her freedom to develop a personality different from your own.
- Enter fully into the world of Susan's feelings and meanings without evaluating or judging it, or trampling on any part of it; extend empathic understanding without limit.
- Accept each facet of Susan as she is, receiving them unconditionally.
- Be sensitive enough not to be threatening to Susan, freeing her as completely as possible to be herself.
- Free Susan from the threat of external evaluation or judgement, good or bad (even a good judgement conveys the power to judge).
- Meet Susan as a person in the process of becoming (not bound in the past) and do not label diagnostically, but confirm her potentiality. People behave as they are perceived, so if we are to have any hypothesis it needs to be positive.

A person-centred approach reminds us that service users are people who have feelings and hopes and are deserving of respect. The principles of practice (unconditional positive regard, congruence, empathy) are all ways of demonstrating such respect and can be useful (if often emotionally demanding) techniques for social workers. They are based on assumptions about people's mechanisms for change, and are more than simply 'being nice' to service users – they have a purpose based on a theoretical understanding of how people function. Magda will need to be aware of the underpinning theorising behind a person-centred approach if she is to practise in a reflexive way.

Values

How we think about or conceptualise disability influences the approaches, interventions and services that have been developed and implemented. Social work with disabled people has been criticised for using approaches that generate and maintain dependency in service users (Priestly, 2004), with damaging and disrespectful consequences. We will highlight two areas that are of special interest to our vignette: anti-disablism and identities.

Anti-disablism

It will be important from the outset for Magda to recognise that there are powerful negative images of disability and disabled people that will have an impact on her work with Susan and her family. Keeping Susan at the centre of the assessment, planning, intervention and evaluation of services will assist in empowering her to recognise her strengths. Magda may have to challenge some of the internalised disablist notions that the family may hold, and allow them to view Susan's situation as one of rights and participation, rather than charity and the 'generosity' of the welfare state. She may also, however, have to engage with her own prejudices and assumptions. Magda will therefore have to maintain a clear sense of Susan in context, avoiding making assumptions about her as a 'disabled person' and seeking to jointly identify the services that she may want with the aim of increasing her independence and self-worth. Although it may seem helpful to refer Susan to a group of other disabled people with the intention of providing mutual support, this may not be her preferred option and indeed has its own potential problems of segregating disabled people. As Knight (1981, pp 9-10) has wryly said: 'One disabled person is a disabled person, two disabled people are a field trip, and three disabled people are a rehabilitation centre.' This takes us into a discussion of identities.

Identities

Magda will need to be aware of how Susan may view herself as a woman, and how her current situation may negatively impact on her self-image. Myers and Milner (2007) discuss how the sexuality of disabled women may be compromised, but also how disabled women can adjust to their circumstances and develop new modes of sexual expression that accommodate their impairments. To assume that impairment automatically restricts and limits sexual behaviour does not accord with the research evidence. Swain et al (2003, pp 105-6) quote Paula, a disabled activist with MS:

> People say 'oh, you're a wheelchair user, this must mean that you can't have sex', and I say 'why' and they say 'you can't walk' and I say 'oh, you walk while having sex?'. Two of the best lovers I had were wheelchair users. They were more imaginative. They were more sensitive and they were not performing.

In order not to assume a completely negative picture, Magda may find it useful to ask questions such as:

- In what ways has your disability made you a stronger person?
- What is good about your body?
- What needs to happen for you to lead a fuller life? (Myers and Milner, 2007, p 98)

The issue of identities also affects Magda herself. She is a social worker and a woman. But she is also a Polish woman, and as such, she is one of the half a million Polish migrants who have come to work in Britain in recent years. Wales has itself seen an influx of Polish workers and other migrants, leading to some local unrest.[4] Magda's ethnicity may mean that she has some experience of discrimination and disadvantage, in her home country and in her adopted country. It is also possible that the family values that she has grown up with may be different from those of Susan and her family. For example, Susan's suggestion that she go into residential care might be a complete anathema to Magda, given her strong Catholic background. She will have to be aware of all this – in a reflexive way – as she engages with Susan and her family.

The identity of other family members is worthy of consideration, particularly given the increasing attention given to the role of men as carers in recent years (Phillips et al, 2006). The majority of carers (in a broad sense) in the UK are women; for example in the age range 45-64, 27% of women are carers compared with 19% of men, but men provide significant care for women in older age (Phillips et al, 2006). The role of men as carers has to a certain extent been ignored, marginalised or understood as different from that of women, yet in the care of spouses in older age the amounts of caring are similar between men and women. Dave, Susan's partner, may find himself in the position of redefining his identity as a carer, a reconfiguring of his masculine identity. Calasanti (2003) discusses how men who provide care for others receive more praise than women for taking on a role that is viewed as 'naturally' female. Rose and Bruce (1995) found that men who looked after their spouses with dementia were less likely to be distressed than vice versa, as they felt useful and productive, whereas the women tended to grieve for the loss of the relationship (Featherstone et al, 2007). The inclusion of men in caring is clearly important, and Magda will need to ensure that Dave has opportunities to become involved that are not based on stereotyped and fixed assumptions of gender.

Underpinning knowledge

Disability has been theorised in two main ways: the medical/individual model and the social model. Both can be seen to have influenced policies and practices with disabled people and both have their strengths and limitations.

The medical/individual model of disability

This model views the impairment of disabled people as being the cause of their problems, based on a normative assumption about the body and illness. Disability is a product of physical difficulties that require addressing to fit into the non-disabled 'normal' world. This can be seen in policies and practices that focus on assisting disabled people to adjust to an idea of normality through the provision of specific supports to achieve reasonable functioning in day-to-day living. Rehabilitation programmes are designed to either correct or change the physical condition towards a normative, able-bodied one. The focus is on the body of the person, rather than their social and environmental situation.

In addition to this are practices that assist the disabled person in 'coming to terms' with their condition, based on assumptions of psychological damage and emotional fragility. Both these approaches are deficit-led, assuming that disabled people have something missing or damaged and this needs correcting. It has been criticised on a number of grounds, not least that it leads social workers and other professionals to take the position of expert in diagnosing and treating the impairment, thus marginalising the views, knowledge and experience of the disabled person (Wilding, 1982).

When someone is facing a change in their non-disabled status, this model presumes that there are psychological adjustments that need to be made to be able to function normally. Psychotherapeutic theories are marshalled to provide an understanding of the processes that people are going through, particularly theories of loss and the ways in which this has emotional effects. This approach has borrowed ideas from the theorising undertaken on death, dying and grieving, especially the notion that people need to work through various stages to achieve a healthy emotional state. Susan may be viewed as struggling to adapt to her deteriorating condition, leading to her depression and mood swings. She is experiencing psychological difficulties in processing her grief at losing her independence and control over her body, requiring assistance in moving through these problems in order to cope with the impairment.

A focus on this internal world of the disabled person can lead to practices that seek to identify how well they have adjusted to their situation; what stage of grieving they are at; how they can be assisted in working through their stages and having a clear aim of being emotionally well adjusted to their situation. Feelings such as anger and depression are viewed as pathological aspects of psychological maladjustment, and the purpose of intervention is to recognise these as such and promote healthy responses. This approach has been criticised on a number of counts. One is that the assumption of stages to be worked through presumes a biological or developmental pattern to loss. Albrecht (1976, in Oliver and Sapey, 2006) identified that such models are premised on factors such as:

- An individual must work sequentially through all the stages to become fully socialised.
- There is only one path through the stages.
- An individual can be placed clearly in one stage by operational criteria.
- There is an acceptable timeframe for each stage and the entire process.
- Movement through the system is one way, that is, the system is recursive.

Fixed-stage models of understanding and working with loss can reduce the complexity of people's situation, marginalising what Thompson (2002b) identified as the cultural and sociopolitical factors that influence how people express and deal with such events. These models can be criticised as being overly deterministic, that is, they propose an absolute template for the process that must be adhered to otherwise there will be problematic consequences, and can lead to a narrowing of practice. Even when disabled people challenge assumptions made about their impairment they can be dismissed as 'in denial', a common psychotherapeutic term used in dealing with traumatic life events. Butt (2004) questions the blanket term 'trauma' to describe a wide range of events and responses, as this tends to reduce a complex series of interactions to a single concept, thus losing the specifics of the individual.

Neimeyer and Anderson (2002) also discussed the ways in which individual psychological dispositions, spiritual beliefs and social support systems combine to reconstruct the meaning of people's lives following loss. They proposed an alternative model of understanding loss – *meaning reconstruction* – where the three aspects of sense making, benefit finding and identity reconstruction are useful to consider. This highlights some of the problems with a stage model that tends to locate the problem within the person and their impairment, ignoring, for example, the importance of family in aiding their changing situation. Rather than focusing on internal pathology, it can be more helpful to think in terms of the changing relationship between the person and their environment.

Linked with this is the notion of disability as a personal tragedy, a view commonly held in the popular imagination, where disabled people are expected to be weighed down by the burden of their impairments, thus warranting concern and sympathy (Swain et al, 2003). Feeling sorry for disabled people is part of this, but they are also expected to be grateful for assistance. If someone manages to lead a life that confounds these expectations (overcoming their disability) then they are praised for their moral courage. These ways of understanding disabled people are patronising at best and have been criticised by disabled people as locking them into a victim status that is unhelpful and dependency-creating. Social work and other services can be experienced by disabled people in this way, with a consequence that if they argue for their rights then they can be dismissed as awkward, demanding or not properly adjusted to their disability.

Finkelstein (1980) articulated the problems caused by the imposition of an able-bodied construction of disability onto disabled people, including an assumption of able-bodied normality that sets the standard for disabled people to be measured by. The notion that disabled people need help is also problematised, as this help is provided through normative judgements about what their problem is and how to respond to it, rather than coming from the disabled person themselves. Oliver and Sapey (2006) also warn of the consequences of the introduction of new technologies that require forms to be completed to assess need based on the individual model. These tend to categorise people through a checklist of impairments, producing assessments that reduce people to a list of factors designed for bureaucratic need rather than engaging with the person. Such approaches are used to define but also limit the services required. Magda will need to reflect on how some of the forms she is required to complete on Susan and the family may limit or influence the outcome of the assessment she undertakes, ensuring that the voice of the service user is not lost or distorted by these protocols.

The social model of disability

The increasing criticisms by disabled people and their allies of the individual model have led to a change in focus away from the deficits of people's bodies to how the social, cultural and environmental context can be in itself disabling. The physical and ideological structures of society limit the freedom, choice and independence of people with impairments, and the social model asks questions about how society can change to include disabled people, rather than requiring disabled people to change to fit a normative able-bodied society.

The Union of Physically Impaired Against Segregation (UPIAS, 1976, p 4) produced a useful position statement that redefined the terminologies used to make this point:

> Thus we define impairment as lacking part or all of a limb, or having a defective limb, organism or mechanism of the body: and disability as the disadvantage or restriction of activity caused by a contemporary social organisation which takes no or little account of people with physical impairments and thus excludes them in the mainstream of social activities.

This encapsulates the change in philosophy; no longer is the person with impairments viewed as the object to change, but society needs to reflect on how it excludes/disables people from full citizenship and participation. An obvious example is access for people with restricted mobility. Aids and adaptations can be given to the person to enable them to access buildings more effectively, focusing on their deficits and rectifying these. However, the social model would identify how such buildings are designed for an able-bodied norm, questioning how their construction can be changed to enable maximum access for all people. Even this can be problematic if there is an assumption that non-disabled people know what is appropriate for disabled people. At one university a lift was installed to facilitate access for people who could not use stairs. Unfortunately the lift was not large enough to accommodate an electric wheelchair, thus excluding some students. This could have been avoided at design stage by proper consultation with disabled groups, rather than imagining (for benign reasons) that a lift was in itself a good idea.

The construction of physical environments to a supposed able-bodied norm has consequences for housing and other services, such as social work buildings (Beresford and Oldman, 2002). Thinking about how to maximise access, safety and utility is a major task that would benefit from disabled service user involvement, ensuring that services are as unrestricted as possible. Because impairments are so varied, it is important to avoid blanket assumptions about disability, including the tendency to see all people with impairments as one category called Disabled. An example of this can be found in the social expectations of employment, where assumptions about disabled people as of limited economic worth can reinforce notions of dependency. This can become self-fulfilling, as work patterns and environments may exclude disabled people from participation, thus forcing reliance on welfare. Rethinking employment policies and practices can provide opportunities for disabled people to participate in economic life, which is a mark of status and engagement in our society.

The social model of disability is helpful in rethinking what the purpose of social work practice is. It assists in remembering that there are consequences of a narrow focus on the individual as the problem, recognising that the difficulties a disabled person encounters are often the product of how disability is thought of, and structural barriers to full participation. This is not to exclude the importance of the individual experience of disability or impairment, but to place this in the context of a society that has traditionally devalued, dehumanised and been discriminatory towards those who have impairments. A consequence of the dominant individual model held by society has sometimes been the internalisation of disablist attitudes by disabled people themselves (Reeve, 2002), which can create misery and reduce personal agency. If you are bombarded by negative images about disability then it is likely that these will affect the image you have of yourself. The social model can provide a useful and empowering counter to these ways of thinking that disabled people have found helpful.

The social model can also provide opportunities to consider how disability is experienced differently through, for example, issues of 'race', class and gender. Disabled people are not a homogenous group, and other structural discriminations need to be taken into account. A black service user may have to negotiate the added complication of services that are geared to an assumed white norm, rather than being appropriate for their specific needs, as well as racist assumptions about who they are (Begum et al, 1994). Recent research in Wales has explored the ways in which gender is constructed locally, with certain expectations of the role of women. Scourfield (2006) identified that there were stereotypical notions of women that were not always helpful for them and benefited from questioning.

Caring

Latest government statistics suggest that around six million people (11% of the population aged five years and over) provided unpaid care in the UK in April 2001. While 45% of carers were aged between 45 and 64, a number of the very young and very old also provided care. Under the age of 65, a larger proportion of women than men were carers. The number of hours of care given was related to age, with a higher percentage of older carers providing 50 or more hours a week. The proportion of carers providing this level of care rose sharply from age 65. The percentage of people aged 16 to 64 providing unpaid care does not vary greatly by social group. However, there was a clear variation across the social groups in the number of hours of care provided. Over a fifth (22%) of carers in routine occupations and nearly two fifths (37%) of carers who had never worked or were long-term unemployed provided 50 or more hours of care per week. This compares with less than one in ten (8%) of carers in the higher managerial and professional group.[5]

Research studies show that people who may require care hold on to their independence for as long as they can, struggling alone at home, or in the marital relationship, before admitting that they need help (Cree, 2000). The older people interviewed by Qureshi and Walker (1989) were acutely aware that they did not wish to become a burden to their children. When care became inevitable, they preferred their care needs to be met in the family, first and foremost by their spouse or an adult who shared their household. This finding has, however, been challenged by research conducted with people with disabilities. Morris (1995) indicates that it may be more satisfactory, and more empowering, to pay an outside person to provide care; the introduction of Direct Payments has been widely welcomed by disabled groups and individuals.[6]

Other forms of knowledge

The social model has been criticised for marginalising the real physical difficulties that people with disability and chronic illness experience. Not all the problems faced by people are the result of social reaction. Pain and physical impairment have real bodily and emotional consequences that cannot be explained away as simply socially constructed. Crow (1996) argues that impairment needs to be recognised within the social model and that this enables the complexities of individual circumstances to be recognised.

Conclusion

The social work role in working with disabled people is currently undergoing change due to legislative and policy changes, not least the creation of Care Trusts by the 2001 Health and Social Care Act (see further implications in Chapter Seven). Nonetheless, Magda will bring her professional value system to work in an empowering way with Susan and her family, marshalling resources that will assist Susan to have the best quality of life possible. Susan may well decide that she would rather manage her entitlements herself, using the cash allowances to purchase care that is within her control. Magda will assist in the monitoring of this and in jointly reviewing with Susan the effectiveness of the care support. Changing circumstances will need to be anticipated and planned for in any evaluation, with Susan's wishes being at the centre of any services. Social work can have a positive impact on people's lives, through maintaining a focus on the service user; taking a holistic approach; and understanding the complexities of what constitutes a positive outcome (Lloyd, 2002).

Notes

[1] Magda's employers have provided her with a laptop computer, and a senior social worker proofreads her reports before they are sent out.
[2] Some service users have chosen to be called 'experts by experience', in recognition of the expert knowledge that they bring by virtue of their experience as users of services. See *Social Work Education*, Themed Issue, 2006, vol 25, no 4.
[3] See www.drc.gov.uk
[4] See 'Don't Misunderstand Us: Agnieszka's Story', www.bbc.co.uk, Wales North East, 5 March 2007.
[5] See www.statistics.gov.uk
[6] See www.carers.gov.uk

Key questions

(1) What is the difference between a 'needs-led' and a 'service-led' assessment?
(2) What does it mean to suggest that it is society that disables individuals?
(3) How does illness and disability affect all family members, and what might social work do to help?

Further reading and resources

- Milner, J. and O'Byrne, P. (2004) *Assessment in Counselling: Theory, Process and Decision Making*, Basingstoke: Palgrave Macmillan.
- Oliver, M. and Sapey, B. (2006) *Social Work with Disabled People* (3rd edition), Basingstoke: BASW/Palgrave.
- Rogers, C.R. (1980) *A Way of Being*, Boston, MA: Houghton Mifflin.
- www.drc.gov.uk

5

Making a difference in advocacy

Introduction

The focus of this chapter is Key Role 3 of the National Occupational Standards – to support individuals to represent their needs, views and circumstances. This is subdivided into two units:

(10) Advocate with, and on behalf of, individuals, families, carers, groups and communities.
(11) Prepare for, and participate in, decision-making forums.

Vignette: social work with an older person

Brenda Jones is a social worker with an Adult Services team in a large, rural English county. Her role is to assess the needs of older people in the community to ensure that they can maintain their independence and dignity. The county has great disparities in wealth, with many people living in poverty, poor housing and excluded from services due to geography, limited public transport and resource limitations. The area her team covers is huge, requiring significant travelling that needs careful planning to ensure that her time is managed well. Brenda is a black woman originally from an urban area who moved to her current position when her partner gained a well-paid position with the armed forces.

Mrs Gray is a white woman of 84. She lives on the outskirts of a small village some 20 miles from the nearest market town. Her husband died some years ago and she has no relatives who live locally. Mrs Gray is dependent on the state pension and a small annuity from her husband's work as a railway employee. Recently, Mrs Gray has become 'absent-minded' and there are concerns that she might be in the early stages of dementia. If this is the case, she may be at risk of harming herself through neglect or accident. Her neighbours have been 'keeping an eye' on her. Mrs Gray's physical health is good and she enjoys growing her own vegetables in her garden. However, this is becoming increasingly demanding for her. She has said she does not want help and that she can manage on her own.

Discussion

There is much for Brenda to consider in this scenario. Mrs Gray's problems are clearly made more difficult by physical and structural factors. Rural poverty is recognised as being a particularly problematic issue, compounded by images of the countryside as inhabited by wealthy people and structured by semi-feudal relations. Travel and access to services are key issues for those who live in isolated areas, and quality of life can be severely compromised by a lack of resources (Best and Shuckworth, 2006). Social isolation has been identified as a common risk factor for depression, anxiety, suicide, delirium and even types of dementia (*UK Inquiry into Mental Health and Well-Being in Later Life*, 2007).[1] Brenda must ensure that Mrs Gray has access to the services she needs and she must also safeguard Mrs Gray so that she is not left 'at risk' of harm to herself.

Legal and social policy context

There have been massive changes affecting the UK population over the last 50 years or so. In 2003, there were 20 million people aged 50 and over in the UK, representing a 45% increase since 1951. The number has been projected to increase by a further 36% by 2031, when there will be 27.2 million people aged 50 and over. Projections have also indicated a more rapid ageing of the population over the next 30 years or so. By 2031, it is predicted that people aged 85 and over will comprise 3.8% of the total UK population.[2] In 2005, 43% (£16 billion) of the total NHS budget and 44% (£7 billion) of the total social services budget was allocated to those aged 65 and above (Healthcare Commission, 2006, p 5).

Demographic change has a number of social and economic implications. As more people are living longer, so more people with poor health (mental and physical) are living longer, and so require treatment for longer. Moreover, there are more older women in poor health.[3] As the age structure of the population changes, so there are proportionately fewer people paying taxes and National Insurance contributions (which fund social and health services). The falling birthrate also means that fewer children are available to care for their elderly relatives. Older women are more likely to live in poverty, relying heavily on state benefits, often without occupational pensions (Crawford and Walker, 2004). And so the list goes on. Successive governments have struggled to manage the consequences of this demographic shift, and social work with older people has been at the nexus of legislative and social policy change.

Historical background

Chapter Two stated that in mediaeval times, sick, older people who had no family to look after them often found themselves in the care of the Church or monastery. By the industrial era, they were more likely to be supported through the Poor Law by the 'parish', the local town or county authorities, which raised money through a mix of local taxes ('rates') and church collections, or, as in the example given in Chapter Two, by the care of a voluntary charitable organisation. For most older people in need of help, assistance would be provided at home (known as 'outdoor relief'). They would be given a small sum of money (a 'pension') each week, and some assistance 'in kind' (this might be coal, clothing or food). The unlucky ones would be forced to turn to the workhouse or poorhouse for 'indoor relief', where conditions were deliberately harsh in order to discourage people from seeking help. This has been called the 'less eligibility principle': the idea that any services that are provided for poor people should be of a standard and quality that is lower ('less eligible') than the conditions of the poorest independent labourer. Of course, older people were not able to work and, arguably, this condition should not have applied to them. They, alongside disabled people, were considered 'deserving' as opposed to 'undeserving' poor (for example, unemployed men, single women with children) and hence were more likely to receive relief at home. But the amount of financial help provided was very low, and many people were unable to manage on the sums given. In addition, there was no free health service for those who were sick or disabled;[4] the infirm wards within the workhouses offered the only means of medical care for many poor people. Because of this, workhouses and poorhouses were full to overflowing by the end of the 19th century with poor, sick, older people (Cree, 2002).

The 20th century, as we have argued, saw a gradual acceptance of the idea that a minimum level of care should be provided by the state. Liberal reforms at the beginning of the century were followed during and after the Second World War by a programme of social legislation that promised to tackle outright the five giants of 'Want, Disease, Ignorance, Squalor and Idleness' (HMSO, 1942) and remove all trace of the stigma attached to the Poor Law. The principal systems of provision included social security and pensions, the National Health Service, education, family allowances, housing and planning, childcare and national assistance, and the aim was to end social inequality for all. It should be emphasised here that social work was not envisaged as one of the mainstream, general services. It was seen, from the outset, as a *residual* service whose task was to rescue and rehabilitate the small number of people who fell through the welfare net. Three separate local authority departments were set up in 1948 to meet social work needs: children's departments for children deprived of a 'normal' family life; health departments for people with mental health problems and people with learning disabilities; and welfare departments for older, physically disabled and homeless people (Cree, 2002).

The new welfare departments were very much 'Cinderella services': they had few staff and their range of coverage was very broad. Meanwhile, there was growing concern for the experience of older people in residential care. Research by Townsend (1962) was highly critical of residential institutions for older people, arguing that they should be closed in favour of care in the community. This was followed soon after by *Sans Everything* (Robb, 1967), which presented a damning indictment of care for older people in general and psychiatric hospitals. The 1970 Local Authorities Social Services Act (England and Wales) and 1968 Social Work (Scotland) Act created new generic social services and social work departments, bringing together the previously disparate services under one roof, offering universal personal social services for all; 'through one door on which to knock' (Seebohm Committee, 1968). It would be wrong, however, to assume that from this point on, older people were given the care they required at home and, where necessary, in institutions.

From the 1970s onwards, the policy driver has been towards community, rather than institutional, care. Large residential homes have been closed as have long-stay hospital wards, in favour of small, locally based units, sheltered housing and home-based care. There have been different reasons for this. At the top of the agenda, inevitably, financial considerations play a part. Care within institutions is vastly more expensive than supporting someone at home. There are also medical explanations, however. Modern medical treatment means that it is now possible for someone to live a relatively independent life at home, and successive research studies have demonstrated that this is where people *want* to live (for example, Qureshi and Walker, 1989; Arber and Ginn, 1992). In 1990, building on the Griffiths Report of 1988,[5] the National Health Service (NHS) and Community Care Act heralded major reforms to community care services, reflecting the then Conservative government's philosophy of 'individual choice, the value of free-market competition and the merits of financial prudence and accountability' (Crawford and Walker, 2004, p 39). One of the biggest changes resulting from this legislation as it affected older people was that the local authority now became responsible for the first time for assessing and arranging residential care for older people in the public and independent (private and voluntary) sectors.[6] Two other key pieces of legislation at this time also impacted greatly on practice. In 1995, the Carers (Recognition and Services) Act gave carers the right to ask for an assessment of their own needs as part of the assessment being carried out on the person being cared for. This was soon followed by the Community Care (Direct Payments) Act of 1996, which gave local authorities the power to provide cash payments to individuals so that they could arrange and purchase their own care services. (See Chapter Four for a fuller discussion of community care legislation.)

Current legislative and policy framework

The New Labour government, elected in 1997, then again in 2001, took forward the initiatives already begun under the Conservative administration, this time under the guise of 'modernisation'. The White Paper *Modernising Social Services: Promoting Independence, Improving Protection, Raising Standards* (DH, 1998a) was quickly followed by three other White Papers, all with the aim of modernising public services. Crawford and Walker (2004, p 40) suggest that the modernisation agenda set out to tackle the following broad areas:

- supporting independence, developing prevention strategies and promoting well-being;
- protecting vulnerable people;
- improving standards and regulation, including staff development, organisational learning and training;
- equality of access to services across England;
- a partnership approach to working across the whole system, including the participation of service users and the wider community.

In 2001, *The National Service Framework for Older People* was published (DH, 2001), promising to 'look at the problems older people face in receiving care in order to deliver higher quality services'.[7] The standards are central to Brenda's work with Mrs Gray; we therefore reproduce them here in full:

> **Standard 1: Rooting out age discrimination:** NHS services will be provided, regardless of age, on the basis of clinical need alone. Social care services will not use age in their eligibility criteria or policies to restrict access to available services.
>
> **Standard 2: Person-centred care:** NHS and social care services treat older people as individuals and enable them to make choices about their own care. This is achieved through the single assessment process,

integrated commissioning arrangements and integrated provision of services, including community equipment and continence services.

Standard 3: Intermediate care: Older people will have access to a new range of intermediate care services at home or in designated care settings to promote their independence by providing enhanced services from the NHS and councils to prevent unnecessary hospital admission and effective rehabilitation services to enable early discharge from hospital and to prevent premature or unnecessary admission to long-term residential care.

Standard 4: General hospital care: Older people's care in hospital is delivered through appropriate specialist care and by hospital staff who have the right set of skills to meet their needs.

Standard 5: Stroke: The NHS will take action to prevent strokes, working in partnership with other agencies where appropriate. People who are thought to have had a stroke have access to diagnostic services, are treated appropriately by a specialist stroke service, and subsequently, with their carers, participate in a multidisciplinary programme of secondary prevention and rehabilitation.

Standard 6: Falls: The NHS, working in partnership with councils, takes action to prevent falls and reduce resultant fractures or other injuries in their populations of older people. Older people who have fallen receive effective treatment and rehabilitation and, with their carers, receive advice on prevention through a specialised falls service.

Standard 7: Mental health in older people: Older people who have mental health problems have access to integrated mental health services provided by the NHS and councils to ensure effective diagnosis, treatment and support, for them and their carers.

Standard 8: Promoting an active, healthy life: The health and well-being of older people is promoted through a co-ordinated programme of action led by the NHS with support from councils. (DH, 2001, pp 12–14)

The National Service Framework made clear statements about the need to change attitudes, policies and practices to reflect the evidence of exclusion from mainstream services. The government has funded several initiatives to promote the aims of the National Service Framework, including Partnership for Older People Projects (POPPs) and Champions for older people (www.ageconcern.org). POPPs are designed to provide local services to improve the health and well-being of older people and can take several forms as long as they meet these aims. Champions are designated people within the local health and social care services and structures who have a specific responsibility to ensure that the needs and wishes of older people are considered in the planning and delivery of services.

These initiatives are already under review, demonstrating the continuing importance attached to the needs of older people and the financial and resource implications of future trends. The Green Paper *Independence, Well-Being and Choice: Our Vision for the Future of Social Care for Adults in England* (DH, 2005); the White Paper *A New Ambition for Old Age: Next Steps in Implementing the National Service Framework for Older People* (DH, 2006); and the report by the King's Fund *Securing Good Care for Older People: Taking a Long-term View* (King's Fund, 2006)[8] all provide further evidence that the issue requires significant planning to ensure a good quality of life for older citizens.

One final piece of legislation merits attention here. The expressed aims of the 2005 Mental Capacity Act[9] are 'to clarify a number of legal uncertainties and to reform and update the current law where decisions need to be made on behalf of others'. It governs decision making on behalf of adults both where they lose mental capacity at some point in their lives, for example as a result of dementia or brain injury, and where the incapacitating condition has been present since birth. The Act replaces previous legislation in this area and covers a wide range of decisions, on personal welfare as well as financial matters. Five principles underpin the Act:

(1) A person must be assumed to have capacity unless it is established that he [sic] lacks capacity.
(2) A person is not to be treated as unable to make a decision unless all practicable steps to help him to do so have been taken without success.
(3) A person is not to be treated as unable to make a decision merely because he makes an unwise decision.
(4) An act done, or decision made, under this Act for or on behalf of a person who lacks capacity must be done, or made, in his best interests.
(5) Before the act is done, or the decision is made, regard must be had to whether the purpose for which it is needed can be as effectively achieved in a way that is less restrictive of the person's rights and freedom of action.

For the purposes of this Act, a person lacks capacity 'if at the material time he is unable to make a decision for himself in relation to the matter because of an impairment of, or a disturbance in the functioning of, the mind or brain'. The Act says it does not matter whether the impairment or disturbance is permanent or temporary, but that lack of capacity cannot be established merely by reference to age or appearance, or physical condition or behaviour. Any question as to whether a person lacks capacity must be decided 'on the balance of probabilities'.

Discussion

There is little doubt that the direction of social policy and legislation over the last 10 years or so has been positive for the care of older people. However, there is a common saying, 'the proof of the pudding is in the eating'. So it is with social work and social care relating to older people. It is evident from recent reports that reforms have not been evenly introduced across the country, and instead a 'postcode lottery' exists, where some counties are better resourced and supported than others. There are specific differences within this broad picture, with mental health, cancer and heart disease being singled out as particularly bad examples of this trend.[10] In addition, Direct Payments have not been introduced across the board and, again, the lowest take-up has been in relation to mental health.[11] There is also some evidence that government targets to decrease waiting lists have led to an increase in emergency readmissions to hospital. Official figures for 2006 revealed that the number of NHS emergency readmissions had risen by nearly a third since 2002, from 5.3% to 7.1%. The consequence is that Brenda Jones's work with Mrs Gray is, in practice, likely to be affected by budgets and resources as much as it is by need and choice.

From policy to practice: advocating with individuals and families

In working with Mrs Gray, Brenda's overall aim will be to enable her to remain as independent as possible, for as long as possible. She will wish to give her support mentally, physically and emotionally. Brenda is, of course, not alone in this work. At the outset, she will work closely with the GP in terms of the assessment of Mrs Gray's health and care needs; a consultant geriatrician may also be consulted. She will engage neighbours and family members (even though they live at a distance) in discussions about supporting Mrs Gray, and she will investigate other possible avenues of care, such as voluntary agencies, day centres and support groups.

Older people often have needs that fall within the responsibility of different service providers, and it has been recognised that this can lead to a range of professionals undertaking their own specific assessments and interventions in an uncoordinated way. Interventions may be duplicated or people can fall between the gaps in service provision. The introduction of a Single Assessment Process (SAP),[12] where one worker undertakes the assessment and shares the information with other relevant agencies, has the potential to provide a more comprehensive and coherent assessment (Sharkey, 2007). The older person is central to this process and all information should be shared with them. A range of assessment tools can be used (see www.cpa.org.uk/sap) and computerised information sharing is key to this.

Models and methods

Advocacy

Advocacy has been described as a 'central skill within social work' (Trevithick, 2005, p 232), although it is a term that covers many activities. Thompson (2002a, p 66) suggests that 'being an advocate involves representing the interests of people who are unable to do so themselves', while Schneider and Lester (2001, p 65) say that 'Social work advocacy is the exclusive and mutual representation of a client(s) or a cause in a forum, attempting to systematically influence decision making in an unjust or unresponsive system(s).' Thus, advocacy can mean representing ideas, groups or individuals where their own ability to do so is restricted. This will be familiar to many social workers, where speaking up for people and arguing for their right to services and just outcomes is common.

Beckett (2006, p 120), developing the ideas of Brandon and Brandon (2001), identifies two main types of advocacy in social work: direct and indirect. Direct advocacy can include micro-work such as writing to a social housing agency making a case for rehousing an individual service user, and macro-work such as arguing for changes to policies and legislation that affect groups of people. Micro-work in indirect advocacy can be supporting individuals or groups to complain about their services and ensuring that the wishes of the individual are being heard in any assessments or planning. Macro-work in indirect advocacy includes having a supporting role in helping communities to organise and argue for change, for example in the provision of youth services.

Beckett makes a useful distinction between acting *at a client's request* and acting *in their best interests* (Beckett, 2006, p 118). The focus on a 'pure' advocacy of only supporting what the service user has articulated as their needs has its limitations, as some service users (for example, a baby) are unable to say what they want, or may not be in a position to make decisions that acknowledge danger. Nonetheless, the notion of advocacy reminds us that acting in the best interests of someone may actually be contrary to their wishes, be disempowering and carry the danger of being the opinion of the worker and agency rather than the person.

Bateman (2000) argues that a central concern of advocacy is the promotion of people's rights, ensuring that people are informed of and supported in acting on their legal and statutory entitlements. If someone is being harassed by a landlord, discriminated against because of their colour or being paid below the minimum wage, then there are certain legal protections that can be called upon. Taking a rights-based approach to practice again assists in ensuring that people are empowered to understand and act as independent citizens, rather than as passive recipients of charity, professional judgement and structural disadvantage. Similarly, advocacy is needed because some people are structurally marginalised and excluded by practices, thus making it more difficult for their voice to be heard (Beckett, 2006, p 121). Systems, organisations and their individual representatives may treat people disrespectfully because of who they are, which 'category' they belong to and how they are perceived. Someone who is older may find that their views are excluded due to images of the capabilities of old age; a child's opinions may be dismissed as being the product of attachment disorder; someone with mental health problems may have their capacity to make judgements questioned; a father may have his wishes for his children dismissed because of assumptions about gendered roles. Advocating for and with people recognises that our society is structured in ways that curtail full participation for some people and seeks to redress this in practice.

Advocating for people is therefore a satisfying and productive role for social workers. However, the opportunity and ability to undertake this is influenced by several factors, including the specific setting in which social workers are employed. Some voluntary organisations have a particular brief to provide advocacy services for people, and this will be the key role for anyone employed by them. Other social work situations may constrain this role, especially those where there are statutory obligations. Beckett (2006, p 123) identifies six factors that complicate the ability of social workers to undertake advocacy:

(1) Where the social worker is a control agent then the wishes of the person may be over-ridden. Child protection work is an example of this, as the wishes of the service users are not paramount.

(2) Where the social worker is a responsibility holder then decisions may have to be made that do not coincide with those of the service user. A child who lives in a children's home may wish to stay out all night, but this may compromise their long-term interests and safety.

(3) Where the social worker is a care manager or almoner with responsibility for limited resource allocation then an effective advocacy for one user may compromise resources for another. In the desire to achieve a good outcome, such advocacy can also exaggerate the 'neediness' of the user and create problems of labelling.

(4) Where the social worker is a direct change agent, undertaking work to modify behaviour through challenging people, then this is unlikely to be defined as advocacy. If someone has behaved badly and requires

intervention to improve the safety of others it is difficult to see how a pure advocacy role can be sustained.

(5) An advocacy role can generate conflicts of interest, particularly when working with families and groups, as advocating for the rights of one person may compromise those of another.

(6) Taking an advocacy stance may bring the social worker into conflict with the duties and obligations of the employer, as the service user may be making a complaint against the employing service, or against another service which works closely with them.

Advocacy has strong connections with community development work, acknowledging that advocacy with an individual may assist in strengthening that person's skills, confidence and entitlements, but that the underlying causes of the disempowerment are still in place. Encouraging the formation and support of self-advocacy groups can be of great benefit to service users, and social workers can suggest to service users that joining such an interest group may be beneficial for them. Such groups are often based on a notion of a shared identity or issue, perhaps a group for single parents or people who have specific mental health problems. Self-advocacy groups help people in 'finding ways to speak for themselves in order to protect their rights and to advance their own interests', and this can be achieved through peer advocacy where people 'work together to represent each other's needs' (Trevithick, 2005, p 233).

Self-advocacy groups can play an important role in ensuring that social welfare services retain the sense of being there for service users. Service user representation is increasingly recognised as being important in the planning and delivery of social work and in social work education. Braye (2000) outlines four ways in which service users can participate in the development of social work:

(1) Individuals can be involved in their own services.
(2) Groups of service users can be involved in planning services.
(3) Service users can develop their own services.
(4) Service users can be involved in research and evaluation.

Service user involvement helps in constructing a service that is 'fit for purpose', as well as being empowering for those who participate. There may be questions about whether those service users who do participate are representative and such participation sits more easily with some groups than others. Nevertheless, one of the potentially positive ways forward for Brenda Jones in her work with Mrs Gray might be to link her to a dementia support group, or instead, to a local history group or community arts project in the village. (See Chapter Three for an exploration of community social work.)

This discussion demonstrates that it will not be easy for Brenda to be Mrs Gray's advocate. While this will be her goal throughout her work, she has responsibilities for Mrs Gray's safety, and if anything should go wrong (for example, Mrs Gray wanders off and gets lost, or has a fall in her garden), her relatives (and the general public) will see her (and her employers) as negligent to some degree. Fook (2002) argues that advocacy can be practised in ways that accept the complicated and often contradictory nature of social work. In accepting that power can be used productively, social workers can take an advocacy stance that recognises that not all agencies are 'unhelpful' and that not all service users are blameless for their situation. Each circumstance requires a particular response that addresses local needs, maintaining a respectful approach that is aimed at gaining what the person wants. This suggests that Brenda will need to be honest and clear in her communication with Mrs Gray and her relatives, so that everyone understands from the outset the nature of the situation (and the risks) in which they are involved.

Task-centred social work

A task-centred approach to social work is often cited as one of the most frequently used problem-solving models that workers use in their practice. Doel (2002) locates the development of the model in North American casework, where Reid and Epstein (1972) built on research that had identified the effectiveness of short-term interventions to create a therapeutic approach that was brief and goal-oriented. Reid and Shyne (1969) had found that when interventions that were originally planned as longer term were shortened, the outcomes were the same as or better than for those who continued in longer-term therapy. Shorter term was defined as lasting about eight sessions, and there was no difference in the sustainability of the outcomes between long- and short-term interventions. The setting of a time limit to work focused attention and generated motivation to achieve the task, rather than a more open-ended approach that potentially allowed for 'loose, diffuse and rambling work' (Epstein and Brown, 2002, p 143).

Healy (2005, pp 111-12) discusses the controversy that this approach created at the time. Social work interventions had been dominated by casework, heavily influenced by psychodynamic theory (Woods and Hollis, 1990), which expected problems to be deep-rooted and to require intensive and long-term specialist input to address these difficulties. Reid and Shyne (1969) in contrast proposed time-limited, structured and focused interventions to solve problems, which challenged the assumptions of psychotherapeutic models where people were encouraged to move at their own pace (with the expert guidance of the worker) to understand 'deep' emotions and experiences. The task-centred approach was aimed at tackling immediate and presenting problems in a business-like way, rather than concerning itself with underlying emotional and psychological states.

Marsh and Doel (2005) is a UK key text in outlining the method, and claims to be an appropriate approach to use in a variety of social work settings and with a range of social work service users. Healy (2005, p 112) provides a synopsis of the 'problems in living' that the method was recommended for:

- interpersonal conflict;
- dissatisfaction with social relations, such as social isolation;
- problems with formal organisations;
- difficulty in role performance;
- problems in social transition, such as entering or leaving an institution;
- reactive emotional distress, such as anxiety provoked by a traumatic experience;
- inadequate resources, such as lack of money or housing.

Although the above list does exclude some issues such as chronic psychiatric illness, proponents have increasingly claimed that the model is useful across all social work interventions.

A task-centred approach is a model rather than a theory in the sense that it does not prescribe what sort of understanding of people is used as long as the intervention abides by the core principles of being short term, focused and structured. A variety of theoretical perspectives can be brought to bear on understanding and dealing with a problem, which could include psychodynamic, behavioural, cognitive or other approaches, thus the model requires an in-depth engagement with a wide knowledge base (Epstein and Brown, 2002). In itself, the task-centred model does not provide a singular and coherent theoretical basis for intervention; it provides the structure in which to apply the most appropriate knowledge to practice. Healy (2005, pp 113-15) usefully summarises the key practice principles of the model; these are represented below, together with some further discussion of what they may mean in practice.

- 'Seek mutual clarity with the service users.' Healy argues that there needs to be mutual clarity about the purpose and processes of intervention, so that the work is open and transparent. Agreeing what needs to be done and how to do it is a joint project between worker and service user, establishing verbal or written contracts and a clear timescale for achieving and reviewing progress.

- 'Aim for small achievements rather than large changes.' What Healy is drawing attention to here is the reality that goals that are about the radical and wholesale transformation of someone's situation are rarely achievable; instead, small but significant changes can be more helpful in building confidence and generating further change.
- 'Focus on the "Here and Now".' Healy reminds us that the focus of work is very much on the immediate situation rather than dwelling on the past. Agreement needs to be made about the priority of problems, focusing on a limited (and therefore more achievable) number of them (a maximum of three is recommended). Exploring the service user's past is not essential, except in thinking how such experiences may affect the solving of the problem.
- 'Promote collaboration between worker and service users.' Collaboration and partnership are central to the model, argues Healy, with active participation from both the service user and the worker. The role of the worker is a directive one, providing advice and guidance on problem solving and in ensuring that the service user is motivated to achieve the tasks agreed.
- 'Build client capacities for action.' Healy indicates that service users often lack the skills or resources to address a problem, and the worker will assist in developing both these areas in a way that is locally relevant to the person. The service user is supported to develop their capacities and capabilities to deal with the here and now, rather than necessarily resolving the structural and personal problems that may have led to the difficulties.
- 'Planned brevity.' Using this approach, interventions should be planned to be brief, so Healy points out that no more than 15 sessions over a three-month period would be a usual pattern. This focuses energies into achieving the tasks and recognises the research into positive outcomes. It also fits the agenda of busy social workers and organisations under resource pressures, as well as providing a minimum intrusive intervention into people's lives.
- 'Promote systematic and structured approaches to intervention.' Again, Healy suggests that the model is systematic and structured, which allows for clarity and accountability, as such an approach can be evaluated through clear boundaries and expectations. It provides a transparent framework that is flexible enough to respond to the specifics of individuals while remaining sufficiently standardised for effectiveness to be measured.
- 'Adopt a scientific approach to practice evaluation.' Healy concludes that the model lends itself to scientific evaluation on effectiveness, and task-centred practice is committed to the rigorous application of outcome research in order to provide the most effective interventions with service users. The model framework includes monitoring and reviewing that lend

themselves to measurement. This is important in a world of organisational performance targets, but also for a genuine desire to provide an effective service for people.

Doel (2002) outlines a framework of task-centred practice, identifying entry, three phases and exit as the preferred structure. Entry into task-centred practice highlights the need to clarify the context of the intervention, including the reasons why the service user is engaging with the worker. Although task-centred practice was developed with voluntary service users, Trotter (1999) discusses how these ideas can be successfully applied to those people who are mandated to social work, such as offenders and those where there are concerns about safety. The worker needs to be explicit about their role, including the limits to confidentiality and any reporting requirements about harm to people. The expectations of the service user can also be elicited, plus any practical arrangements about the location and timing of meetings.

Phase 1: Exploring problems

Doel suggests that this first phase consists of a series of stages, to begin to be clearer about the nature of the problems. Problem scanning encourages the service user to identify all the problem areas in their life in a descriptive way, without providing any explanations or analysis of these. The worker can also contribute to this by suggesting other problems that the service user may be unaware of or reluctant to discuss, particularly where they are mandated for problematic behaviour. The worker can then ask for more detail about the problems to begin to clarify the nature and seriousness of them, and their significance for the person.

When the problems have been discussed, the worker and the service user agree to prioritise them in order to identify which ones they want to work on. Epstein and Brown (2002, p 155) recommend that no more than three problems should be selected. Selection is influenced by the feasibility of working on a particular problem, which will be considered, and whether this is the appropriate problem to address the reasons for the referral. If someone has been referred for being violent but wishes to work on their problem with filling in forms, the worker may raise questions about the relevance of such a strategy in achieving the purpose of the intervention. Healy (2005, pp 119-20) discusses some of the issues this raises about service user self-determination, as people may not share the professional concerns about them. Where there is potential harm to themselves or others, the worker will have to ensure that this is raised as a problem for targeting.

Phase 2: Agreeing a goal – the written agreement

Once problems have been selected, the next step is to identify and agree goals to address them. This needs to be explicit and clear, based on what the person wants, and linked directly to alleviating the problem. Task-centred practice often includes a written agreement (recommended by Doel, 2002), although this may be more necessary with mandated service users and a verbal agreement may be sufficient in some other cases (Epstein and Brown, 2002). Other media of communication can be used as appropriate for the abilities and skills of the service user. Doel (2002, p 195) identifies that goals should be 'within the clients' control to achieve; one which they are well motivated to work towards and which workers consider ethically desirable'.

An agreement (or contract) lends itself to clarity about the purpose of the work undertaken and promotes accountability. Healy (2005, p 121) suggests that the agreement should contain information about the practical arrangements of the work, such as the duration, frequency and location of meetings, so that both service user and worker can be held to account. Once these practicalities are established, attention can then be turned to identifying how problems can be prioritised and what goals need to be achieved to address them. In order to achieve the goals, the service user and worker agree a series of tasks that will move towards the goal. These tasks need to be detailed and explicit, clarifying who will do what, when, where and how. As task-centred practice is interested in developing the skills and capacities of service users, there will be an expectation that the service user will have a major role in deciding on and undertaking the tasks. As a counterbalance to this, Healy recalls Dominelli's (1996) caution that a mutually agreeable contract may not be achievable, as service users may feel obliged to enter into an agreement to receive resources, thus agreeing to work on areas that are not necessarily of their choosing. Practitioners need to be aware of the potential for disempowered people to appear to agree to joint initiatives, yet not feel in a strong enough position to assert their true wishes. The term 'contract' is loaded with legal ramifications, and service users need to be informed of the status of this contract and agree consequences for not achieving it.

Phase 3: Implementing the tasks

Doel (2002, p 195) makes the point that 'tasks' in task-centred work are not simply about doing something, a confusion that is often found in social workers' accounts of their practice. Tasks are 'carefully negotiated steps along the path from the present problem to the future goal. They build in a coherent fashion, sometimes completed in the session itself, sometimes completed between sessions, some for the user, some for the worker'. They have coherence and an aim, to achieve the agreed goal.

Setting tasks is the start; a key element of task-centred practice is to refine the problem and tasks as the work progresses to ensure that these are still relevant. Situations and circumstances change, so problems may disappear (financial problems may be dealt with by a win on the Lottery), be changed or be superseded by new problems. The worker has an important role in supporting the service user to achieve their tasks and goals. This can include a range of approaches, such as educational through providing information about resources, and confidence-building through encouraging the rehearsal of situations the user finds particularly difficult. The object is to enhance the skills and motivation of people to become stronger in dealing with their problems, skills that can be learned and transferred into other problem areas. There will be some tasks that are better, more appropriately or can only be done by the worker. These will be agreed and the rationale for doing this will be explained.

Task-centred sessions review the progress of tasks to ensure that they are relevant and working. If a task has been set and it has not been achieved, then there will be a discussion about this to learn new ways of working towards the goal, or enhancing the skills needed to achieve the task. Failure to achieve can be useful in developing understanding about the person and their life, although it may be emotionally difficult to fail. As the tasks are concrete and measurable it should be easy to know if they are achieved, although in some circumstances this may require third parties to provide evidence. This will have been agreed earlier in the process. If a boy says that they are managing their task to go to school, but the school informs the worker that this is not the case, then this communication with the school should not have been a surprise to the boy. Evidence sources should be made explicit.

Exit

The contract will have been explicit about the length of time of the intervention; therefore, the service user and worker will be fully aware of the deadline for completion of the tasks. As task-centred work is premised on the motivational impact of deadlines, it is only in rare cases that this timeframe will be extended, and in such situations the extension will again be time-limited and focused. This provides discipline for both the worker and the service user in achieving the goals, thus preventing drift, dependency and disempowerment.

The last session needs to review what has been achieved; how the tasks have been completed; to what extent the goals have been met; and what the service user has learned (skills and knowledge) from the process that can be usefully taken into their future lives.

A task-centred approach may, on the surface, seem a surprising model for Brenda to adopt in her work with Mrs Gray, given that she may have a long-term, progressive illness. However, Brenda's decision to use this approach comes about from an awareness that this will allow her to work in a positive, focused way with Mrs Gray. She will therefore work with Mrs Gray to identify what problems she wishes for help with (her memory, her isolation and her garden spring readily to mind). She will then seek to put in place resources to help with these problems, with the explicit understanding that when she does so, Mrs Gray will do her best to make use of them. Resources may include a way of remembering day-to-day things, such as use of a dictaphone, attendance at a weekly support group or day centre and someone to help with the garden. Brenda will then withdraw for the meantime, with the agreement that if Mrs Gray's mental health deteriorates, she will need to re-engage with her at a future point.

Values

User empowerment

Empowerment is a term that is used frequently in social work, yet it is not uncontested. Thompson (2002a, p 91) considers that the aim of working in an empowering way is to assist service users to 'gain greater control over their lives and circumstances', while Clark (2000) stresses the importance of ensuring that people have 'meaningful choice' and 'valuable options' in any social work intervention. Sharkey (2007, p 137) identifies two main approaches: consumerist and democratic.

A consumerist approach is concerned with providing a wider range of choice of services, based on the principles of the market. People are made aware of the different services on offer and make informed choices about which are the most suitable for their needs. There is a clear division between the purchaser (consumer) and the provider (service) that in theory should make services more responsive to people's needs. Inappropriate or poor services will not be used, whereas efficient and useful services will emerge from the consumer-led demand. In practice, there are difficulties with this model, as it assumes a free market in purchasing services (similar to shopping around for the best product to suit the individual), but what services are on offer may be limited and there may not be the resources available to purchase them. Service user choice may be illusory, as there is no involvement in the design of appropriate services and resource limitations can reduce options. Service user empowerment is limited to buying what is made available.

The democratic model (Carter and Beresford, 2000) is much more concerned with the involvement of service users in the planning, design and implementation of services. In the consumerist model, Mrs Gray may have a choice of purchasing care from two organisations in her locality, but she will have no say in the way they are established or in how they are operated. Her choice is about which service to use. In the democratic model she will ideally have been consulted about what sort of service would be appropriate and how she can be involved in the delivery of this. Participation is key to the operation of services in this model, with a sense of ownership and 'meaningful choices'. Rather than organisations providing services which people then choose (or not), service users (as experts by experience) are involved in constructing the service itself.

Barr and Hashagen (2007) reproduce the idea of a 'ladder of empowerment', suggesting a series of steps to achieving a democratic model, identifying how various approaches can be seen as working towards full participation. These can be used to assess how initiatives are really underpinned by a commitment to empowerment:

- manipulation – creating an illusion of participation resulting in disempowerment;
- informing – telling people what is planned;
- consultation – offering options and listening to feedback;
- deciding together – encouraging others to provide additional ideas and join in decisions about the best way forward;
- acting together – deciding together and forming partnerships to act;
- supporting independent community interests – helping others to do what they want.

If user empowerment is to have meaning, then practitioners need to consider how their policies and practices enable service users to be at the heart of planning and delivery, rather than an afterthought. Of course, this may throw up some ethical dilemmas, as service users may prefer services that have consequences for others. If Mrs Gray decided that she did not want her respite care home to be open to black and minority ethnic or non-Christian users, then service user choice conflicts with values of anti-discriminatory practice. Service user choices may well be made within the context of oppressive discourses, and this complexity will need to be negotiated.

Anti-ageism

Social, theoretical and professional discourses about the lifecourse often make assumptions or stipulations about how we should think, feel and behave within particular age groupings. Thus our expectations of a six-year-old are different from those of a 16-year-old and a 60-year-old. Ageism is the term used to describe the 'social processes through which negative images of and attitudes towards older people, based solely on the characteristics of old age itself, result in discrimination' (Hughes and Mtezurka, 1992, p 220). This discrimination has significant effects on the quality of life of older people, resulting in marginalisation and particular expectations of 'growing old'. These tend to be notions of increasing frailty, lack of capacity and dependence on others, with a consequent lack of hope for any future. However, these discourses of age deny the complexities of individual situations and circumstances, as older people are not a homogenous group but have as varied mental and physical capabilities as younger adults. Older people can become ill and recover; they have a past, a present and a future, although this latter aspect is often neglected.

Images and expectations of older age are reinforced by theoretical and professional ways of thinking, so for example a strong belief in the inevitable and progressive biological decline of older people can reduce hope for the future and lead to questions about the usefulness of some medical and welfare interventions. Erikson's (1995) lifecourse theory makes certain assumptions about the psychological well-being of older people, proposing that older people need to come to terms with their life history in order to achieve integrity, rather than despair and a fear of death. Such an expectation can lead to older people being pathologised if they do not demonstrate that they are comfortable with their life circumstances (Crawford and Walker, 2004).

Ageism is complicated and compounded by other structural factors such as ethnicity. The tendency to create a category called 'old age' can reduce the differences within this, and there are consequences for those service users from a non-majority ethnic heritage. Perceptions that minority ethnic groups have strong family networks that provide for older people can lead to professional expectations that affect service delivery. Katbamna et al (2004) studied the experiences of carers in Asian communities in the UK and found that they were no more likely to receive wider family or social support than the majority white population. Assumptions about how minority ethnic families operate can lead to discriminatory practices and prevent individuals from receiving appropriate services. However, it is important to bear in mind that minority ethnic groups will have pressures on them that the majority do not, and immigration and asylum/refugee laws are an example of factors that may contribute to a wariness of engagement with state services.

Brenda will be committed to promoting the independence of Mrs Gray and in making sure that she is aware of the services and choices available. In this context, ageism, location and poverty will all have to be taken into account.

Underpinning knowledge

Dementia

Dementia is a term used to describe various different brain disorders that have in common a loss of brain function that is usually progressive and eventually severe. There are over 100 different types of dementia; the most common are Alzheimer's disease, vascular dementia and dementia with Lewy bodies. People with multiple sclerosis, motor neurone disease, Parkinson's disease and Huntington's disease can be at an increased risk of developing dementia. Symptoms of dementia include:

- loss of memory (for example, forgetting the way home from the shops, or being unable to remember names and places);
- mood changes (these happen particularly when the parts of the brain that control emotion are affected by disease; people with dementia may feel sad, angry or frightened as a result);
- communication problems (a decline in the ability to talk, read and write).[13]

A 2007 report provides a full picture of the extent of dementia in the UK (Knapp and Prince, 2007). It indicates that there are currently 700,000 people with dementia in the UK, and it predicts that this will rise to 950,000 by 2021. The report states that dementia is most common in older people. One in five people over the age of 80 has a form of dementia; dementia affects one in 20 people over the age of 65. It is also disproportionately experienced by women: two thirds of those with dementia are women. Most of those with dementia are cared for at home; again, the broad figure for this is around two thirds. The authors state that £17 billion is spent on care and informal care on dementia every year, and they estimate that carers for people with dementia save the government about £7 billion a year. The authors conclude that more support needs to be given to carers, and that the government needs to make dementia a priority, setting aside money for dementia care in its comprehensive spending review. They also propose that staff working in this field need to have adequate knowledge of legislation, signs and symptoms, and principles of care.

One of the report's key recommendations has particular relevance to Mrs Gray's situation. It argues that people with dementia need improved home care support packages, including low-level support to retain their independence and dignity. The authors state:

> Stated national policy focuses on early identification and intervention. However, local authorities across the country have been skewing access to home care support towards people with the highest levels of need. It is now very difficult for people not classed as having substantial or critical levels of need to access services. As the population ages and the number of people with dementia increases, this situation will worsen. (Knapp and Prince, 2007, p 83)

They recommend that the number and extent of home care packages must be increased, and that home help services such as help with cleaning, shopping, DIY and gardening must be brought back. Moreover, the opportunities for people with dementia and carers to access Direct Payments and individual budgets must be increased. This mirrors the approach that Brenda Jones is using in her work with Mrs Gray.

Structural perspective

It is important in approaching her work that Brenda Jones does not see Mrs Gray's problems simply as individual or medical ones. We have already explored the social model of disability in Chapter Four. This suggests that it is society which disables people, by excluding them from full citizenship and participation. Mrs Gray's situation therefore needs to be considered in its social context. It also, however, needs to be considered in its structural context.

Research indicates that poorer people tend to live shorter and have less healthy lives than wealthier people (McLeod and Bywaters, 2000). Older women are subjected to the sexism of society through specific images of how they should be, resulting in health and welfare practices that marginalise and exclude them (Orme, 2001). The specific difficulties faced by minority ethnic groups have been known for some time. For example, Norman (1985) described the 'triple jeopardy' faced by older people of minority ethnic background of low socio-economic status, racism and ageism, which has been reinforced by subsequent research (DH, 1998d). Older people are therefore not a homogenous group, although they are often treated as such.

In reviewing theories around age, gender and class, McMullin (1995) notes that mainstream sociological theorists, by fore-fronting class, have overlooked gender and age relations. Subsequently, feminist theorists who set out to explain women's experience paid little attention to age, just as ageing theorists tended to underplay gender relations. The result has been an incomplete theorising of the connections between age, gender and class. McMullin rejects an 'add-on' approach to theory-building, where gender is added to an analysis of age; or where age is added to a feminist analysis. Instead, she argues that social class should be understood as being structured through age-based and gendered (and, we would argue, 'race' and ethnicity-based) relations of distribution and production.

Mrs Gray is an older person and also a woman. In addition, she is a white, working-class woman, with no financial 'nest-egg' on which to rely. Her experience will therefore be structured by her age, gender, class and ethnicity, as it will be by her sexuality and, of course, her illness. This does not suggest any hierarchy, where one factor 'tops' the other. Rather, her experience should be understood as one of interconnecting and interlocking structures.

Other forms of knowledge

Research has consistently shown that older people do not want to be 'a burden' to others, either to family members or to others in their community. They want to look after themselves, and significant numbers are involved in care for others – for partners, children and grandchildren (see the discussion of caring in Chapter Four). Studies have also shown that friends play an important role in the social networks of older people, substituting for family in situations where no such help is available (Phillipson et al, 2001).

In interviewing older people for their study, Cree and Davis (2007) found that older people were clear about what they liked and did not like from their social workers and carers. They did not like to be patronised (to be called 'flower', for instance) and they wanted choice. They also wanted workers to live up to their promises; as Annette describes, 'It was wonderful. I expected them to do things and they did and they anticipated what I wanted from them' (Cree and Davis, 2007, p 133).

Conclusion

This chapter has explored the complex challenges inherent in supporting an individual who may be 'at risk' so that she can live an independent life for as long as possible. We have argued that Mrs Gray, like all people with whom social work interacts, must be treated as an individual, not as a 'problem'. Her illness must therefore be given proper attention and care, but at the same time, her circumstances and situation must be analysed in their social and structural context. The *National Service Framework for Older People* (DH, 2001) provides a good starting point for supportive, enabling work with older people. It is only to be hoped that funding can turn this rhetoric into reality.

Notes

[1] See www.mhilli.org
[2] See www.statistics.gov.uk/focuson/olderpeople
[3] See www.statistics.gov.uk
[4] The wealthy paid for private medical treatment; others who could afford it (that is, those in regular paid work) set aside a sum of money each week or month as part of a contributory scheme to pay for medical care.
[5] The Griffiths Report envisaged a new role for social services departments, as purchasers rather than providers of care. Care managers would allocate resources and set priorities; practitioners would assess individual cases. See Griffiths (1988).
[6] Up to this time, a higher level of income support funded care, without the requirement of an assessment by a social worker.
[7] See www.dh.gov.uk
[8] Also known as the 'Wanless Report'.
[9] See www.opsi.gov.uk/acts/acts2005/en
[10] See www.heartstats.org
[11] See www.pssru.ac.uk; Davey et al (2007).
[12] The language of 'Single Assessment Process' is in an English context. In Scotland the terminology is 'Single Shared Assessment' and in Wales 'Unified Assessment' (Sharkey, 2007, p 73).
[13] See www.alzheimers.org.uk

Key questions

(1) How do the ways that older people are presented in the media affect our views of old age?
(2) What does it mean to suggest that society is experiencing a demographic time-bomb?
(3) How far is dementia an individual, a medical or a social problem?

Further reading and resources

- Brandon, D. and Brandon, T. (2001) *Advocacy in Social Work*, Birmingham: Venture Press.
- Crawford, K. and Walker, J. (2004) *Social Work with Older People*, Exeter: Learning Matters.
- Sharkey, P. (2007) *The Essentials of Community Care*, Basingstoke: Palgrave.
- www.dh.gov.uk

Making a difference in risk assessment and management

6

Introduction

The focus of this chapter is on managing risk to individuals, families, carers, groups, communities, self and colleagues, as outlined in Key Role 4 of the National Occupational Standards. This Key Role is subdivided into two units:

(12) Assess and manage risks to individuals, families, carers, groups and communities.
(13) Assess, minimise and manage risk to self and colleagues.

Vignette: social work in a Youth Offending Team

James Brown has been a social worker for 25 years, with a background of working with children who offend. He is currently employed in a Youth Offending Team (YOT) in a town in the North East of England with responsibility for providing intervention with children and young people who become involved in crime.

Kyle is 14 years old and lives with his white mother, Sarah, two younger sisters and his younger brother in social housing on an estate on the outskirts of the town. The area has a reputation for being deprived, with poor services, a history of poverty and unemployment, low educational attainment, high crime and disorder and significant drug problems. Kyle's father, Jack, is black and lives locally. He has regular contact with the children. The relationship between him and Sarah ended several years ago. Communication between the parents is difficult, and the children often 'play off' one against the other.

Kyle received an Anti-Social Behaviour Order (ASBO) a year ago following complaints about playing football against a neighbour's house wall with a group of other boys. This was set for three years and the conditions included not playing noisy games on the estate. Due to high levels of crime and disorder, the estate is subject to a Section 30 Order (2003 Anti-social Behaviour Act), which allows the police to disperse groups of more than two people who may be acting in an anti-social manner between the hours of 5pm and 11pm. Recently, Kyle has been convicted of an offence of racially aggravated assault when he hit a shopkeeper who accused him of stealing goods. The shopkeeper was Asian and Kyle verbally abused him with racial insults during the assault, which left the shopkeeper with slight injuries. Kyle appeared in Youth Court and received a Referral Order.

Discussion

Youth crime has been the subject of increasing political and social concern and anxiety since the early 1980s. Images of young people as 'feral', 'out of control' and warranting restrictive interventions have been compounded by political debates about the nature of such behaviour and how to respond to it, with party political positions claiming solutions and vying for the votes of a worried electorate (Goldson and Muncie, 2006; Smith, R., 2007). Despite the fact that all methods of recording crime have demonstrated that criminal behaviour has reduced during this period, there is still a strong public perception that society is becoming more threatened by lawlessness, making rational argument problematic when such evidence is dismissed. A consequence of the increased focus on crime and 'getting tough' has been a rise in the use of imprisonment generally and for children and young people in particular, with England and Wales having one of the highest rates (and possibly the highest rate) of custodial sentences in comparative industrialised countries (Smith, R., 2007).

Practice with children and young people who break the law has changed significantly during this time, and in our scenario, James will have seen new laws, policies, initiatives and guidance that have influenced how he practises and what he is allowed to do. These changes have been led by political initiatives that have focused on England and Wales but have also influenced practice in Scotland (Whyte, 2000) and Northern Ireland, which have different legislation and structures to respond to children and young people's criminality.[1]

Risk is at the centre of many initiatives in youth crime, from identifying young people who are likely to become involved in criminal behaviour to managing those who are already seen to pose a danger to society. This chapter will discuss the ways in which risk is assessed and responded to, and offer an approach that can help to make sense of criminal behaviour and so reduce the harm that this may pose for others.

Legal and social policy context

It is axiomatic that criminal behaviour by children and young people (that is, youth crime) has always been an issue of concern; Pearson (1983) has identified that such anxieties have been a recurring theme in social commentary since recorded history began. The 'bad' or criminal behaviour of young people has also been subject to various explanations and remedies, influenced by what Hendrick (2006, pp 3-4) outlined as:

- 'change' (particularly social, political, economic and personal);
- 'order' (cultural, social and political);
- the influence of professional and administrative class agendas;
- party political programmes for the content and management of governance;
- age and generational relations.

Historical background

Our current understandings of youth crime are heavily influenced by the historical reformulation of young people's behaviour in the 19th century (Shore, 1999), when the social and economic upheaval of industrialisation created new ideas and environments that generated the notion of the 'juvenile delinquent' as a separate category of societal investigation. Social change and perceived threats to the existing social order created the conditions for the recognition of children as warranting specific attention to stem their potential for destabilising society. Coupled with this was the development of notions of childhood (Jenks, 1996), where children and young people were increasingly viewed as a separate category of *becoming* adults, with debates about their 'innocence' and/or 'sinfulness' leading to regulatory frameworks to order their proper transition into adult society.

In practice, concerns about the behaviour of children were translated into concerns about the behaviour of *poor* children (Muncie, 2004), where class anxieties about threats to the moral, social and political order led to legislation to deal with such young people. Explanations for bad behaviour were explicitly located in a lack of morality, but also in wider concerns about the welfare of children, as is demonstrated in the following quote from the 19th century about the causes of delinquency: '... the improper conduct of parents; the want of education; the want of suitable employment;

and the violation of the Sabbath; habits of gambling in the public streets' (Shore, 1999, p 20).

Interestingly, the first three explanations have been consistently used up to the present day and figure in contemporary debates about the nature of youth crime, demonstrating a continuity of concern. Youth crime became the site of arguments about the nature of society, arguments that were much broader than the individual misbehaviour of children, and this has continued to dominate public and political debate about what the problem is and how to respond to it.

Legislation was developed to respond to the changing perception of youth crime, and the first laws specifically to address young people as a separate entity were the 1854 Youthful Offenders Act and the 1857 Industrial Schools Act.[2] Both Acts saw residential education as the way to provide support, guidance and control for (pre-)delinquent children. The late 19th century saw an increase in the reported rates of offending by children, which fuelled social concerns about children (especially poor children) being out of control. However, Gillis (1975) claimed that this can be accounted for by the criminalisation of behaviour that was more aptly described as 'nuisance' rather than dangerous, and by policing policies that targeted young people in a more focused way. These social, structural and administrative reasons for the increase in youth crime have been argued to be relevant to current perceptions of the problem, and we will return to these later.

Changing approaches to young people led to the introduction of the 1908 Children Act, which attempted to make sense of the varying needs of children by establishing a juvenile court. The purpose of this was to deal with all matters relating to children and young people, be they welfare (neglect, abuse, deprived) or justice (criminal behaviour). The juvenile court was to deal with all children, whether they needed rescuing from harm or punishing for doing harm (or both), which led to some ambivalence and conflicts when faced with young people who were before them for very different reasons (Gelsthorpe and Morris, 1994). However, the Act was intended to provide rehabilitation for young people through treatment, based on developing notions that people could be scientifically dealt with through emerging initiatives in medicine and psychology. On a wider level, 'adolescence' as a category had been accepted with consequences for how children were viewed as in need of (firm) guidance, protection and regulation, and there were major social movements focused on providing support and (self-) control to ensure that they grew up into moral and law-abiding adults. The Scout movement is one example of this, originally designed to harness the potentially dangerous energies of boys into constructive, patriotic and militarily useful activities (Pearson, 1983).

Increasing concern for the welfare of children and young people resulted in the 1933 Children and Young Persons Act, a significant piece of legislation that still resonates today. It established the principle that courts dealing with young people should have regard for their welfare, whatever the reason for which they have come to the attention of the court. It has been argued that this legislation was the result of developments in the general welfare of children, for example the provision of child guidance clinics, and also theoretical influences (such as psychodynamic) that questioned the role that parenting styles had in producing delinquent behaviour. Children who behaved badly were often seen as victims of families, requiring expert guidance or removal into institutions that could provide a 'correct' nurturing environment. Indeed, the government specifically accepted recommendations that stated that 'there is little or no difference in character and needs between the delinquent and the neglected child' (cited in Hendrick, 2006, p 9).

This focus on welfare continued to be debated in subsequent decades, influencing further legislation such as the 1963 Children and Young Persons Act[3] and the 1969 Children and Young Persons Act. The latter attempted to move responsibility and action in dealing with young people's criminal behaviour away from formal justice systems to children's services located in social services departments and regulated by the Department of Health and Social Security, where children and families could receive treatment for their perceived difficulties. Contradictions in the legislation and policies had the effect of increasing the numbers of young people who were either imprisoned or incarcerated in residential provision during the 1970s (Gelsthorpe and Morris, 1994). A concern for welfare led to the removal of young people into care provision for offences that would not warrant custody, although the experience for young people may well have been similar (that is, removal from home; living far away from their community; under residential restrictions). The 1980s saw new developments from the neoliberal Conservative governments, which used anxiety about crime as one of their political platforms. Goldson (1999) describes the approach taken as one of 'diversion, decriminalisation and decarceration', influenced by the need to reduce the costs of the youth justice system. Initiatives were introduced that quietly produced a more liberal outcome, reducing the numbers of children coming before the formal justice processes, avoiding early labelling as 'criminals', and significantly reducing the use of custodial and residential sentences. This coincided with a reduction in recorded juvenile crime, although whether this was due to the policies or broader economic and social factors is debateable.

The 1990s saw an unparalleled politicisation of youth crime, where the main political parties vied for credibility in their explanations for and responses to young people's behaviour. There is little doubt that the killing of James Bulger in 1993 by two 10-year-old boys provided the stimulus for broad social discussions about the nature of children, childhood and crime (Jenks, 1996; Newburn, 1996), leading to an increased punitiveness and intolerance towards young people in general, and those who commit crime in particular. The Conservative government of the early 1990s introduced a series of legal initiatives to demonstrate its 'tough' approach to the issue, and youth crime became a central election battleground in 1997. The Audit Commission's 1998 report *Misspent Youth* identified severe shortcomings in the youth justice system and also social deprivation factors that contributed to young people becoming involved in crime. The incoming Labour government of 1997 produced the White Paper *No More Excuses* (Home Office, 1997), the title of which encapsulated a view that youth crime was out of control, that previous policy had failed and that there had been a shift to an ineffective 'liberal' practice approach that minimised the problematic behaviour of young people.

Current legislative and policy framework

The 1998 Crime and Disorder Act introduced a raft of changes to the way in which the criminal behaviour of young people was responded to. The Act established the Youth Justice Board for England and Wales, a quasi-autonomous agency which regulates policy and practice and has the aim of reducing youth offending.[4] Multi-agency YOTs, local agency partnerships and statutory planning to deal with youth crime were created. In reviewing the Act, R. Smith (2007) argues that it introduced a micro-management approach through prescriptive guidance on the assessment and processing of young people.[5]

The Crime and Disorder Act brought in a graded approach to managing and responding to youth crime (Smith, R., 2007). First, there were a range of orders aimed at preventing crime through targeting pre-delinquent children, including the Child Safety Order, the Curfew Order, the Parenting Order and the ASBO (subsequently amended by the 2003 Anti-social Behaviour Act). Second, there were pre-court or diversionary disposals for more minor offences and those young people who had little previous concerning behaviour, including Reprimands, Final Warnings and Referral Orders (introduced by the 1999 Youth Justice and Criminal Evidence Act).[6] Third, where young people were seen to be failing the previous disposals through further criminal behaviour, more intrusive sentences could be used, including Reparation Orders, Attendance Centre Orders and Supervision Orders.[7] Finally, custodial sentences (Detention and Training Orders; Section 90/91 Orders) were available for those deemed to have committed offences that were so serious and/or frequent that they required imprisonment.

The Crime and Disorder Act also introduced the legal concept of 'racially aggravated offences', where an offence is motivated by, or includes, hostility to the victim based on their membership of a racial or religious group

(Webster, 2007). This has the effect of making an offence of, for example, violence, more serious than if it did not include such elements, and it attracts a more severe penalty. The defining of any incident as 'racially motivated' is based on the perceptions of the victim or witnesses, rather than by the police as previously.

'Anti-social behaviour' has become a common term to describe low-level disorder in communities that does not always meet the more prescriptive definitions of crime. ASBOs can be applied for in civil courts and the standard of proof required is not of the same quality as in a criminal court. Evidence can be given that does not require witnesses to be identified, thus preventing reprisals against them. An ASBO can be made if a person acts in 'a manner which causes or is likely to cause harassment, alarm or distress to one or more persons not of the same household' (Home Office, 2006, p 10), and is aimed at behaviours such as verbal abuse, criminal damage, vandalism, noise, graffiti, smoking or drinking alcohol while under age, prostitution, begging and threatening behaviour in large groups (Home Office, 2006, p 9). The ASBO has been subject to criticism as being widely drawn and having a peculiar legal position. In practice, someone can receive an ASBO for relatively minor non-criminal behaviour, breach this, and find themselves in prison (Hughes and Follett, 2006).

R. Smith (2007) observes that there is an increasing divergence between the approaches taken to respond to youth crime in the nations of the UK. Scotland has retained a criminal justice system distinct from that of England, Wales and Northern Ireland, with a structure of 'children's hearings' that ensure that children under the age of 16 are dealt with in a diversionary way, rather than subjected to the more punitive sanctions available elsewhere. This commitment to diverting children away from formal court systems has been maintained (Scottish Executive, 2004), and such 'welfare' initiatives are influencing policies in Wales (Cross et al, 2003) and Northern Ireland (Schrag, 2003). England appears to be the only UK nation that considers children to warrant a more punitive approach, although the picture is complicated by the low age of criminal responsibility in Scotland (eight, one of the lowest in the world) and its high rate of custodial sentencing for those who are eligible for it (Muncie and Goldson, 2006).

Discussion

This review of the legal and social policy context shows that the legislative framework for youth justice has been amended and changed considerably during the last 10 years or so, with new laws appearing on a regular basis to respond to the perceived nature of crime and disorder. This rapidity of change means that anyone working within this system will need to update their knowledge on a regular basis. The Youth Justice Board has a Practitioner's Portal on its website, which they will find useful in considering the impact of these changes.[8]

In our vignette, James has seen radical developments in the way the youth justice system deals with young people. His previous role was to undertake direct work with children, young people and their families with a strong welfare approach and a wariness of the potential damaging consequences of children becoming enmeshed in the criminal justice system. The new developments have changed the expectations of his role and focused his work on completing the required assessment forms and managing resources to address the identified criminogenic needs of the young person (discussed more fully in Chapter Eight).

Kyle finds himself in a difficult position where he is already subject to an ASBO that can be used to indicate that he is a 'problem'; an order that may be seen as providing evidence that he is a danger to others. He may have needs through structural issues such as poor environment, but the focus of the ASBO is to control his misbehaviour rather than provide services for him. He is facing a serious charge of violence and racism that could lead to a custodial sentence. Kyle may well be unaware of the consequences of some of his actions for himself, as there are popular perceptions that the criminal justice system cannot do anything to young people – this is mistaken and Kyle could face strict punitive sanctions.

From policy to practice: risk assessment and management

In our vignette, James has to manage the organisational requirements of completing assessments with the values of working with often-disadvantaged children who have extensive needs. Kyle has multiple needs that would warrant intervention, yet these may be viewed as further indicators of risk. James is faced with maintaining a child-centred approach within processes that increasingly demand that his role is to focus on the criminal behaviour. He will be aware of the concerns that have been expressed about the prescriptive methods of working, which may stifle his creativity, skills and knowledge, leading to what Pitts (2001) called the 'zombification' of youth justice. The turn to a rational-technical approach (Parton and O'Byrne, 2000) in youth justice has consequences for James and Kyle, and James will need to retain a reflexive stance (Taylor and White, 2000) to the system he works in, ensuring that he understands the opportunities and limitations of his role.

Models and methods

Risk assessment

Two methods are currently used in assessing risk in social work: actuarial and clinical methods. The actuarial (or statistical) method has its roots in the insurance industry; it involves statistical calculations of probability, in which an individual's likely behaviour is predicted on the basis of the known behaviour of others in similar circumstances (Cree and Wallace, 2005). Clinical assessment is the traditional (and, arguably,) more familiar method used in social work practice, and employs diagnostic assessment techniques relating to personality factors and situational factors relevant to the risky behaviour and the interaction between the two (Prins, 1999). Actuarial methods have become increasingly popular in recent years in the assessment of criminal behaviour, informing decisions about who should receive what type of intervention, based on assumptions about their level of dangerousness. The Youth Justice Board has developed the Asset, Onset and Risk of Serious Harm protocols, which consist of lists of factors to explore and allocate a numerical value; the outcome of which leads to a particular intervention.[9]

Silver and Miller (2002) identify three key elements of an actuarial assessment:

(1) Decisions are grounded in statistical relationships. Statistical algorithms are used to categorise individuals into population subgroups with shared characteristics and similar levels of risk. Individuals can be given a numerical score based on high and low risk attributes, where certain risk factors can be weighted to gain the numerical score. As a consequence of this process, individuals can be grouped into homogenous risk classes based on shared high or low risk attributes.

(2) Actuarial prediction moves decision making from professional knowledge and expertise to the actuarial model. Relevant information is inputted into a risk assessment algorithm, similar in principle to the introduction of data into a computer. This information may be gathered from a variety of sources by a variety of techniques. In this process the professional–client relationship becomes a one-way exchange of information, as all that is required is the accurate gathering of relevant information in a format that can be processed by the algorithm.

(3) Actuarial prediction uses aggregate data in prediction. As in motor insurance, risk is determined by individuals who share characteristics. Aggregate data allow for estimating the likelihood that a certain group will commit violence. It is claimed that actuarial algorithms tend to be more accurate and consistent than human decision makers, therefore

> there is an ethical imperative to use them, particularly when predicting harm against people.

The history of actuarial risk assessments has been subject to various developments and reflects the social and political context of the time (Auerhahn, 1999). There have been two recurring criticisms of this approach: that of false-positive predictions (predicting cases to reoffend that do not do so) and false-negative predictions (predicting cases not to reoffend that do so). The ethical consequences of this are obvious, with large numbers of people being dragged into a net of stringent social control based on a mislabelling. Because of this, actuarial approaches have changed to a less definitive and certain way of predicting behaviour with a 'probabalistic' model. This again explores characteristics that place people within a category, but the category is deemed to have a certain percentage of them who will go on to reoffend (see Beaumont, 1999; Craig, 2004).

Major questions remain about the purpose to which such approaches are applied. Feeley and Simon (1992) assert that they are responding to a social and political context that demands increasing predictive accuracy to allocate limited resources more effectively. Not only do they assist in providing for effective management of offenders, they also have the potential to marginalise those professionals who have skills in working with people, as the required data can be collected and codified through computer programs, claiming to reduce the variable of individual interpretation to produce a 'purer' outcome. Moreover, actuarial risk assessments are not designed to explain, judge or question the causes of youth offending, but are there to predict the likelihood of offences, thus ignoring the moral decisions about social and political change and diverting the problem back onto the individual. Risk markers may include poverty, poor education and unemployment; however, actuarial risk assessments provide no imperative to deal with these issues – they simply treat people who are victims of these circumstances as 'a high-risk group that must be managed for the protection of the larger society' (Feeley and Simon, 1992, p 467). In this sense, actuarial risk assessment is an inherently political process, focusing as it does on the shortcomings of the individual and marginalising the social context. Webb argues that risk assessment and management have developed within the context of neoliberal political agendas. In consequence, risk is 'understood as a form of governmentality that undermines traditional practices of value and relationship-building' (Webb, 2006, p 47). These warnings strike at the heart of the values of social work, and trying to maintain compassion, care and the humanity of practice may be severely compromised by a preoccupation with risk.

Turning to our vignette, James will have to make use of risk assessment tools including Asset.[10] According to the *National Standards for Youth Justice*

(Home Office, 2000), Asset must be completed for all young people who are subject to:

- bail supervision and support;
- a request for a court report (pre-sentence report and specific sentence report);
- community disposals during the assessment, quarterly review and closure stages;
- custodial sentences at the assessment, transfer to the community and closure stages.

The Asset form collates information about the background, education, lifestyle and personal characteristics of young people. The following topics must be discussed:

- offending behaviour;
- living arrangements;
- family and personal relationships;
- education, training and employment;
- neighbourhood;
- lifestyle;
- substance use;
- physical health;
- emotional and mental health;
- perception of self and others;
- thinking and behaviour;
- attitudes to offending;
- motivation to change;
- positive factors;
- indicators of vulnerability;
- indicators of serious harm to others.

Replies are scored to indicate the risk of further offending, and recommendations for intervention are then made.

We have already discussed the use of an assessment framework in Chapter Three, in the context of children and families' social work. In that chapter we acknowledged that such a framework can be useful for those using and delivering services, but identified that there is a need to practise in a reflective way to maintain the sense of the individual within this. The Asset tool likewise has the potential to be useful for both Kyle and James in ensuring that all relevant areas are considered. However, in conducting his assessment, James will wish to hold on to what is useful in both clinical and actuarial approaches, fore-fronting the importance of professional judgement rather than simply checking boxes and adding up problematic factors.

Risk management: using a solution-focused approach

In analysing the evidence from research, Stephenson et al (2007, p 242) identify that some approaches seem to be more effective than others in reducing reoffending. These include:

- individual counselling;
- interpersonal skills training;
- multiple services;
- restitution and probation;
- employment and education programmes;
- advocacy and casework;
- family and group counselling.

They also identify those approaches that seem to be less effective. These are vocational programmes, deterrence programmes and wilderness experiences. (It should be noted that these categories are very broad and allow for a wide range of interventions to achieve reductions in reoffending.) Stephenson et al also identify the most effective ways of responding to the risk factors commonly found with young offenders. These include:

- providing community-based support for parents through home visiting;
- organisational change in schools;
- pre-school education;
- social skills education;
- providing information for parents.

With this in mind, James's preferred method of intervention in working with Kyle is to make use of a solution-focused approach.

A solution-focused approach shares some of the values of the humanist models of counselling and has some features in common with cognitive-behavioural therapies in that it uses cognitive and behavioural questions and frequently leads to tasks to be carried out (Milner and O'Byrne, 2004). However, the focus is quite different. While other approaches focus on understanding *problems*, classifying them, and identifying each category to match up treatment models, solution-focused practice (or solution-focused brief therapy, SFBT) focuses on understanding *solutions* (Milner and Myers, 2007). Solution-focused practitioners consider that people have the capacity to discover their own, workable solutions to their problems. It is deeply sceptical about the ability of the 'grand', modernist theories and explanations to deliver truth, holding instead to a plurality of truths, especially including those contained in the 'local' theories of service users. It avoids any form of diagnostic labelling and sees professional categorisation of people as disempowering. As people are viewed as essentially capable, there is a constant search for competencies; for example, a young person who could be classified as suffering from attention deficit disorder is viewed from a solution-focused point of view as being a person with many strengths (energy, creativity, individuality), all of which can be used in solution finding.

Solution-focused practice takes a deliberately 'not-knowing' stance towards people's problems, preferring to remain curious about people's stories and views, about their strengths and potential, about occasions when the problem was less, and about how that happened. There is a preoccupation with difference, with what was different when things were better and what needs to be different for them to be better again. Each problem-free aspect of the person is utilised to this end. The therapeutic relationship is built by engaging in problem-free talk, engaging the person, rather than the problem. Solution-focused practice thus sees the problem as outside the person: the person is not the problem; the problem is the problem. The practitioner joins with the service user *against* the problem and creates a different story. Therefore this approach avoids pathology and the identification of deficits. This solution-focused approach seeks to find the seeds of solution in a service user's current situation, seeking those occasions or *exceptions*, however small or rare, when the problem is less of a problem in order to identify when and how that person is doing or thinking something different that reduces the problem. This involves listening carefully to, and then using, what the person brings to the encounter, focusing on problem-free moments, imagining a problem-free future, and getting a very detailed description from the service user of what will be different then and whether any of that is already beginning to happen. In partnership, the service user and the practitioner build a picture of a possible future without the problem (Myers, 2007).

Language is seen as powerful enough to construct life; talk of life with the problem constructs a problem-laden life; talk of life without the problem constructs a problem-free life. Talking in detail of what will be happening, what people will be saying, what effect this will have on relationships and so on provides the experience of a glimpse of that life; that life then becomes a possibility and the person experiences a sense of personal agency in setting out to construct it. The new story can even include a changed or different self, especially an accountable self. Assessments that fix people's identities, conflating the person and the problem, are avoided as new possibilities become viable.

One of the key techniques within SFBT for assisting in the creation of goals and a problem-free future is the 'miracle question'. This has developed from therapeutic approaches that have posed hypothetical questions, and there have been variations of this for some time. Ansbacher and Ansbacher (1998) describe the use of the 'magic wand' question, where someone will be asked: 'If I had a magic wand or pill that would eliminate your symptom immediately, what would be different in your life?' The key elements of the miracle question are that, because it is a miracle, it invites people to imagine limitless possibilities for their lives to enable them to identify what changes they would want to achieve these. It is also future-oriented, moving away from rumination on past and present problems to thinking about what a problem-free life would look like. The question invites people to consider the actions and behaviours that would be happening when their problems have disappeared, which allows for more detail to be developed and a richer picture to emerge. Initially, people may describe more of a photograph of the future, and the worker can assist them in developing a video of the ways in which this will be happening. The miracle question is used to generate goals that can then be worked towards and those goals are from the person rather than imposed assumptions by the worker.

A further technique of SFBT is that of 'scaling' questions, where people are invited to rate their perceptions of the problem and their capacities, confidence and willingness to deal with this. The scale is structured so that the numbers are all pointing towards solutions, as even a 1 is a move forward from 0. Of course, these scales are not an absolute or scientific measure; they are the product of the subjective experience of the person and do not have any meaning outside what the person gives them. This is unlike some psychometric measures that claim to have a true numeric value of a thought, feeling or event. Scales in SFBT provide a relative value for the person (and the worker), because if it is at 8 then this is better than 7, much better than 4, and getting towards 10.

Scaling safety and progress

Using scales makes it possible for people to acknowledge when they are not making sufficient progress without making them feel like complete failures. The range of points on a scale means that they are rarely condemned and recognises their aspirations to 'do better'. The scales can be constructed in such a way as to make it easier for people to discuss what they need to be doing differently even when the subject is emotionally charged. Again this places the responsibility for developing a safety plan, and putting it into effect, on the person whose violence led to safety concerns in the first place.

Assessing willingness, confidence and capacity to change

Although it is important for offenders to take responsibility for their behaviour in the future, Turnell and Edwards (1999) make the point that practitioners have a responsibility for setting the scene so that motivation can be improved. Adversarial relationships with professionals reduce the possibility of this, causing unnecessary frustration and increasing feelings of powerlessness at the same time as the offender is expected to exercise self-control. Willingness to change can be increased by assessing whether the person needs help with motivation or ability to change. This is done by creating separate scales for each behaviour. For example, 'If 1 means you can't be bothered and 10 means you will do anything it takes, where are you on this scale?' And 'If 1 means you have no confidence in your ability to change and 10 means you have complete confidence, where are you on this scale?' The lower of the two scores becomes the focus of the work, that is, 'What will you be doing differently when you are one point higher?' It is also important to ask: 'If 1 means you haven't a clue about what to do differently and 10 means you know exactly what to do to change, where are you on this scale?'

This means that practitioners need to be aware of, and explicit about, their values and meanings. They do have influence by the nature of the questions they ask; hence the importance of only asking questions to which one does not know the answer, and not mentally framing 'the next question' until the answer to the previous one has been fully heard and acknowledged.

The solution-focused practitioner thus holds offenders appropriately responsible for finding their own solutions to their behaviour, particularly what their futures will be like when they are violence-free. These solutions can include the actions and behaviours of others, particularly in the case of a young person where autonomy is limited and where their family, social workers and teachers may be able to assist in building safety. But there is no assumption made that this will be easy; Myers (2007) describes a solution-building process that requires discipline and effort. The role of the solution-focused practitioner is, therefore, one of helping the offender define a goal that is achievable, measurable and ethical; helping them find exceptions to the behaviour, and solution behaviours; and then amplifying, supporting and reinforcing these. Exceptions are not discovered simply to be praised, nor are solution behaviours regarded as 'positives'; rather they are examined as possible competencies that the person can utilise in the search for a satisfactory and enduring solution. For example, if a person can give an example of a time when they were calm in a situation that has led to violence previously, they are asked where and how they did this, and whether they can do it again.

In our vignette, Kyle has committed a serious offence that has elements of racism. Violence is clearly not acceptable and James has the task of intervening to address this behaviour. However, social work is complex, and Kyle presents not just as an offender but as a child with needs and James will seek to understand the interactions between these and Kyle's offending to ensure that his welfare is promoted as well as reducing the chances of the behaviour reoccurring. James has to complete forms such as Asset and Risk of Serious Harm, a 'tick-box' approach that appears to be authoritative but requires subjective interpretation of factors, which is where his skills and experience will be invaluable. James will be faced with decisions about levels of seriousness that will have a direct impact on the services that Kyle will receive, placing him in the difficult position of maintaining a balance between an actuarially based outcome and appropriate services.

Values

Respect

The notion of 'respect' has been adopted by government in England and Wales as a key instrument in its initiative to control antisocial behaviour in communities. The 'Respect Task Force', established as a cross-governmental organisation in September 2005, is responsible for coordinating and delivering the 'Respect Action Plan', which seeks to target issues such as problem families, poor parenting, truancy and poor behaviour in schools, and unresponsive services.[11] As part of this campaign, neighbours are encouraged to 'take a stand against anti-social behaviour'; to fight back to reclaim their communities. At the same time, those working in communities (police officers and community workers) are applauded for their successes in controlling anti-social behaviour.

This is a very different understanding of 'respect' to that which is central to social work practice in the UK. Social work's professional association, the British Association of Social Workers (BASW), suggests in its Code of Ethics that social work is committed to five basic values: human dignity and worth, social justice, service to humanity, integrity and competence.[12] Respect is seen as fundamental to human dignity and worth in the following ways:

- respect for human rights;
- respect for all persons, and respect for service users' beliefs, values, culture, goals, needs, preferences, relationships and affiliations;
- respect for service users' rights to make informed decisions, and ensuring that service users and carers participate in decision-making processes.

Respect will be at the heart of James's work with Kyle and his family. He will, of course, be acutely aware of the government's agenda here. But he will also wish to work with Kyle and his family in ways which show that he has respect for them, for their own efforts in dealing with their problems, and for the positive choices that they have made, however small these may seem. The family may well be experiencing multiple stresses and James may be able to offer support and resources in assisting them to achieve what they want (if this is ethical), rather than imposing expectations from outside. Adopting a solution-focused approach will enable James to put this into practice.

Respect will also be important in another way, however. Kyle has been found guilty of an assault with a racist element to it. This suggests not only that he has racist attitudes that need to be challenged, but also, possibly, that he has internalised some feelings of oppression himself, as a youth with a white mother and black father. Because of this, James's work with Kyle will benefit from a prosocial approach (Trotter, 1999), in which he challenges some attitudes and, at the same time, models good behaviour and attitudes, with the aim of helping Kyle to learn to respect others (including himself) better. (A prosocial approach is discussed more fully in Chapter Eight.)

Justice

In introducing the subject of justice, Clark (2000) suggests that it plays a similar theoretical role to the principle of respect. While respect is said to be the 'key to right interpersonal relations, justice is held up as the key to right action for the public sphere and its institutions' (Clark, 2000, p 146). He identifies five notions within the idea of justice:

- *Justice as due process*: this assumes that decisions should be taken according to rules and procedures which have authority.
- *Justice based on desert*: this is the notion that people should deserve their rewards and punishments.
- *Justice as human rights*: the idea that individuals have certain fundamental rights or entitlements.
- *Justice as fair shares*: this assumes that people should be treated fairly in comparison with others.
- *Justice as liberation*: this starts with the premise that some people have been disadvantaged in society so that society needs to change to create justice.

The term 'justice' is frequently used today prefaced by the word 'social'. 'Social justice' is a popular mantra of politicians from all parties. Those on the left tend to see social justice in terms of redistribution (this is 'justice as liberation' in Clark's typology), whereas those on the right are more likely to claim that social justice is best achieved through the workings of the free market and philanthropic endeavour (this lends more to the notion of justice in terms of fair shares). Our scenario shows how problematic the notion of justice is in the real world of social work practice. As we have demonstrated throughout this book, social work is intimately involved in the processes of social control. As individual social workers, we may have personal views about the lack of justice in specific legislation and government ideologies. But if we work in statutory agencies as employees of government, or even in voluntary agencies that are dependent on government for funding, we may find ourselves acting within rules and procedures that we do not think are 'fair' or 'right'. This means that James, with 25 years in practice, may believe that Kyle and his mother are best supported using a welfare approach, but in the context of his practice today, the discourse is much more likely to be couched in terms of punishment and community protection. The challenge for him will be to find ways of managing this effectively, so that he meets the requirements and, at the same time, acts in a way that he sees as 'just'.[13]

Underpinning knowledge

As in all the previous chapters, the models and methods discussed draw explicitly, and sometimes implicitly, on theoretical ideas. Risk assessment and solution-focused approaches draw primarily on psychological approaches, including learning theory, which is examined more fully in Chapter Eight. We will examine two different theories here: risk and postmodernism.

Sociology of risk

Beck (1992, 1999) has famously said that we live in a 'risk society'. He argues that there has been a major shift in the way that we view risk. In pre-modern societies, natural disasters were viewed as acts of God, or accidents of fate, and because of this, it was thought that there was little anyone could do either to prevent, or to protect themselves from, adversity. Industrialisation brought a new, 'modern' outlook, which presumed that human beings could and should seek to control such misadventure (Cree and Wallace, 2005). But, Beck argues, industrial society did not remove risk; instead, it created new and more damaging risks, including environmental problems such as pollution, and social problems such as unemployment and family breakdown. In the postmodern world, Beck asserts that more and better knowledge often leads to more uncertainty; 'expert' and lay voices compete with one another as the outcomes of modernity are challenged on all fronts (Beck, 1999, p 6).

Commentators have argued that Beck has understated the complexities and contradictions inherent in the idea of risk. For example, Tulloch and Lupton (2003) argue that pre-modern notions about 'fate' still have meaning in people's lives, as do early 'modernist ideas' about the possibility of controlling risk. They also point out that risk is not necessarily negative; that people need to take risks to be alive. They argue that a life without risk may be perceived as 'too tightly bound and restricted, as not offering enough challenges' (Tulloch and Lupton, 2003, p 37).

Both ways of thinking about risk have something to offer James in his work. Beck's analysis is helpful in giving him a way of understanding the context within which risk assessment and risk management takes place. They are, in Beck's conceptualisation, 'modern' mechanisms designed to demonstrate that risk is under control – or at least, under the semblance of control. But risk can never be removed, and it will be important for James, for his professional association and for his managers to give clear messages to the public and to politicians alike about what can, and cannot, be achieved in risk assessment and management. This takes us into a discussion of postmodernism.

Postmodernism

Postmodernism assumes that we are living in a 'post' era (from the Latin meaning 'after'): our ways of thinking about society and the world in which we live are seen as qualitatively different from a time when it was believed that social order and social progress could be achieved through the application of reason and science (a 'modernist' approach). Although postmodern approaches are varied, they view society as pluralistic and individualistic, having a 'multiplicity of voices' where everything is fluid and changing. There is no single, 'true' theoretical perspective, no 'grand theory' that can explain and interpret our experience. Likewise, we are not bound to a single identity; instead we have a range of identities to choose from. The consequence is that life feels fragmented; we do not always know who we are and how to behave (Cree, 2000, p 20).

The related concept of poststructuralism (a rejection of underlying structural explanations of the world) similarly views meanings as multiple, unstable and changing. Foucault (1977) argues that there is no such thing as set or objective meaning, but instead power, language and institutional practices come together in 'discourse' at specific moments in time to produce particular ways of thinking. Discourse is presented as more than simply verbal representation or even a way of thinking and producing meaning.

It is a way of regulating knowledge: 'practices that systematically form the objects of which they speak' (Foucault, 1977, p 49). Foucault's work has been highly influential in demonstrating that the various institutions of the modern era (for example, prisons, schools, hospitals) have become sites for the ever-more detailed operation of power over subject populations. For example, the drive to find the characteristics of someone called 'the criminal' presupposes that such a category exists and that they are different from a presumed norm. In making sense of people through this presumption we can work in limited ways that marginalise other ways of thinking about the person. Healy (2005, p 196) argues that Foucault's work encourages us to be cautious in our claims to 'help', 'empower' or 'emancipate', as these practices are themselves associated with the 'will to power' over others.

Postmodern and poststructural approaches have had a growing impact on social work literature since the 1990s (for example, Howe, 1994; Parton, 1994; Cree, 1995; Featherstone and Fawcett, 1995). What these authors share is an acceptance that social work is a product of 'modernity': it was formed alongside the social sciences as a way of explaining and improving the human condition (Cree, 2000). Social work therefore needs to be alert to the contradictions within this; to the control through care dichotomy that we explored in Chapter One.

Returning to our vignette, postmodern ideas underpin both solution-focused practice and sociological theories of risk. They offer a useful way of thinking about some of the contradictions inherent in youth offending policy and practice, and they offer a positive (although inevitably contingent) way of moving forward. They illuminate the ways in which 'help' for Kyle is also controlling, and that dominant approaches to understanding criminal behaviour are often psychological and deficit-led, leading to practices that fix an identity for him (damaged, criminal, violent, racist). Postmodern ideas accept that people are complex and influenced by the social environment, rather than having fixed patterns and one way of being. This opens up possibilities for change in ways different from a modernist perspective, as those unwanted aspects of his behaviour can be seen as only part of his story; he will have other more helpful qualities that can be obscured by fixed thinking.

Other forms of knowledge

The voices of young offenders have been largely absent from much of the rhetoric around anti-social behaviour and young people. One longitudinal research study has identified that the peak age for offending by both boys and girls is 14 years; after this time, most reduce their offending or stop completely (Smith, D., 2007). Moreover, the study demonstrates that being an offender and being a victim of crime are very closely linked, so much so that one of the best ways to predict which young man is going to be an offender is whether he has been a victim of crime (see McAra and McVie, 2005). This was expressed graphically by one girl interviewed for the study:

> The hurt and the pain its not going to go away is it, you just want to hurt and give someone else pain, you pass it on and they'll probably pass it on to someone else, they pass it on till they pass it on, all these people get hurt.[14]

This research suggests that it is not helpful to draw a line between young people as offenders and young people as victims; rather, they should be treated as both troubled and troublesome, and given support to enable them to make positive choices in their lives. The study also suggests that, since most young people desist from offending of their own volition, interventions should be targeted and proportionate.

Conclusion

This chapter has focused on an increasingly important issue in social work, that of risk. Risk is not an uncontested term, with various claims made about how it is thought of, constructed and acted on, and social workers need to be aware of the potential consequences of engaging with particular risk assessments. Organisational demands for effective risk management impact on practice and, in our vignette, James needs to engage with the prescribed protocols, frameworks and models with a commitment to ensuring the best holistic outcome for Kyle. In order to do so, the knowledge base of postmodernism and the sociology of risk will help him to understand some of their strengths and shortcomings, and his values of respect and justice will enable him to maintain a clear perspective on Kyle as a complex individual not easily reduced to a series of factors.

Notes

[1] Scotland has a distinctive legal structure that has taken a different approach to managing youth crime, with consequences for young people and practitioners. See Whyte (2000).

[2] The Youthful Offenders Act established reformatories for those young people who had committed crimes, and the Industrial Schools Act established schools for neglected and vulnerable children who were potentially 'at risk' of becoming criminal.

[3] This Act raised the age of criminal responsibility in England and Wales to 10; it remains eight in Scotland.
[4] For an outline of the systems in Scotland and Northern Ireland, see www.youthjusticescotland.gov.uk and www.youthjusticeagencyni.gov.uk
[5] For example, the use of Reprimands and Final Warnings (introduced to replace the prior Cautioning system) is highly regulated with little space for discretion.
[6] The Referral Order directs the young person by an order of the court to a youth panel comprised of lay volunteers, where a programme of reparation and work is agreed to prevent further offending. It is the main response to those young people who are appearing in the Youth Court for the first time.
[7] For a full list of available sentencing options, see R. Smith (2007).
[8] See www.yjb.gov.uk
[9] *Ibid.*
[10] Asset has been used since April 2000 throughout England and Wales by Youth Offending Teams. See www.yjb.gov.uk
[11] See www.respect.gov.uk
[12] See www.basw.co.uk
[13] For a fuller discussion of the philosophical debates about the nature of justice relevant to social work, see Banks (2006).
[14] Taken from a BBC Scotland interview in July 2007, in which Professor David J. Smith, who headed the research study, relates this story.

Key questions

(1) In what ways has the behaviour of young people *always* been a subject of concern?
(2) What does it mean to suggest that we live in a risk society?
(3) What is the difference between actuarial and clinical assessment of risk, and why does good social work practice need both?

Further reading and resources

- Goldson, B. and Muncie, J. (eds) (2006) *Youth Crime and Justice*, London: Sage Publications.
- Myers, S. (2007) *Solution Focused Approaches*, Lyme Regis: Russell House Press.
- Smith, R. (2007) *Youth Justice: Ideas, Policy, Practice* (2nd edition), Cullompton: Willan Publishing.
- www.yjb.gov.uk

7 Making a difference in your practice in your agency

Introduction

The focus of this chapter is Key Role 5 of the National Occupational Standards: it expects social workers to manage and be accountable, with supervision and support, for their own social work practice within their organisation. This Key Role is subdivided into four units.

(14) Manage and be accountable for your own work.
(15) Contribute to the management of resources and services.
(16) Manage, present and share records and reports.
(17) Work within multidisciplinary and multi-organisational teams, networks and systems.

We will outline the case scenario on which the work of this chapter is based, before going on to explore the issues that it raises in relation to the units.

Vignette: social work in hospital

Bill McIlroy is a social worker attached to a specialist renal unit based in the fictional Royal Infirmary, a large general hospital in Northern Ireland. He is 30 years of age. He works in the hospital's Social Work team, which is made up of eight social workers, only two of whom work with renal patients and their families. His post is funded for three years by a charity that supports kidney patients.

Bill has been working with Samantha Hughes over the last 18 months. Samantha (known as 'Sam') is a 32-year-old, white, single parent who works in an office and cares for her young son, Harry, now aged 10 years. She also acts as primary carer for her elderly grandparents who live nearby. Sam experienced renal failure unexpectedly 18 months ago. She had experienced flu-like symptoms for a week or two, and then collapsed and was admitted to hospital as an emergency patient with acute renal failure. Bill met her at this time. He carried out a psychosocial (that is, influenced by psychodynamic theory) assessment to see how she was likely to cope with her illness, and explored options for treatment and support with her. Since then, Sam has been managing well on three-weekly dialysis, and Bill has seen her when she has come to the hospital for treatment. Unfortunately, Sam's condition has worsened suddenly, and she has been admitted to hospital again. Bill wants to help Sam as she faces an uncertain future. He also needs to make arrangements quickly for Harry's care and for the care of Sam's grandparents.

Discussion

On the face of it, this is a very specialist scenario, set in an extremely specialised environment. To work effectively, Bill will need to have 'expert' knowledge and understanding about renal illness and its possible progression, and awareness of the impact of illness on individuals and families. He will need to have highly developed skills in bereavement counselling and in multidisciplinary practice. He will need to be familiar with the complex values issues that inevitably go together with helping people to prepare for death and its aftermath. Nevertheless, we believe that it is basic social work knowledge, skills and values that will make a real difference in this work. The 'bottom line' is that Bill needs to have a good sense of his own identity; an understanding of what he, as the social worker, has to bring to this situation. He also needs to have respect for those with whom he is working, and rely on them to tell him what they think and feel. In this, he includes not only the various medical 'experts' (the consultant urologist, chaplain, nurses and so on), but also Sam herself. What does she want, and need? What is *her* understanding of her choices and of the decisions she has to make? And what does Harry think and feel? He is old enough to have a view and to be allowed to express this, as are Mr and Mrs Hughes (senior) – what are their perceptions and wishes about their long-term care? Who else needs to be consulted in the wider family or community? Reaching a good outcome in this scenario will be as much about basic social work practice as it is about specialist knowledge. As in previous chapters, Bill will need to start with a good grounding in the legal and social policy context within which he is working, and it is to this that we now turn.

Legal and social policy context

Social work has played an important role within healthcare almost since the beginning of hospitals, as a brief historical overview indicates.

Historical background

The Royal Infirmary, the fictional hospital within which Bill works, is likely to have begun its life in the late 1830s as a union workhouse, established as a result of the 1838 Poor Law Act 'for the more effective relief of the destitute poor in Ireland'. In the years after the Act was passed, workhouses were built across Ireland, taking the poor, sick and unemployed adults and children and, wherever possible, setting them to work (see O'Connor, 1995). The workhouse would have had an 'infirmary' block and an 'idiots' ward' for those with serious mental health problems, and for many of Ireland's poor, this would have offered the only free healthcare services that were available to them (those who could afford it would have paid for private healthcare). After the partition of Ireland in 1921 and the introduction of the National Health Service (NHS) after the Second World War, the workhouse would have become managed by the new Hospitals Authority. (See Chapter Two for a fuller discussion of workhouses in the UK.)

Health-related social work has a long history, not all of it celebrated today. Histories of hospital social work suggest that it began in 1895 with the appointment of Miss Mary Stewart as almoner to the Royal Free Hospital, in Gray's Inn Road, London. She was paid by the Charity Organisation Society (COS), and her task, in common with other COS visitors of the day, was not (as might have been expected) to provide services or alleviate distress. Instead, she was appointed to tackle the 'abuse' of outpatients' departments in voluntary hospitals. The term 'abuse' was used because it was believed that some patients who could afford to pay for medical treatment were not doing so, while others were 'so poor as to be unable to benefit from it'; as a result, outpatients' departments had become 'scandalously overcrowded' (Willmott, 1996, p 1). Miss Stewart was appointed to act as a 'gatekeeper', to encourage those who were able to do so to join a provident medical association (a kind of insurance scheme), which would pay for their care; others would be referred to private charity or the Poor Law. (See Chapter Two for a fuller discussion of the role of the COS.) Although Miss Stewart's was a new appointment, the idea of almoning was not itself new. In 1546, four of the original governors of St Bartholomew's Hospital in London had been designated as 'almoners'. They were responsible for interviewing all applicants for admission and deciding whether to admit or reject them.[1]

This does not, of course, suggest that the almoners of the late 19th and early 20th centuries were cruel or uncaring people. On the contrary, they believed that the best way to help people (and society) was to encourage them to help themselves. This notion is expressed well in a famous quotation from a book on self-help, published in 1859: 'Heaven helps those who help themselves.... Help from without [that is, from the outside] is often enfeebling in its effects, but help from within invariably invigorates.'[2]

Nor does it suggest that the almoners of the past were unique in their 'gatekeeping' role. Social workers today in all settings (whether health, education or criminal justice) must make decisions about who should, and should not, receive their services. In hospital settings, social work assessments play a critical role in deciding if and when a patient is discharged; the so-called problem of 'bed-blocking' seems highly reminiscent of the 'scandalously overcrowded' outpatients' department of a century ago. Social workers also routinely carry out financial assessments to decide eligibility for services that are free or at a reduced rate.

The history of medical social work is told in detail in a volume by Baraclough et al (1996). This narrates the spread of almoning, first to other voluntary hospitals, and then, after the 1929 Local Government Act transferred responsibilities for Poor Law infirmaries to local authorities, to municipal hospitals. With the founding of the NHS in 1948, the number of almoners increased across the UK, and a small number were taken on in general practice, gradually being recognised and renamed as social workers. At the same time, specific psychiatric social work expanded throughout the UK. With the 1970 Local Authority Social Services Act and the 1968 Social Work (Scotland) Act, social workers in hospitals and health-related areas came to be employed by the new local authority social services and social work departments; in Northern Ireland, they remained part of the Health Boards. Osborn (1996) suggests that social workers working in hospitals in the 1970s and 1980s often felt that their skills and expert knowledge were not fully understood or appreciated in the new world of generic social work. The pendulum has, of course, shifted again in recent years, and there is much greater acknowledgement today of the need for specialist knowledge across all spheres of social work practice.

Current legislative and policy framework

Concerns about the NHS and its future have dominated the domestic political agenda since the beginning of the 1990s (Annandale, 1998). The changes introduced by the Conservative government's 1990 NHS and Community Care Act were taken forward by New Labour over two terms in office, and, in the process, Annandale (1998, p 198) argues that:

> ... patients have been reborn as consumers who are theoretically empowered to make health-care choices (through contracts placed on their behalf by purchasers) and to hold health-care professionals to account through new citizens' rights embodied in the Citizens' and Patients' Charters.

Soon after its election to Parliament, the New Labour government, as part of the White Paper *The New NHS: Modern, Dependable* (DH, 1997), made a commitment to encourage more 'joint working' between health and social services. *Partnership in Action* (DH, 1998b) promoted more extensive joint working across three areas: planning, commissioning and providing services. The government also published a Green Paper – *A Healthier Nation: Our Contract for Health* (DH, 1998c) – in which the links between ill-health and social exclusion were explicitly made. An improvement in living conditions and health were portrayed as part of a 'contract' – a partnership – between government, local organisations and individuals. This was followed up by another White Paper, *Saving Lives: Our Healthier Nation* (DH, 1999) and then in 2000 *The NHS Plan: A Plan for Investment, A Plan for Reform* (DH, 2000b), which set down the government's longer-term strategy for the reorganisation of health and social services. *The NHS Plan* proposed that social services and the NHS would come together with new agreements to pool resources, and Care Trusts would be established to commission health and social care in a single organisation. New legislation (the 1999 Health Act and the 2001 Health and Social Care Act) translated these ideas into practice.[3] More recently, the input of those who use services (patients and carers) has also been acknowledged as an important and necessary part of the partnership process in a consultation exercise – 'Making Partnership Work for Patients, Carers and Service Users' – which took place between August and November 2003.

For our vignette it is important to recognise that this raft of legislation does not apply to Northern Ireland, where hospital and community care services are shaped by a range of policy papers.[4] Health and personal social services in Northern Ireland have been provided as an integrated service since as far back as 1973. The four Health and Social Services Boards planned and commissioned services for the residents of their own areas. As part of the Review of Public Administration in April 2008, the Boards were replaced with five Local Commissioning Groups, and discussions are under way about the shape of a single Health and Social Services Authority. Eventually it is proposed that health and social care services will be mapped onto new district councils and, it is asserted, will be 'demand led by patients and driven by GPs and primary care professionals'.[5]

Alongside the structural and organisational developments, National Service Frameworks (NSFs) have been introduced across Britain (although again, not in Northern Ireland) for a range of conditions and patient groups. These comprise a series of policy documents on reform of services, procedures and workforce structures; the NSF for Renal Services was published in 2004. It promised that by 2014, the NHS would need to deliver on the following five areas:

- Standard 1: a patient-centred service – all adults and children should have access to information to enable them with their carers to make informed decisions and encourage partnership.
- Standard 2: preparation and choice – everyone should receive timely preparation and their options should be maximised.
- Standard 3: elective dialysis access surgery – everyone should have access to timely and appropriate surgery.
- Standard 4: dialysis – services should be designed around individual needs and preferences and available throughout people's lives.
- Standard 5: transplantation – those who will benefit from transplantation should receive the best support to manage the transplant and to achieve the best quality of life.[6]

Whether the standards will be met by 2014 remains an open question. With the shortage of donor organs, and the continuing pressure on routine treatment, it seems unlikely that many patients will feel that their needs have been fully met. Meanwhile, although social workers have applauded the idea of 'client-centred approaches' and 'needs-led services', the British Association of Social Work Renal Special Interest Group wrote in 2000:

> We deplore the fact that underfunding and a finance-led approach has resulted in an overwhelming and time-consuming bureaucracy, which has diverted social workers from skilled psychosocial intervention into repetitive paperwork. (BASW Renal Special Interest Group, 2000)

Discussion

In reviewing the historical legacy and current policy context, it is abundantly clear that the notion of almoners as 'gatekeepers' has not disappeared from 21st-century social work. Social workers today, whether in hospital or community settings, often find themselves in the situation where their assessments may (or may not) lead to the provision of resources (economic, practical and emotional) for individuals and families. This puts them in an extremely influential, but at times ethically difficult, position, especially when resources are scarce, having to negotiate often competing professional and organisational demands. A hospital social worker interviewed by Cree and Davis (2007, p 138) said that she regularly had to bend the rules and spend longer with service users than expected; she could not provide the service that people needed within the parameters set. She described hospital social work as task-centred, not person-centred. This suggests that a gap exists between the rhetoric of government policy and the reality of practice. This provides a good starting point for our exploration of practice.

From policy to practice: managing and being accountable for your practice within your agency

We have already argued that, to make a difference, social workers (whatever their occupational setting) must, first, have a good understanding of their own identity and function and, second, understand this in relation to others: their managers, other professionals, service users and carers. As a social worker working in a renal unit, Bill in our vignette is likely to be constantly building up his specialist medical knowledge in relation to kidney failure and treatment. He will be learning about the different kinds of kidney disease, their symptoms and problems, the commonly prescribed drugs and their side-effects, and the likely progression of the illness. He will also, however, be learning that a patient's experience of illness is affected, in large part, by their own individual differences and by the social context within which the person and their illness are located. In our vignette, Sam may be facing death; a kidney transplant seems unlikely, given her poor physical condition. She will be feeling extremely ill, and may (or may not) wish to engage with what the future holds for her and her family. As a consequence, it is likely, from Sam's point of view, that there is no concrete 'problem' to be solved, or 'solution' to be focused on, or 'task' to be centred on, although these methods may all, of course, be helpful in making arrangements for Harry's care and for the care of Mr and Mrs Hughes (senior). What Sam needs most is for someone to 'be alongside' her, to be prepared to listen and, when appropriate, to advocate on her behalf. Currer (2002) proposes that two factors are essential in working with people who are dying: first, confidence in the social work role, and second, reflectivity, that is, a willingness to recognise and manage your own strong feelings. Currer argues that this cannot be sustained and developed without adequate training and supervision, as well as appropriate policies and structures.

In continuing to work with Sam through this difficult phase of her life, Bill will therefore seek to build on the relationship of trust that they already share (see Chapter Eight for a fuller discussion of relationship). As Sam's mediator, he will probably also find himself as arbiter and manager in the multidisciplinary team. We will focus now on two key areas – interprofessional collaboration and supervision – before going on to explore the values issues and the contribution of social science ideas to this practice situation.

Models and methods

Interprofessional collaboration

All social work practice requires the ability to work with others from different professional backgrounds. This has been a consistent finding of public inquiries into failures of practice, as demonstrated in the Laming Inquiry (2003) into Victoria Climbié's death. The inquiry found that, although a whole range of professionals had had contact with Victoria, not enough had been done to bring their concerns together. Our discussion of legal and policy frameworks has already outlined the push in government policy towards 'joint working'. However, how this is played out in the real world of practice is highly variable, and a topic of much controversy. Gregson et al (1992) set down a taxonomy of collaboration:

- no direct communication;
- formal, brief communication;
- regular communication and consultation;
- high levels of joint working;
- multidisciplinary working.

In their research conducted in the early 1990s, Gregson et al acknowledge that at that time, the highest level of collaboration – multidisciplinary working – was quite rare, even between doctors and nurses. Leathard (2003, p 95) suggests that if Gregson's study had been replicated 10 years later, higher levels of cooperation would have been seen across the board, and, significantly, a sixth level would have been added, under the title 'integration'. There have always, of course, been specialist settings where integration has been a priority for professional staff, and there has been some blurring of boundaries as a consequence. Hurdman (1995) provides the example of hospice care, where *all* team members spend part of their time counselling individuals and their families. She suggests that the social work role in such teams sometimes provides the dual function of supporting other team members as well as patients. This does not, of course, suggest that there is never any conflict in the team. Nor does it suggest that such cooperation is routine or easy to achieve.

O'Connor et al (2003) explore the difficulties in teamwork for social workers in a secondary setting such as a hospital. They suggest that difficulties may arise because of differences in training and values. They may also, however, be based on differences in status, with the medical profession holding the greatest power. O'Connor et al assert that in all teams, the social worker has to balance the interests of individual service users and the groups he or she works with against the interests of individual team members and of employers. This balance, they continue, poses a number of questions:

> How do we balance the need for service user confidentiality with the need to share information in the team? How can you time your work with service users so that you don't overrun other team members? How do you handle conflict in the team? How do you involve the agency service users in decision making? (O'Connor et al, 2003, p 154)

O'Connor at al suggest that the aim of conflict resolution, from a social work perspective, should be to seek to achieve a 'win-win' outcome rather than a 'win-lose' outcome, as far as possible. They suggest that to achieve this, the worker must:

- Identify and describe the ground rules for interaction;
- Stick to the issues at the heart of the conflict rather than focus on the personalities involved;
- Stick to the issues in a process sense rather than try to achieve a predetermined outcome;
- Recognize that there are multiple solutions to a conflict. (O'Connor et al, 2003, p 130)

To return to our vignette, Bill, as a renal social worker, works in a multidisciplinary team. If he is to make a difference in this work, he will have to, first, know his own work well, and second, be able to work effectively with all those involved in Sam's care. This suggests that he will have to be able to build and maintain good working relationships; contribute to the identification and agreement of goals for each partner in working with Sam; maintain and share records and reports; and play a part in evaluating the effectiveness of the team's work. More specifically, he will have to come to his own assessment about the risks facing Sam, both psychological and social. While the consultant will have greater knowledge of the physical risks that she has to face, he or she may be less in tune with the world in which Sam is living: it will be up to Bill to ensure that Sam's views about her family life, and her hopes and fears for the future, remain at the centre of the decision-making process. Advocating on Sam's behalf may bring Bill into conflict with other professionals. If this happens, it is important that he is sure of his own ground and able to deal constructively with disagreement.

Supervision theory and practice

'Supervision is both central and marginal to the practice of social work,' write Sawdon and Sawdon (1995, p 3), 'central because the main resources which social work has are the personal resources of its workers; marginal because its potential efficacy is undervalued and undermined by low commitment' (1995, p 3). They assert that ambivalence about supervision has been reinforced by the political context and its increasing influence on the nature of practice. A combination of factors, including critical inquiries into child protection practice, legislative change and a recurring emphasis on the need for business skills to provide value for money, have led supervision to become 'synonymous with bureaucratic control (Sawdon and Sawdon, 1995, p 3). Yet supervision is, as Tsui (2005) suggests, as old as social work itself; almost from its inception, the COS offered administrative and educational support to its visitors. The COS even sponsored the first course in fieldwork supervision in the US in 1911, under the leadership of the social work pioneer, Mary Richmond (Tsui, 2005). Kadushin and Harkness (2002) argue that the aim of social work supervision today is to provide efficient and effective services to clients. Beyond this:

- Administrative supervision provides social workers with a context that allows them to do their jobs effectively.
- Educational supervision aims to improve their capacity to do the work effectively, by helping them to develop professionally and maximising their practice knowledge and skills.
- Supportive supervision aims to ensure that social workers feel good about the job they are doing.

This brief introduction makes it clear that supervision is commonly understood to have three basic functions: administration, education and support. Some commentators have added a fourth dimension – mediation – to take account of the need to work in partnership with other agencies, while others have added a fifth – assessment – since performance appraisal has now become a routine part of supervision. Given the anxieties generated by successive child abuse scandals, the above functions will also underpin concerns about protection, as workers need to demonstrate that they are neither a risk to service users nor at risk from service users within their practice. The controlling element of appraisal in particular will need to be made clear in any supervision arrangement. Our introduction also signals the complexities, ambiguities and tensions that are inevitably part and parcel of the experience of supervision. Sawdon and Sawdon (1995) point out that the very many different ways of writing and thinking about supervision tend to reflect the time at which they were written. Interestingly, Tsui's (2005) text on social work supervision does not consider institutional oppression at all; issues of power are dealt with primarily at the level of individuals, not institutions, reflecting a wider shift that has taken place in recent years in the discourse on oppression.

Much of the supervision literature to date has focused on how the practice of supervisors might be improved. There has been less consideration of what supervisees might do to make better use of supervision. Using our vignette as an exemplar, we will unpack the five elements in supervision, giving attention within this to the need for Bill (as employee) to manage and be accountable for his work.

Administration

Critics (for example Hughes and Pengally, 1997) argue that over many years the management of service delivery has overtaken the other, equally important aspects of supervision. Nevertheless, supervision provides a vital context within which key administrative matters can be discussed and resolved, including workload, time management and staffing. Faced with the unanticipated crisis in Sam's life, Bill has to manage and prioritise his workload. If he is to give Sam and her family the attention they require, he will have to give up something else; another service user/patient will not get the service they require, unless he can find some other way of dealing with this. This will require some strategic thinking on his part, as well as careful discussion in supervision with his senior social worker. The scenario also throws up inevitable questions of resources and services. In taking this case forward, Bill will have to make arrangements not just for Sam's son, but also for her grandparents. He will have to find out what help can be provided by Harry's father (if he is still in contact with the family); by other family members (if there are any); and by friends and neighbours. He will then need to identify what services are available, from statutory, voluntary and private organisations, and make a judgement about which will be best suited to this particular situation. Bill will have to follow the systems and procedures that accompany the application to delivery and review of these services. In doing so, he will have to keep his senior social worker (and other team members) up to speed with what he is doing, in order to avoid any overlap or confusion.

Education

Bill has never worked with a person facing death before. It will be important that he is not afraid to ask questions, to seek out information and guidance, and in this, his senior social worker will play an important role. The senior social worker may also wish to encourage Bill to undergo some postqualifying training in, for example, counselling or stress management. Research has demonstrated that senior social workers in the past have shown a lack of appreciation or interest in their staff members' experiences of training. Hughes and Pengally (1997) see this as a missed opportunity, while reminding us that training can never be a substitute for supervisory attention in all areas. However, as a social worker committed to improving his professional practice, Bill will be able to independently access current research and practice guidance from organisations such as the Social Care Institute for Excellence (SCIE),[7] which can be a valuable resource across the range of social work areas.

Support

Bill is relatively new to the hospital setting and this is a new situation for him. Moreover, he has had little experience of dying and death in his personal life. He has built a close relationship with Sam, whom he respects greatly, and he fears for her future, and is unsure how he is going to manage his own emotions over this period of uncertainty. Supportive supervision will be crucial to a good outcome here, as will the identification of other avenues of support, for example colleagues in the social work (or wider multidisciplinary) team, or a mentor inside or outside the team.

Mediation

It is possible that Bill's senior social worker may need to advocate on his behalf with some of the other professionals involved in the work, especially if he disagrees with the approach of a more powerful person, such as the consultant. One possible way forward here might be for Bill and his senior to do some joint work on an aspect of the case. Bill will be supported to recognise his strengths and that he has professional powers and authority appropriate to his role, rather than being disempowered through the handing over of all responsibility to his supervisor.

Assessment

It is important that Bill sets in place from the outset a mechanism for reviewing his practice: what has he learned from this, and what could he have done better? This should not be seen as a narrow appraisal of performance or competence. Rather, supervision should provide Bill with an opportunity to reflect critically on his practice, as is discussed below. He should also be free to reflect critically on supervision, to explore what is working and not working in his supervision arrangements.

Evaluation

Evaluation is, Watson and West (2006, p 147) argue, an integral activity in social work, not just for managerial purposes (analysing need and assessing outcomes) but also for professional practice, allowing social workers to 'learn from their experiences and enhance the quality of service being delivered'. A study of social workers' views of evaluation confirms this perception (Shaw and Shaw, 1997). Practitioners interviewed for the study distinguished between two types of evaluation: what they called 'evaluation proper' and 'self-evaluation', representing two distinctive sets of commitments, activities and attitudes. 'Evaluation proper', or 'Evaluation with a capital E', was seen to originate in legal or administrative requirements, and was led by managers. It tended to be quantitative in nature and reduced activities into small units that could be counted. Self-evaluation, in contrast, was 'fundamentally about quality, not quantity'; it was often done 'on your feet' rather than in a pre-planned way; its meaning was 'essentially fuzzy' (Shaw and Shaw, 1997, p 857). Shaw and Shaw (1997, p 862) conclude that to build an alternative approach to evaluating in practice, we need to 'start from the realities of day-to-day practice and with social workers' experiences and accounts of how they evaluate their work, rather than impose an abstract and decontextualized framework of evaluation'. In other words, we need to work 'from the bottom up', not the 'top down'. They therefore suggest that the following issues need to be taken into consideration:

- Start with the tacit knowledge of social workers.
- Cultivate reflexive evaluating in practice.
- Evaluating will rest on plausible and falsifiable evidence.
- Evaluating will be for and with the service user.
- The methodology of evaluating in practice will have at its core qualitative research methods 'translated' for practice (Shaw and Shaw, 1997, pp 863-6).

Watson and West (2006) develop this further, suggesting that an inclusive approach to evaluation can help to consolidate empowering practice for both the social worker and the service user. They recommend that the worker should be explicit from the outset about the reasons for their involvement, and that they should explore with the service user *what* is to be evaluated, *how*, *why* and *by whom*. This offers a useful model for Bill in his work with Sam. Sharing with the service user what research evidence supports particular interventions will allow for more informed decision making and a greater opportunity to work in partnership.

Values

Mind–body–spirit interconnectedness

We start from the premise that a medical model of illness cannot give us a complete understanding of the complex values issues that are likely to be faced by the social worker and service user in our vignette. (For a fuller critique of the medical model, see Chapter Four.) In other words, if we focus only on Sam's physical problems, we will fail to give her the service she needs. Bill knows that Sam must be treated as a whole person – she is much more than simply a damaged kidney, or a needy single parent. As a result, her mind, body and spirit must all be given due respect and attention. Social work has, in the past, shied away from discussion of spirituality as a legitimate part of its practice; this has been left to the chaplain, the minister, the rabbi or the religious leader. But increasingly, academics and researchers have been highlighting the relevance of spirituality and religion to service users in social work. Research studies have suggested that religious observance and faith may be particularly significant for those from minority ethnic backgrounds (for example, Furness, 2003; Gilligan and Furness, 2005).

Ng and Chan (2005) recommend the 'mind–body–spirit approach', inspired by traditional Chinese medicine and philosophies. This approach has a number of basic assumptions:

- Everything is connected: human existence is a manifestation of physical, psychological and spiritual being.
- Life is the eternal dance of 'yin' and 'yang': life is ever-changing; and the interflow of energy maintains a harmonious, dynamic equilibrium. Problems in life are caused by disruption of harmony.
- Healing comes from within: therapy aims to 'ignite the client's innate healing power to bring them back to a state of balance'.
- Restoring harmony 'not only cures illness and solves problems, it also opens up opportunities for growth and transformation' (Ng and Chan, 2005, 73).

Looking at Sam's situation from this perspective offers fresh insight. Sam's illness (and her recent deterioration) inevitably brings a host of questions, for Sam and for those in her family (and, of course, for Bill). They have probably found themselves going round in circles, asking 'Why me? Why did this have to happen to me (or my loved one)?' This turmoil is expressed well by the rabbi Harold Kushner in his classic book *When Bad Things Happen to Good People* (1981).[8] A mind–body–spirit approach will allow Bill to ask a different set of questions, which are much more focused on what can be done to help Sam to come to terms with (and so find harmony in) her current situation.

Inequalities in health

It is impossible to think about physical illness without acknowledging that physical health is a site of social inequality. As McLeod and Bywaters (2000, p 1) assert, 'Unequal social relations create unequal chances of staying alive, unequal possibilities of health across lifetimes and inequalities in the experience of ill health. Profound, unjust suffering results.'

Sociologists first drew attention to the ways that class and poverty affected health and life chances in the 19th century. Edwin Chadwick's *Report on the Sanitary Conditions of the Labouring Population of Great Britain* was published in 1842. It showed that the average age at death in Liverpool at that time was 35 years for gentry and professionals but only 15 years of age for labourers, mechanics and servants. Friedrich Engels' (1892) account of the lives of the industrial poor in Manchester, written between 1842 and 1844, came up with similar findings. Although life expectancy has improved for all classes since this time, inequalities have remained. In 1980, the Black Report (DHSS, 1980) showed that although there had been an improvement in health across all the classes since the introduction of the NHS in 1948, there was still a correlation between social class and infant mortality rates, life expectancy and inequalities in the use of medical services. In 1997, soon after it was elected, the New Labour government commissioned a review of research to look at this issue again. The Acheson Report concluded that unacceptable inequalities in health persisted, and that 'the weight of scientific evidence supports a socio-economic explanation of health inequalities' (DH, 1998e, p xi).

To return to our scenario, it will be vital that Bill keeps the question of social inequality on his agenda in his work with Sam. In keeping with anti-oppressive practice aims (see Chapter Three), he will wish to do everything he can to reduce the impact of inequality on her, while recognising that her social position (in terms of her class, age, gender and, particularly in Northern Ireland, her religion) will inevitably affect her experience of illness, as well as the strategies that she is able (and not able) to use to cope with the illness.

Underpinning knowledge

Loss and bereavement

Psychologists have had a major influence on how we think about chronic illness and bereavement. Elisabeth Kubler-Ross first published her seminal book *On Death and Dying* in 1970. Since then, it has remained one of the key texts for professionals in all branches of healthcare. Her insights have had a major impact on the care and treatment of terminally ill patients in hospitals, in hospices and at home. Kubler-Ross's work has also, however, had more widespread application, and her concepts have been used to explain people's reactions to all kinds of loss: of health, of loved ones, of status, of identity, of self.

One of her first observations was that, in spite of medical advances, death remains 'a fearful, frightening happening'; she argues that what has changed over time is not death, but rather our ways of coping with it (Kubler-Ross, 1970, p 4). So, she continues, death has become a taboo; we fear and deny the reality of death; death has become a lonely and mechanical event, a dying person is treated as less than human. Kubler-Ross goes on to argue that given the news of their terminal condition, patients typically go through a number of stages:

- *First stage: denial and isolation* – the patient's first reaction is often denial: 'no, it's not true'. It is usually a temporary defence, which is soon replaced by partial acceptance; however, some patients use denial through most of their lives. Kubler-Ross does not see denial as a problem; she sees it functioning as a buffer, allowing 'the patient to collect himself, and with time, mobilize other, less radical defenses [sic]' (Kubler-Ross, 1970, p 35).
- *Second stage: anger* – the question now becomes, 'why me?' This anger is displaced in all directions – towards family, medical staff, counsellors and anyone else, seemingly at random.
- *Third stage: bargaining* – the patient tries a different approach; they try to postpone the inevitable outcome by making promises, to themselves, their family, their doctors, God. These promises may be associated with guilt, and bring with them irrational fears or a wish for punishment. Kubler-Ross indicates that the hospital chaplain may be of particular help during this stage.
- *Fourth stage: depression* – a patient, in facing up to the future, also has to face loss at many levels. The patient will also experience anticipatory grief, as they prepare for final separation from this world.
- *Fifth stage: acceptance* – if a patient has enough time and support, they will reach a stage where they are neither depressed nor angry about their fate;

they will contemplate the coming end 'with a certain degree of quiet expectation' (Kubler-Ross, 1970, p 99).

It has been suggested that Kubler-Ross's view of death and dying may be rather naïvely optimistic, but this is to misunderstand the complexity of her argument. She does not suggest that the stages mark a linear process through which all people travel. On the contrary, she asserts that the stages that she has identified last for different periods of time, and will replace each other, or may exist, at times, side by side (Kubler-Ross, 1970, p 122). Moreover, she believes that what persists through all the stages is hope; she urges that as helpers, we should 'never give up' on a patient. In addition, she urges that more people should talk about death and dying as an intrinsic part of life; she writes: 'we do more harm by avoiding the issue than by using time and timing to sit, listen and share' (Kubler-Ross, 1970, p 125).

Thompson (2002b) reviewed current developments on grief and loss. New approaches work from the starting point that the idea of universal stages misses the complexity of people's experiences. For example, Stroebe and Schut (1995) have argued that we experience sadness and loss *at the same time* as we struggle to move on and rebuild our lives. Moreover, Klass et al (1996) emphasise the importance of holding onto the relationship with the person who has died, rather than letting go. They argue that grieving is a process of maintaining ties *despite* the loss, not severing ties. Thompson finds approval with this approach. He concludes that when a loved-one dies, it is not only the beloved person that we lose, but also what they mean to us; that part of our identity which was wrapped up with them. Grief is, he writes, 'the price we pay for love' (Thompson, 2002b, p 17).

Theoretical ideas about loss and bereavement are vital for Bill's work with Sam. Sam (and her family) will already have undergone a kind of bereavement when she first learned about her kidney disease and started dialysis. Now, this process will be reawakened all over again. Sam is bound to have a million questions to ask, not all of which will have answers, and it will be essential that Bill is clear what help he can give, and what belongs with others in the professional team (see the section 'Interprofessional collaboration' earlier in this chapter). He will have to give Sam the time and space she needs. He will also have to deal with his own feelings of loss and bereavement as he confronts his own fears and uncertainty about Sam's future.

Coping

Psychology has also made a significant contribution to our understandings of ways of living with chronic illness, that is, to answering the question: how do people cope? Radley (1994) indicates that 'dispositional' theories (which focus on stable personality differences as an explanation for people's coping) have been generally abandoned in psychology for research that explores the different coping mechanisms that people might use: cognitive (that is, a way of thinking) or behavioural (in the form of a course of action). In addition, psychologists have noted a distinction between emotion-based coping (where the individual attempts to minimise the emotional impact of the situation by adopting a specific attitude) and problem-based coping (where the individual tries to do something practical about the situation).

Cognitive and behavioural approaches will be extremely helpful in Bill's work with Sam. It will be important for him to explore with her what she is thinking, as well as how she is behaving. What messages has she internalised about herself, as a woman, a mother, and now, possibly, a dying person? Can Bill and Sam, together, find more positive ways of facing the future? (Chapter Eight considers cognitive-behavioural approaches in more detail.) Bill will also have to keep Sam's feelings to the fore. She may, as outlined above, 'put a brave face on it' and refuse to acknowledge the severity of her situation. This may be helpful in the short term, affording her some respite from psychological pain. It seems unlikely to be productive in the longer term, however, as decisions will have to be made about longer-term care for Harry and Sam's grandparents. Here a problem-solving approach may be most useful (see Chapter Five). Whichever approach is adopted, psychologists agree that ways of coping are related not only to individual temperament and personality and to the illness itself but also to social factors, including poverty and social class. This takes us from social psychology to sociological explanations.

Sociology of health and illness

One of the main contributors to the development of a sociological approach to health and illness is the structural functionalist writer Talcott Parsons. Writing in 1951, he insisted that health and illness should be seen as *social* phenomena, not physical entities or the property of individuals. He saw health as an essential resource for individual achievement and for the smooth running of society; ill-health, in contrast, made it impossible for individuals to fulfil their social roles as breadwinners or parents. More particularly, Parsons claimed that when people become ill, they adopt a 'sick role', which allows them to be exempted from their normal responsibilities; they are not, therefore, blamed for being ill. But, Parsons argues, there is an obligation on the sick person that goes along with this setting-aside of day-to-day duties. The sick person must seek help from the professional in the 'physician role'; they must also promise to get better as quickly as possible. Parsons' analysis has much to offer our understanding of the ways in which society behaves towards chronically ill people. Those who have lifelong conditions such as multiple sclerosis or HIV (and, of course, kidney disease) cannot meet their side of this ideal contract and therefore do not fit the 'sick role' as Parsons has conceptualised it:

- They cannot promise to get well as quickly as possible.
- One period of sick leave will not provide a cure.
- Conventional medicine may not provide the answer, since medication designed to control symptoms may itself carry debilitating side-effects.

Because they are unable to meet the expectations of the 'sick role', chronically ill people experience personal blame and institutional discrimination from family members, employers, social welfare systems and society in general. This takes us to a discussion of power.

Conventional Marxist and feminist analyses have pointed out the importance of class and gender in medicine, arguing that it is middle-class men whose interests have been served by the growth in medicine's hegemony. Foucault offers a different approach. He argues that power is diffuse; it operates from the bottom up, not just the top down. It is 'a multiple and mobile field of force relations where far-reaching, but never completely stable, effects of domination are produced' (Foucault, 1980, p 102). Power is not, therefore, simply held by individuals, once and for all time; instead, it operates through the norms and technologies that shape the body and the mind. Moreover, Foucault (1980) argues that where there is power, there is always resistance. This provides a useful way of thinking about our scenario. It suggests that Bill, as social worker, and Sam, as patient, both have power in this situation; they are not simply beholden to a faceless NHS or an all-powerful consultant. Instead, they create their own 'expert' knowledge: practitioner knowledge and service user/patient knowledge. They also, paradoxically, in a very subtle way, recreate medical power, by taking on board and developing medical discourses (that is, the ideas and practices that permeate everything that goes on in hospitals). This suggests the need for careful reflection, as Bill and Sam respond to the new situation in which they find themselves. This can be incorporated into any evaluation undertaken by Bill and Sam, and by Bill in his supervision.

Other forms of knowledge

Patients have been in the vanguard of the service user movement in recent years, particularly through the work of disabled people (for example through the Coalition for Disabled People and People First) and mental health survivors' movements (such as Mind). In this, they have acted as a major influence on the delivery and organisation of health services (Taylor and Vatcher, 2005). There is an active patient-led group for those with kidney disease in the UK. The National Kidney Federation (NKF)[9] aims to promote both the best renal medical practice and treatment, and the health of persons suffering from chronic kidney disease or established renal failure. It also supports the related needs of those relatives and friends who care for kidney patients. It is very likely that Bill will have told Sam about the NKF and encouraged her to join. Through the federation, she will get access to best evidence on new treatments and also have an opportunity to lobby politicians on important subjects such as organ donation. As an 'expert by experience', Sam will have much to contribute to her own care and to health and social services more generally; in turn, Bill (and all the other hospital staff) will have much to learn from Sam. However, it must be remembered that experience is often constructed and made sense of through dominant discourses within society, and claims that service user knowledge is 'pure' need to be reflected upon. Sam may well have absorbed medicalised views of her situation that can have consequences for how she lives her life, and she may be encouraged to explore her understanding of her experiences.

Conclusion

The focus of this chapter has been on how social workers can make a difference in their own agencies, through being accountable for their work, and through working collaboratively with others. The context of our discussion has been a multidisciplinary setting (a renal ward in a busy hospital) but we have argued that all social workers need to see themselves as working alongside others (other professionals, service users and carers), whatever their specific agency or setting. We have suggested that social workers need to develop specialist knowledge as it relates to their working environment. But we have also argued that good social work is about basic social work knowledge, values and skills that transcend setting or agency. Social work is about valuing individuals, about seeing them as 'whole people', about acknowledging the impact of individual, social, political and economic factors on their lives and experiences. Social work is about speaking on behalf of others when they are unable to speak for themselves; and about encouraging service users to find their own 'voice'. We have proposed that supervision plays a key role in supporting and facilitating social workers to do their jobs effectively. Being self-critical – being prepared to step back and evaluate your own practice – is also essential, since this is a fundamental precursor to moving on to new ways of thinking and acting.

Notes

[1] See www.bartsandthelondon.org.uk

[2] From Smiles, S. (1859) *Self Help*, quoted in Fraser (2003).

[3] There are no Care Trusts in Scotland; instead, Health Boards run hospital services, and hospital social workers are employed by local authority health and social care departments.

[4] See www.belfasttrust.hscni.net

[5] Written Ministerial Statement, Northern Ireland Office Review of Public Administration, Future Health and Social Care Structures (www.archive.rpani.gov.uk/health211105.pdf).

[6] Standards are paraphrased from www.dh.gov.uk

[7] See www.scie.org.uk

[8] Kushner wrote this book as a reaction to personal tragedy – the premature ageing and death of his son.

[9] See www.kidney.org.uk

Key questions

(1) What impact do class and poverty have on health, and to what extent has this changed in the last 100 years, if at all?
(2) What does it mean to suggest that social work with adults is primarily about 'gatekeeping'?
(3) What is the social work role in a health team?

Further reading and resources

- Leathard, A. (2003) *Interprofessional Collaboration: From Policy to Practice in Health and Social Care*, Hove: Brunner-Routledge.
- McLeod, E. and Bywaters, P. (2000) *Social Work, Health and Equality*, London: Routledge.
- Shaw, I., Greene, J. and Mark, M. (eds) (2006) *Sage Handbook of Evaluation*, London: Sage Publications.
- www.dh.gov.uk

8

Making a difference in demonstrating professional competence

Introduction

The focus of this chapter is Key Role 6 of the National Occupational Standards: that is, demonstrate professional competence in social work practice. This is subdivided into four units:

(18) Research, analyse, evaluate and use current knowledge of best social work practice.
(19) Work within agreed standards of social work practice and ensure own professional development.
(20) Manage complex ethical issues, dilemmas and conflicts.
(21) Contribute to the promotion of best social work practice.

Vignette: a formal complaint

Clare McLeod works as a criminal justice social worker in a city in Scotland. She is 24 years of age, white, and qualified with a BSc (Social Work) 18 months ago. She chose to apply for a position in criminal justice social work because she had a most enjoyable and challenging practice placement in this field while undergoing her training. Clare sees herself as an open and friendly person; she works hard to treat her clients with respect and to value them for who they are. Clare's life has been turned upside down because one of her clients has made a complaint against her to the Chief Executive at the Scottish Social Services Council (SSSC).[1]

The service user is Sharon, a 26-year-old unemployed white woman who is on a probation order following her conviction for shoplifting and being in possession of a small amount of cannabis. At the time of the complaint, Clare had been working intensively with Sharon for about nine months. Following the guidelines set by the National Objectives and Standards for Social Work Services in the Criminal Justice System,[2] she had seen Sharon on an individual basis once a week for the first three months, and since then, once a fortnight. In addition, Sharon had been attending a group for women offenders which Clare runs, along with a senior social worker. Their work together was initially offence-focused; Clare had explored with Sharon why she had been shoplifting, and she had helped her to consider other, more positive options for her life, including education and work. She had also discussed Sharon's use of cannabis, which was clearly causing problems for her. As Sharon got to know Clare, she had disclosed that she had been sexually abused by an uncle when she was a child; since that time, she had found it difficult to trust men, and all her relationships with men had been characterised by violence. Clare had felt privileged that Sharon was prepared to share her story with her, and she felt it was important that she did not let Sharon down, as so many people had done in the past. Clare therefore had readily agreed when Sharon suggested that they meet in a café, rather than the office, and this had become the pattern for their regular meetings. Sharon gave Clare a present of a silver locket at Christmas time, and Clare gave her a small gift in return. On one occasion, they met by accident at a club in town and had a drink together. Then one day, while they were having lunch in the café, Sharon expressed her love for Clare, and Clare was shocked: she had not expected this. She quickly apologised and ended their meeting abruptly. In discussion with her senior social worker, it was agreed that the case should be transferred to another social worker. Soon afterwards, Sharon telephoned the SSSC to make a complaint, claiming that Clare had abused her position of trust in their relationship.

Discussion

This vignette raises a number of perplexing questions for social workers, whatever their area of practice. Social work is all about building relationships with people – but what happens when these relationships break down? Did Clare overstep the boundaries in the helping relationship? If so, at what point did this happen? What should and could Clare have done to protect Sharon (and indeed herself) from disappointment and from what was ultimately experienced as mistreatment and perhaps even exploitation? These and other questions will now be explored in some depth.

Legal and social policy context

This vignette throws up a number of legislative and social policy issues. First and foremost, because it is located within probation services in Scotland, we must give attention to the historical background and legislation and policy as it affects criminal justice social work in Scotland. The subject matter of the scenario, however, is not specifically related to criminal justice social work. Instead, it addresses much broader questions in relation to professional conduct, and so must be considered within the context of workforce regulation, professional codes of practice and complaints procedures.

Historical background

Probation services in Scotland, unlike those in the rest of the UK, are envisaged uniquely as social work services (McNeill and Whyte, 2007).[3] The 1968 Social Work (Scotland) Act abolished the Scottish Probation Service and brought together the full range of social work services (including criminal justice social work) into one, all-purpose, local authority department, under the principle of 'promoting social welfare' (Moore and Whyte, 1998, p 3). This Act located probation as a social work service, 'a welfare rather than primarily a punishment exercise, where the object is to "help" the offender change as a means of protecting the public and the victims of crime' (Moore and Whyte, 1998, p 211). The underlying belief was that people would be less likely to offend – and hence the public would be better protected – if offenders were rehabilitated into the wider community. The notion of rehabilitation was not, however, a new one. Probation began in the UK in the 1870s with the appointment of 'missionaries' to the courts by the Church of England Temperance Society. The objective of the so-called 'police court missionaries' was 'the saving of souls through divine grace' and 'the restoration and reclamation of individual drunkards appearing before the criminal courts' (McWilliams, 1983, p 134). This is described colourfully in an entry in a Police Court Mission book of 1922:

> What a blessing it is then that the Saviour of men lived our life, and knowing all our frailties is able to help us to overcome. I am learning more and more to recommend Him to my fellows as their only hope of overcoming the evil around us and in us, and helping us to walk a clean, straight path.[4]

The first legislation to institute probation was the 1887 Probation of First Offenders Act, later extended by the 1907 Probation of Offenders Act. This legislation made it possible to 'hold back' punishment for a period of time, to allow the person in trouble to be supervised by someone responsible to the court. Successful completion of probation would result in the avoidance of punishment and the person 'living down' or 'making good' for the offence (Moore and Whyte, 1998, p 210). The duties of probation workers were defined in the 1907 Act as being to 'advise, assist, and befriend' those in their charge.

In their history of the probation service in England and Wales, Whitehead and Statham (2006) chart the developments in the probation service from 1876 to 2005. Drawing on Garland's (1985) analysis, they argue that probation has never existed in a vacuum; instead, it can only be understood within its wider political, social and economic context. Hence the notion of 'saving souls' fitted with the 'laissez-faire' approach to economics; a minimalist state and freedom of the individual fitted in a political system dominated by a free market. As it became accepted that the state *should* have a greater role in individual and family lives, so probation itself changed: casework, diagnosis and rehabilitation became the order of the day from the 1930s until the 1970s, when the rehabilitative ideal collapsed. By the 1980s and 1990s, the emphasis was firmly on alternatives to custody, punishment in the community and evidence-based practice. Whitehead and Statham (2006, p 13) conclude that probation should not be seen as a humanitarian movement designed to counter the repressive nature of the Victorian penal system. Instead, it is one of the ways of 'managing, containing and controlling "problem" populations on behalf of the state'. The establishment of the National Offender Management Service (NOMS) in 2005, bringing together probation and prison services, reflects this reality. (The idea of care/control is explored more fully in Chapter Two.)

McNeill's (2005) analysis of 100 years of probation in Scotland tells a similar story. He identifies four phases in its history:

- from punishment to supervision (1905-1931);
- from supervision to treatment (1931-1968);
- from treatment to welfare (1968-1997);
- from welfare to public protection (1998-2005).

McNeill argues that criminal justice social work must be much more than simply efficient management of offenders; instead, it must continue to be concerned with improving justice and helping offenders to change.

Current legislative and policy framework

The framework for current probation legislation in Scotland is provided by the 1995 Criminal Procedure (Scotland) Act and the 2005 Management of

Offenders etc. (Scotland) Act, which set up Community Justice Authorities. The Criminal Procedure Act states that a probation order is made 'instead of sentencing', in both summary and solemn procedure (section 228). In consequence, an offender is not 'sentenced to' probation, but is 'placed on' a probation order (literally, they are placed 'on test' or 'on proof'). The difference may, however, feel more semantic than real, because, as Moore and Whyte (1998, p 220) suggest, 'for all practical purposes, probation counts as a conviction'. Subsequent legislation has not changed this situation (McNeill and Whyte, 2007).

Criminal justice social workers in Scotland work within the framework set by the National Objectives and Standards for Social Work Services in the Criminal Justice System, initially published in 1991.[5] The priorities for probation include 'those whose current offending behaviour places them at risk of custody, who have significant underlying problems and who seem likely to re-offend, particularly young adult offenders' and 'repeat offenders with significant underlying problems whose offending history places them at risk of custody, even if the offence is trivial' (Social Work Services Group, 1991, p 1). The standards were updated in 2001 and again in 2004, with greater emphasis placed on public protection as the overarching goal for community-based criminal justice interventions, and a stronger commitment to assessment of risk and the risk management of offenders (Justice Department, 2001). Figure 8.1 demonstrates the interdependence of the intended outcomes of criminal justice social work.

Probation orders are used flexibly by the courts for almost all crimes and offences, for people of all ages, from every kind of background. They can last for anything between six months and three years. Some requirements are standard to all probation orders. The probationer must:

FIGURE 8.1

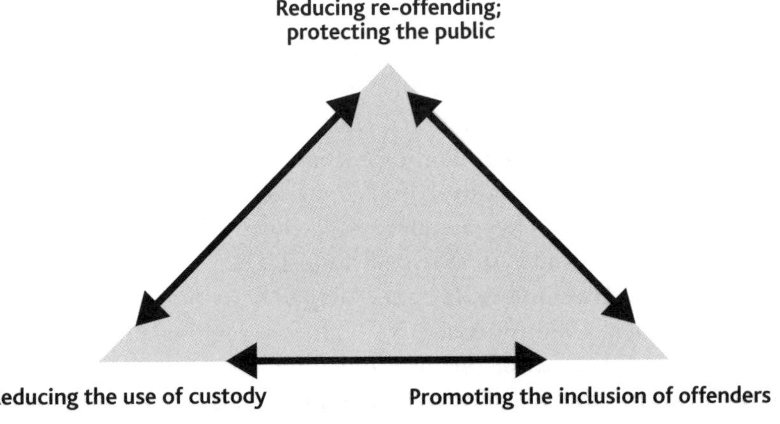

- be of good behaviour;
- conform to the directions of the supervising officer;
- inform the supervising officer if he/she changes work or employment.

Additional conditions can also be attached, for example requiring that the offender undertakes unpaid work. Moreover, stipulations can be made on the offender's place of residence, and probation orders may include curfews (including electronic monitoring), financial recompense to the victim or attendance at a specialist programme such as alcohol or drug treatment. Before an order is made, the offender must agree to address their offending behaviour and its underlying causes. According to recent statistics, the use of probation orders is increasing across Scotland. A total of 8,465 orders were made in Scotland in the year 2004/05, corresponding to 23.5 per 10,000 population; this compares with just under 20 per 10,000 population in 2001/02. The vast majority of those placed on probation were male: 82% were male, while only 18% were female. Probation orders were used with all ages of offender, but most frequently with those between the ages of 21 and 40. Most orders issued in the year 2004/05 were between one and two years in duration. The overall rise in probation orders reflects a general increase in the number of people convicted in Scottish courts. This figure fell from an all-time high of 155,000 in 1995/96 to 113,000 in 2000/01; since then, there has been a steady increase in numbers to 134,000 in 2004/05.[6]

Repeated studies have demonstrated that those on probation tend to have high social, economic and psychological needs (also known as 'criminogenic' needs; they, in effect, cause crime) (McNeill et al, 2005). They are likely to be unemployed and living on state benefits, having problems with debt, low educational attainment, health and drug problems and problems in family and childhood. Interestingly for our case scenario, there is some evidence that women offenders are treated differently by the criminal justice system. Research conducted by the Home Office and the Scottish Office and reported in 1998 (Social Work Services Inspectorate, 1998) indicated that magistrates tended to see women as 'more troubled than troublesome', and so sentenced them in such a way that women would receive assistance.[7] Pullar's more recent research (2007) in Fife in Scotland shows that very little has changed in the last 10 years. Women offenders are still likely to be viewed as 'in need of care and protection' and hence to be given a probation order, often for relatively minor offences or at an early stage in their offending 'career'. They are also less likely to be given community service, for familiar, gender-stereotyped reasons. There has been extensive discussion in the criminology literature about the nature of gender and crime (see Carlen, 1988; Walklate, 2001). It is recognised that although women commit all kinds of offences and share characteristics with men who offend, there are key differences too. Most fundamentally, women are less likely to offend than men. Beyond this, women appear less frequently in some categories of offence than others. For example, they are more likely to be found guilty of crimes of dishonesty (for example, shoplifting and fraud), and are less likely to commit 'serious' crimes such as sexual offences or murder. There is evidence too that women tend to give up offending earlier than men, at the point where they set up their own homes and have children. For those women who continue to offend, there are found to be strong associations between abuse as a child, drug misuse, homelessness and abusive relationships as an adult; self-harm and suicide also feature (Social Work Services Inspectorate, 1998, p 43).

Workforce regulation

It is significant that workforce regulation came much later to social work than to other professional groups in the UK. Social work only became a registered profession for the first time in 2005; the title 'social worker' became protected by law from 2006. The first professional body to be created in the UK was the General Medical Council (GMC), which registered doctors, as a result of the 1858 Medical Act. Nursing councils were established in 1921 for England and Wales, Scotland and Northern Ireland, with duties and responsibilities for the training, examination and registration of nurses and the approval of training schools. Following the passing of the 1943 Nurses Act, it became compulsory to be a State Registered Nurse (called a Registered General Nurse in Scotland). In 2001, the three councils amalgamated to become the UK body the Nursing and Midwifery Council. The first teachers' council in the UK was set up in 1965 in Scotland. The General Teaching Council (GTC) was established after the 1965 Teaching Council (Scotland) Act.[8]

Social workers' tardiness to embrace workforce regulation is not surprising given the diverse nature of the profession as it has evolved over the last 100 years or so. We have already made it clear that social work in the UK emerged in the late 19th and early 20th centuries as a response to the social problems that had accompanied rapid industrialisation and urbanisation (see Chapter Two). A range of statutory and voluntary initiatives grew up at this time, each with their own job titles and training programmes for staff. It was not until 1970 that medical social workers, psychiatric social workers, probation officers, moral welfare workers, childcare officers and mental welfare officers joined forces to form the British Association of Social Workers (BASW). Soon afterwards, a new Central Council for Education and Training in Social Work (CCETSW) was established in 1971, and with it, a new generic Certificate of Qualification in Social Work (CQSW). This might have seemed the ideal time to capitalise on the new cohesion in social work and move towards registration. However, this was not a settled time for social work. Just as the professional association was gathering members, so social work across the UK, with its growing number of local government employees, was becoming unionised (Payne, 2005a). At the same time, many of those working in voluntary agencies, as community workers, residential workers, day-care staff and group workers, did not see themselves as 'social workers' as it was becoming defined in local government agencies. Many argued against professional registration, claiming that professional bodies were self-serving, and protected middle-class, professional interests at the expense of the community that social workers served.

A number of different forces came together in the 1980s and 1990s, changing the status quo and making professional registration inevitable. These are summarised below:

- A series of high-profile tragedies and scandals, focused on the deaths and abuse of children and vulnerable adults, repeatedly placed public sector workers in the spotlight; doctors, nurses, health visitors, teachers and social workers were all singled out for examination and blame. The outcome was a call for greater regulation and standardisation of services across private and public agencies (Adams, 1996).
- The idea of 'more open government' was at the heart of New Labour's 'modernisation' agenda. Hence professionals, and, in particular, public sector professionals, were under increasing pressure to be more open to public scrutiny.
- 'Modernisation' also brought with it moves towards the integration of services ('joined-up' services). This highlighted social work's non-registered status relative to other professional groups. If teachers, health visitors and psychiatric nurses were registered, why not social workers?
- Integration was not simply targeted at public sector workers. As managerial and market mechanisms were introduced into state-run services, including the NHS, so there has been an increasing involvement of the private sector in providing education and social care. Again, this precipitated the need for greater control of social service workers and their work.
- Membership of the European Union brought with it free movement of workers between member states, and in this way, drew attention to the different educational requirements for social workers across Europe. While the minimum requirement for a social worker in other parts of Europe was an undergraduate degree of three years, the UK two-year diploma looked increasingly out of step.
- Movement of workers has also taken place on a much wider scale, as social work agencies in the UK have sought to fill vacancies by recruiting staff from developing countries, and from other English-speaking countries.

In consequence, employers have had to find new ways of regulating the workforce.

- Registration was not only endorsed by government and professional bodies. From the 1980s, the growing service user and patient lobby pushed for improvements in the training and practice of social workers; registration became one part of this wider programme of demands for reform (Beresford and Croft, 2004).

The 1998 White Paper *Modernising Social Services* (DH, 1998a) set the scene for workforce regulation in England and Wales; a consultation paper with an equivalent title was published the same year in Scotland (Scottish Executive, 1998), soon to be followed by the White Paper *Aiming for Excellence* in 1999 (Scottish Executive, 1999). These papers identified a number of key deficiencies in personal social services associated with protection, coordination, flexibility, clarity of role, consistency and efficiency. They promised to ensure that, in future, services would be more geared towards the needs of service users and, at the same time, more consistent for all. The 2000 Care Standards Act (England and Wales) and the 2001 Regulation of Care (Scotland) Act created new bodies with responsibility for inspecting and regulating care services across the UK. At the same time, new agencies to oversee workforce regulation were instituted: the General Social Care Council (GSCC) in England, accountable to the Secretary of State for Health; the Scottish Social Services Council (SSSC), accountable to the Scottish Parliament; the Cyngor Gofal Cymru/Care Council for Wales (CGC/CCW), accountable to the National Assembly for Wales; and the Northern Ireland Social Care Council (NISCC). The message throughout is that registration and regulation is about protection of the public, not of the profession per se (see Cornes et al, 2008). The four councils are thus responsible for the registration and regulation of those working in social services; the register of social service workers in Scotland opened on 1 April 2003. The internet 'home page' of the SSSC lays out its purpose in the following way:

> The SSSC is responsible for registering people who work in social services in Scotland and regulating their education and training. Our role is to increase the protection of people who use social services, to raise standards of practice and to increase public confidence in the sector.[9]

Registration requirements

It also states that six requirements must be met for a social worker to become registered with one of the care councils. An applicant must show evidence that they:

- have the required qualifications;
- are of good character and conduct;
- are committed to complying with the SSSC's Code of Practice for Social Service Workers;
- understand and accept that the SSSC will investigate allegations of misconduct against a registrant;
- are willing to undertake the equivalent of 15 days post-registration training and learning and to provide evidence of having met this requirement if asked to do so by the SSSC;
- have paid the relevant fee.

Codes of Practice

Uniquely for a professional body in the UK, social work has Codes of Practice for both employees and employers, which are common throughout the four nations.

The Code of Practice for Social Service Workers is a list of statements that describe the standards of professional conduct and practice required of social service workers. The intention, as outlined on the SSSC's website, is 'to confirm the standards required in social services and ensure that workers know what standards of conduct employers, colleagues, service users, carers and the public expect of them'. Social service workers are said to be responsible for making sure that their conduct 'does not fall below the standards set out in the code and that no action or omission on their part harms the well being of service users'. Finally, it is stated that the Councils will take account of the standards set in the Code of Practice for Social Service Workers 'in considering issues of misconduct and decisions as to whether a registered worker should remain on the register' (www.sssc.uk.com). The Code of Practice for Social Service Workers lists six rules for social service workers, who must:

(1) protect the rights and promote the interests of service users and carers;
(2) strive to establish and maintain the trust and confidence of service users and carers;

(3) promote the independence of service users while protecting them as far as possible from danger or harm;
(4) respect the rights of service users while seeking to ensure that their behaviour does not harm themselves or other people;
(5) uphold public trust and confidence in social services;
(6) be accountable for the quality of their work and take responsibility for maintaining and improving their knowledge and skills.

In the context of our vignette, paragraphs 4 and 5 are of particular interest. Beyond the general exhortation to 'uphold public trust and confidence', paragraph 5 states that social service workers must not:

> 5.1 Abuse, neglect or harm service users, carers or colleagues;
> 5.2 Exploit service users, carers or colleagues in any way;
> 5.3 Abuse the trust of service users and carers or the access [social service workers] have to personal information about them, or to their property, home or workplace;
> 5.4 Form inappropriate personal relationships with service users;
> 5.5 Discriminate unlawfully or unjustifiably against service users, carers or colleagues;
> 5.6 Condone any unlawful or unjustifiable discrimination by service users, carers or colleagues;
> 5.7 Put [themselves] or other people at unnecessary risk; or,
> 5.8 Behave in a way, in work or outside work, which would call into question [their] suitability to work in social care services.

The Code of Practice for Employers of Social Service Workers presents a complementary package of duties and obligations. To meet their responsibilities in relation to regulating the social service workforce, social service employers must:

(1) make sure people are suitable to enter the workforce and understand their roles and responsibilities;
(2) have written policies and procedures in place to enable social service workers to meet the SSSC Code of Practice for Social Service Workers;
(3) provide training and development opportunities to enable social service workers to strengthen and develop their skills and knowledge;
(4) put in place and implement written processes and procedures to deal with dangerous, discriminatory or exploitative behaviour and practice;
(5) promote the SSSC's Code of Practice to social service workers, service users and carers and cooperate with SSSC's proceedings.

With regard to our vignette, paragraphs (3), (4) and (5) are likely to be of special relevance. Has Clare received adequate induction and training to allow her to carry out her professional responsibilities safely and judiciously? The employer has a role not only in training but also in supporting staff (see paragraphs 3.1, 4.4 and 4.5 below). The employer is also centrally implicated in reporting misconduct and following through on investigations (paragraphs 5.5 and 5.6):

> 3.1 Providing induction, training and development opportunities to help social service workers do their jobs effectively and prepare for new and changing roles and responsibilities;
> 4.4 Supporting social service workers who experience trauma or violence in their work;
> 4.5 Putting in place and implementing written policies and procedures that promote staff welfare and equal opportunities for workers;
> 5.5 Informing the SSSC about any misconduct by a registered social service worker that might call into question their registration and inform the worker involved that a report has been made to the SSSC; and
> 5.6 Co-operating with SSSC investigations and hearings and responding appropriately to the findings and decisions of the SSSC.

Paragraphs 5.5 and 5.6 remind us that the focus of workforce regulation in social work is primarily on the public and on public protection. It is not peer regulation or protection of the profession; this is seen as the task of the professional body, the British Association of Social Workers.[10] Workforce regulation in social work is, in effect, a key demonstration of regulation by government.

Misconduct

In 2005, the SSSC published its Conduct Rules. Here it is stated that:

> … misconduct means conduct, whether by act or omission, which falls short of the standard of conduct expected of a person registered with the SSSC, having particular regard to the Code of Practice for Social Service Workers issued by the Council under Section 53(1) a of the Act and the SSSC (Registration) Rules 2005, both as amended or substituted from time to time.

It is stated that it is the duty of the Conduct Sub-committee to consider:

a) Any charge of Misconduct against a Registrant referred to it, and to decide … what happens next;
b) Any criminal convictions or acquittal on the grounds of insanity referred to it, and to decide … what happens next.

Discussion

Returning to our vignette, Sharon is, in many ways, a typical probation client. She was placed on probation, in part, because it was thought that she would probably reoffend: her drug use had led her to shoplift on previous occasions, and she would do so again unless it was tackled now. She was also given probation because it was felt that she might benefit from it: her high 'criminogenic needs' suggested that this was so. Sharon is, however, not just a typical probation client; she is also a typical female probation client. As we have indicated, research shows that women offenders' profiles tend to be different from those of men, and Sharon's offences and background are characteristic of women who become involved in the criminal justice system.

What is unusual about this scenario is that Sharon has written to the SSSC. Evidence suggests that service users across all public sector organisations are becoming more consumer-oriented and hence more likely to seek to shape the service they receive (see Malin, 2000). They are therefore more likely to complain about what they perceive as a poor service. Yet few probation clients will have heard of the SSSC. Moreover, given the highly personal nature of her complaint, it would have been difficult for Sharon to write her letter. It will therefore have been taken seriously by SSSC. Its officers will wish to investigate the case thoroughly, raising questions about Clare's in-service training and supervision as well as her professional conduct. The vignette also invites questions about how the topics of sexuality, gender and professional boundaries were tackled (if at all) on Clare's social work degree programme. Trotter and Leech (2003) argue that social work education has consistently failed to address difficult personal issues around gender and sexuality.

From policy to practice: demonstrating professional competence in social work practice

Our vignette allows us to explore social work practice from a number of different angles. First, we will consider the offence-focused nature of criminal justice social work, and the cognitive-behavioural principles that underpin much of this practice. (Note that evaluation, another key part of this standard, is explored in Chapter Seven.) Second, we will look at the values issues in the scenario, focusing on relationship and the contribution of feminism to social work. Finally, we will explore the knowledge that underpins practice.

Models and methods

Offence-focused work

Moore and Whyte (1998) assert that the only legitimacy for intervening in the life of the individual within the criminal justice process is their offending behaviour. Put simply, 'no-one should be drawn into the criminal justice process in order to receive social work help' (Moore and Whyte, 1998, p 24). Two explanations are offered for this stance. First, it is argued that it is discriminatory to pull individuals into the social work net inappropriately (so-called 'net widening'). It is also claimed that previous social work interventions with offenders, by focusing on wider psychosocial needs and not on offending behaviour, were ineffective in changing that behaviour. Offence-focused social work is therefore exactly what it suggests: it starts with the offence (the causes of offending behaviour and the risks of future offending) and it sets out to determine what needs to be put in place to contain and reduce offending behaviour in the future.

In our vignette, Sharon has benefited from two different, but complementary, services as part of this approach. She has had individual sessions with Clare during which she has had the opportunity to explore her past and also begin to make plans for her future (including enrolling at a local further education college). She has also attended the Criminal Justice Social Work Centre's women offenders' group, which has also encouraged her to think about her offending behaviour, but this time in a wider societal context. Both the individual's and the group's work draw on cognitive-behavioural principles (discussed below); they are also strongly influenced by feminist values.

Motivational interviewing

Motivational interviewing starts from the premise that we only change our behaviour when we are ready to do so; thereafter, our motivation to change goes through a series of recognisable stages, often presented as a cycle that is repeated over time. The model that is most frequently used in criminal justice social work (and in other settings in which drug and alcohol abuse is the focus of concern) is that of Prochaska and DiClimente (1984). This proposes that there are five stages in the change process:

- *the precontemplation stage*, where change may not be desired, but circumstances have caused the person to consider change (for example a court appearance or an overdose);
- *the contemplation stage*, where the person is willing to consider the pros and cons of changing their behaviour;
- *the action stage*, during which there is a concerted effort to change behaviour;
- *the maintenance stage*, where alcohol or drug use is under control, and cognitive and behavioural strategies are used as a way of resisting temptations to drink or use drugs;
- *the relapse stage*, when the person resumes the addictive behaviour.

Returning to our scenario, Clare will have been helping Sharon through the various stages. She may have encouraged Sharon to use a diary or tape-recorder to record the patterns of her thoughts and feelings in relation to her cravings and desire for cannabis. She will have praised Sharon for her successes, and also sought to build mechanisms into her life that are supportive of non-drug-using behaviour. This might include making new friends who are not cannabis users, rediscovering family connections or taking up a college course. Most of all, she will have wanted Sharon to have a better awareness of the consequences of her behaviour – for good and ill – so that she can make positive choices. The focus in this approach is therefore not on the past, on why Sharon became involved in cannabis use in the first place, but on the present and on the future.

Values

Relationship

As our examination of social work history demonstrates, relationship has been at the heart of social work practice since its very beginnings. We learned in Chapter Two about the unequal relationship that characterised the 'friendly visiting' of early social work. Middle-class lady visitors were in no doubt that the purpose of their 'friendship' with poor people was their moral and spiritual betterment. But they were also aware that this relationship was a two-way process; that they had much to gain from the act of giving. This is expressed vividly in a classic social work text published in 1979. Perlman says that social work is often taxing, but is never boring. She continues:

> So it is that the helper who is open and resonant to the lives of others is himself [sic] the recipient of a variegated and expanded life experience. This is no small reward, that our own inner world becomes livened and enriched by our relationships with so many different human beings in so many different life situations. (Perlman, 1979, p 206)

Trotter (1999) is especially interested in relationship as it affects 'involuntary' clients, that is, those who have not chosen to receive the services they are being given. Users of criminal justice social work services are predominantly involuntary clients; they have social work involvement because the court has deemed this to be so, rather than because they wish it. Trotter contrasts this with other professional relationships such as counselling and psychotherapy where there is no such enforcement, and asks whether the quality of the relationship still matters in this setting. His overall assessment is that it does; he agrees that an empathetic relationship is valuable. But he suggests that a good relationship is not enough to change an offender's behaviour. Instead, relationship must be accompanied by other practice skills, including the use of a prosocial approach, problem solving and role clarification.

Relationship comes high on the list of motivating factors in recent criminal justice research into desistance from offending, including Farrall and Bowling (1999) and Rex (1999). Around two thirds of the probation clients interviewed in Rex's study felt that being supervised reduced their criminal activity and made them less likely to offend. More than this, they reported that they were more likely to *sustain* a decision to stop offending where they felt committed to, and positively engaged in, the supervisory relationship. McNeill et al (2005) return to this topic in their review of criminal justice social work in Scotland. Here they indicate that a good working relationship and trust in the professional play a crucial part in generating change. They also argue that the 'working alliance' is dependent not simply on the worker, but on a set of processes related to both the worker and the client.

Feminism

Feminist ideas have made a significant contribution to criminal justice social work practice over the last 20 years or so. A key starting point was the realisation that criminology and victimology (the study of victims) had traditionally been 'gender blind': the world had been presented and explored as if it were made up only of men; where women appeared, it was as an afterthought or an exception to the rule. Early feminist studies of crime (for example Smart, 1977) sought to put women in the picture; to explain their different experiences and histories. But understanding gender blindness is not just about fore-fronting women. Walklate (2001, p 18) argues that:

> ... it is only through a consideration of the way in which structure their lives, and how we theorise about that process, that we can really appreciate the power that domain assumptions about gender possess.

Adopting feminist values therefore requires a fundamental examination of patriarchal systems, and the ways in which they impact on both women and men. (See Dominelli, 2002b, and White, 2006, for further exploration of feminism and social work.)

Criminal justice social work has translated feminist values into practice in both group work and individual work with both male and female offenders. This has been seen in work with men who have been violent towards women, in domestic violence probation projects[11] and in work inside and outside prison with men convicted of sexual assaults (for example Cavanagh and Cree, 1996). As part of a prosocial approach, it would be seen as good practice to challenge an offender's sexist attitudes, since this would be consistent with the overall goal of reduced offending. Similarly, a prosocial approach would seek to make a female client 'aware of her disadvantage as a woman and challenge comments which reflected an acceptance of patriarchal values' (Trotter, 1999, p 80). A feminist approach might also seek to promote a more equal client–worker relationship, which might involve meeting the client in their home, and some level of self-disclosure as a way to encourage empathy (Fook, 1993).

In our vignette, Clare was working from a feminist value base. Her work with Sharon in the group and in their individual meetings could broadly be defined as 'consciousness-raising': she hoped that, through their work together, Sharon, by having a better understanding of herself as a woman, would be able to make more sense of her own experiences. In this way, her 'private' world would become 'political', allowing her to make more informed (and more positive) choices for the future. Clare also hoped that by working in a more egalitarian way with Sharon (such as meeting her in the café), she would be able to minimise the inevitable hierarchy in their relationship. Their shared experiences of gender oppression as young, white, Scottish women provided a good basis from which to build new understandings of themselves and society (and hence offending within this).

What Clare did not, however, take cognisance of was difference. By concentrating on only limited shared identities (gender, 'race', nationality), she did not recognise the complexities of difference, choosing only to validate the more obvious categories and making global assumptions about these shared labels. The differences in lived experience through class, educational attainment and expectations of life eluded Clare, as well as her own experience of sexuality. As a heterosexual woman, and given Sharon's own sexual history, Clare had felt free to build a relationship with Sharon without considering issues of sexuality and power, as she would probably have done if her client had been a man. Clare did not behave in a homophobic way; she did not discriminate against, or oppress Sharon on the basis of her sexuality. Instead, she simply made heterosexist assumptions, which led her to underestimate the messages she was giving and receiving from Sharon. This, in turn, meant that she put herself and her client at risk. Fish (2006) argues that the public sphere is overwhelmingly heterosexual; that our public institutions (including the criminal justice system) are founded on the concepts of heterosexuality. She concludes: 'Lesbians, gay men and bisexuals did not choose the closet; they were forced into it' (Fish, 2006, p 17).

Underpinning knowledge

All the models and methods and values explored in this chapter draw implicitly and explicitly on social science theories. As we have discussed, offence-focused practice and motivational interviewing draw on predominantly psychological theories; feminist approaches, in contrast, draw more heavily on 'social' and sociological explanations and practices. The idea of 'criminogenic' needs, central to criminal justice social work practice, assumes that both individual/psychological background and current social/structural/economic situation are necessary for understanding behaviour and improving outcomes. Two further theoretical approaches must be examined in more detail here: the influence of cognitive-behavioural theories and labelling theory.

Cognitive-behavioural theories

In reviewing the development of cognitive-behavioural theories, Payne (2005b) explains that cognitive and behavioural ideas come from two related streams of psychological writing. Learning theory (or, more accurately, learning theories, since there is no single pure learning theory, but rather a collection of different, overlapping and sometimes contradictory theories)[12] asserts that most behaviour, with the exception of some inborn reflexes, is learned; we learn how to behave through experience, from influences outside ourselves. The important implication of this viewpoint is that it suggests that we can learn new behaviour or replace existing behaviour if it is causing us problems. Payne states that social learning theory extended these ideas by arguing that learning happens because of what we think and feel about what we are experiencing. Cognitive theory builds on both learning theory and social learning theory. It proposes that behaviour is affected by perception or interpretation of the environment during the process of learning; inappropriate behaviour arises because of misperception and misinterpretation, both of which must be corrected if our behaviour is to react appropriately to the environment.

Payne argues that the main aims of behavioural social work are increasing desired behaviours and reducing undesired behaviours, so that people respond to social events appropriately (Payne, 2005b, p 120). This may be achieved by the social worker reinforcing desired behaviour, identifying small steps towards change ('home work') and modelling good behaviour. Cognitive therapy, in contrast, encourages individuals to change not their behaviour, but their *thinking* (and, as a consequence of this, it is believed, their behaviour).[13] Cognitive therapy thus begins by encouraging the person to identify their 'automatic' thoughts in particular situations. These are then tested out in discussion, allowing the person to see situations more broadly and from different perspectives. The worker may then suggest alternative ways of thinking. Payne identifies the 'Reasoning and Rehabilitation Programme' commonly used in probation settings as one influential application of cognitive therapy.[14] This programme follows a prescriptive schedule of sessions on self-control techniques, thinking skills, social skills, victim awareness and critical reasoning, and is usually located within the context of group work, thus allowing offenders to learn about their own behaviour from others in the group. Cognitive-behavioural approaches are also visible within the concept of 'prosocial modelling', much favoured in individual criminal justice social work practice. As Trotter (1999, p 19) outlines, prosocial modelling involves workers

> identifying and being clear about the values which they wish to promote, and purposefully encouraging these values, through praise and other rewards. It also involves appropriate modelling of the values the worker seeks to promote, and challenging anti-social or pro-criminal expressions and actions.

However, there have been concerns raised about the introduction of cognitive-behavioural models of working, partly because they tend to provide quite prescriptive programmes of work that do not fit the needs of all their participants. Offenders are individuals with different histories, motivations, circumstances, offences and behaviours, but often cognitive-behavioural group work assumes similarities and homogeneity, providing one answer (Milner and Myers, 2007). As cognitive-behavioural work with offenders has developed it has been subjected to rigorous evaluation, which has questioned previous assumptions about the success of the model. For example, research undertaken by the Home Office on prison programmes found that there was no statistical reoffending difference between men (Falshaw et al, 2003), young offenders (Cann et al, 2003) and women (Cann, 2006) who attended a programme and matched groups who did not.

Returning to our vignette, we have said that Sharon attended a women offenders' group run by Clare and another criminal justice social work colleague. At this group, she will have followed a programme much as described by Payne above, in which she will have been encouraged to think and talk about her offending behaviour, and about its impact on herself, her family and the wider community. As cognitive-behavioural models are psychologically based approaches, Clare will have attempted to maintain a social perspective that recognises the structural pressures that some individuals are faced with in society. Over and above this general programme, the group will also have explored women's offending behaviour, and the place of women in society. In her individual work with Sharon, Clare (using the approach outlined above) will have sought to model the values and behaviours she wishes to foster, including self-respect, coping and optimism about the future. She may have used self-disclosure as one method of modelling and encouraging particular behaviour. This will be discussed further when we look more closely at what went wrong in this scenario.

Labelling theory

It would be impossible to write a chapter on criminal justice without drawing attention to the contribution of labelling theory to social work practice. Labelling theory begins with the insight that state intervention is itself 'criminogenic': that is, it causes crime, by labelling certain behaviours as criminal and then taking action against them. Society's approach to drugs is one of the main examples of this. Because certain drugs are deemed to be illegal, people have to resort to illegal means to get hold of them; they then become criminalised in the process.

Labelling theorists (for example, Lemert, 1951; Becker, 1963) argue that there is a distinction between primary deviance, which we all engage in with relatively few consequences, and secondary deviance, in which the reaction to the deviant action creates a 'master status' of deviance for some people. In other words, they begin to see their identity only in terms of their deviant status; they effectively 'become' criminals. This does not, of course, suggest that they do not then go on to commit further deviant acts. Many do, and we can see a self-fulfilling prophecy both in the way they behave and in the ways that others behave towards them. So Sharon will have experienced the negative impact of labelling in various ways, as a drug user, a shop lifter and a person on probation. She may have found it difficult to get others to see her in a more positive light. She may also, however, have told herself that she deserves no better; she may have internalised views of herself as a 'bad person' or a victim, based on the abusive incidents in her childhood. Much of Clare's work with Sharon will be about trying to encourage her to see herself differently; to understand the connection between 'personal troubles and the public issues of social structure' (Mills, 1959, p 8).

Other forms of knowledge

In reviewing the experiences of women on probation, Worrall (1996) indicated that the women offenders in her 1989 study did not see themselves as 'real criminals'. They felt that they had committed their crimes out of economic necessity or as a response to severe emotional stress. They saw themselves as lonely, afraid, lacking in self-esteem, angry and bewildered, and frequently depressed: 'The help that they appeared to appreciate most was friendship, material help and the opportunity to make some real choices for themselves – however trivial these might seem to others' (Worrall, 1996, p 74).

Worrall continues that for many women offenders, their only experience of relationships is oppressive and exploitative:

> Whether in personal or official dealings their expectations have been of hierarchical relationships in which they are told what they should do and how they should behave in order to please other people.... Probation officers who listen and encourage and avoid judging are more likely to motivate women to re-direct their lives than are those who insist on hierarchy and the strict application of National Standards. (1996, pp 74-5)

This gives strong clues as to why Clare's openness and warmth had such an effect on Sharon, and why Sharon interpreted it in terms of love. It also reminds us just how vulnerable Sharon was to exploitation.

Conclusion

One of the striking aspects of our vignette is that Sharon's complaint did not arise out of bad, neglectful or unethical practice. Clare's conduct was, on the whole, careful, respectful, supportive and well intentioned. It was also, however, potentially naïve, and in consequence, Clare put herself, and the service user with whom she was working, at risk. Chapter Seven explored the importance of being a self-critical practitioner, of standing back and asking: 'What is going on here? What are the possible implications of, and consequences of, my actions?' Chapter Seven also examined evaluation and stressed the significance of supervision in enabling social workers to review practice and safeguard standards. Criminal justice social work emphasises the importance of 'role clarification'; that is, having open discussions about 'what we are here for', and, most crucially, what is negotiable and what is not negotiable (Trotter, 1999). Addressing all of these areas would have allowed Clare to be more circumspect in her intervention with Sharon and, hence, more protective of herself and her client. This does not, however, suggest that we will always get it right. We acknowledged in Chapter Six that we can never eliminate risk from professional encounters. Given that social work is about using ourselves and building relationships, personal feelings (positive and negative) are bound to intervene. As Hochschild (1983) has accurately observed, 'emotional labour' is an essential element in increasing numbers of human service jobs, including nursing and social work. Advances in technology over the last 10 years have introduced a whole new raft of challenges for workers in maintaining boundaries, argue Gillen and Sale (2007). Mobile phones, text messaging and emails have all made communication between service users and practitioners easier, thus opening up new opportunities for communication to be misconstrued. It is critical therefore that we confront the ambiguities and complexities within professional relationships; that we make boundaries explicit and hence open to dialogue and negotiation.[15] This should help us to get the balance right, so that we use best available knowledge to inform our practice; we work within agreed standards; we manage dilemmas and conflicts; we contribute to the promotion of best practice. In other words, we demonstrate professional competence.

Notes

[1] The bodies that are responsible for inspecting and regulating social work and social care services across the UK are: the Commission for Social Care Inspection; the Scottish Commission for the Regulation of Care and the Social Work Inspection Agency; the Care Standards Inspectorate for Wales; and the Northern Ireland Commission for Social Care Inspection.

[2] National Objectives and Standards for Social Work Services in the Criminal Justice System (1991), revised in December 2004.

[3] Since 1995, probation officers in England and Wales have not been required to have a social work qualification. See www.probation.homeoffice.gov.uk

[4] Police Court Mission report book entry for December 1922, quoted in Whitehead and Statham (2006).

[5] See www.scotland.gov.uk/Publications/2004/12/20471/49283

[6] See www.scotland.gov.uk/stats

[7] This research found that family relationships and responsibilities were viewed as significant in sentencing women, and children were seen as mitigating factors. In contrast, paid employment was viewed as mitigating for men (Social Work Services Inspectorate, 1998).

[8] The GTC maintains a register of teachers, and looks at cases where registration might be refused or withdrawn on grounds of professional conduct. It also accredits all programmes of teacher education courses.

[9] See www.sssc.uk.com

[10] The British Association of Social Workers (BASW) is the largest association representing social work and social workers in the UK. See www.basw.co.uk

[11] The 'Duluth' model of working with domestically violent offenders is an example of a pro-feminist approach (Pence and Paymar, 1990).

[12] For further information see Sheldon (1995).

[13] In her review of theory, Trevithick (2005, p 263) points out that the differences between cognitive and behavioural approaches have become increasingly blurred, and most practitioners draw on both simultaneously.

[14] This builds on the work of Canadian criminologists Ross and Fabiano (1985).

[15] This is explored further in Shardlow (1995).

Key questions

(1) To what extent is it fair to say that the registration of social workers is primarily about protecting the public, not the profession?

(2) What does it mean to suggest that issues of sexuality have been largely ignored in social work education and practice?

(3) What are the six rules for social service workers?

Further reading and resources

- Cornes, M., Manthorpe, J., Huxley, P. and Evans, S. (2008: forthcoming) 'Developing wider workforce regulation in England: lessons from regulation in social work, social care and education: a review', *Journal of Interprofessional Care*.

- Fish, J. (2006) *Heterosexism in Health and Social Care*, Basingstoke: Palgrave Macmillan.
- Trotter, C. (1999) *Working with Involuntary Clients*, London: Sage Publications.
- www.basw.co.uk

Bibliography

Adams, R. (1996) *The Personal Social Services: Clients, Consumers or Citizens*, London: Addison Wesley Longman.

ADSS (Association of Directors of Social Services) (2005) *Social work in Wales: A profession to value*, Bridgend, Wales: ADSS (www.allwalesunit.gov.uk).

Albrecht, G.L. (ed) (1976) *The Sociology of Physical Disability and Rehabilitation*, Pittsburgh, PA: University of Pittsburgh Press.

Allender, S., Peto, V., Scarborough, P., Boxer, A. and Rayner, M. (2006) Coronary Heart Disease Statistics, London: BHF.

Annandale, E. (1998) *The Sociology of Health and Medicine: A Critical Introduction*, Cambridge: Polity Press.

Ansbacher, H.L. and Ansbacher, R.R. (eds) (1998) *Individual Psychology of Alfred Adler: A Systematic Presentation in Selections from his Writings*, New York: HarperCollins.

Arber, S. and Ginn, J. (1992) '"In sickness and in health": care-giving, gender and the independence of elderly people', in C. Marsh and S. Arber (eds) *Families and Households: Divisions and Change*, Basingstoke: Macmillan.

Audit Commission (1998) *Misspent Youth*, London: Audit Commission.

Auerhahn, K. (1999) 'Selective incapacitation and the problem of prediction', *Criminology*, vol 37, no 4, pp 703-34.

Baldwin, M. (1996) 'White anti-racism: is it really "no go" in rural areas?', *Social Work Education*, vol 15, no 1, pp 18-33.

Banks, S. (2006) *Ethics and Values in Social Work* (3rd edition), Basingstoke: Palgrave.

Baraclough, J., Dedman, G., Osborn, H. and Willmott, P. (1996) *100 Years of Health-Related Social Work 1895–1995: Then–Now–Onwards*, Birmingham: BASW.

Barclay, P. (1982) *Social Workers: Their Roles and Tasks*, London: Bedford Square Press.

Barr, A. and Hashagen, S. (2007) *Working with ABCD: Experience, lessons and issues from practice*, London: Community Development Fund.

Barr, A., Drysdale, J. and Henderson, P. (1997) *Towards Caring Communities*, Brighton: Pavilion.

BASW (British Association of Social Workers) Renal Special Interest Group (2000) *Renal Social Worker's Job Description*, BASW Renal Special Interest Group, February (unpublished booklet).

Bateman, N. (2000) *Advocacy Skills for Health and Social Care Professionals*, London: Jessica Kingsley Publishers.

Beaumont, B. (1999) 'Assessing risk in work with offenders', in P. Parsloe (ed) *Risk Assessment in Social Care and Social Work*, London: Jessica Kingsley.

Beck, U. (1992) *Risk Society: Towards a New Modernity*, London: Sage Publications.

Beck, U. (1999) *World Risk Society*, Cambridge: Polity Press.

Becker, H.S. (1963) *Outsiders: Studies in the Sociology of Deviance*, New York: Free Press.

Beckett, C. (2006) *Essential Theory for Social Work Practice*, London: Sage Publications.

Begum, N., Hill, M. and Stevens, A. (eds) (1994) *Reflections: The Views of Black Disabled People on their Lives and on Community Care*, London: CCETSW.

Beresford, P. and Croft, S. (2004) 'Service users and practitioners reunited: the key component for social work reform', *British Journal of Social Work*, vol 34, no 1, pp 53-68.

Beresford, B. and Oldman, C. (2002) *Housing Matters*, Bristol: The Policy Press.

Berg, I.K. (1994) *Family-Based Services: A Solution-Focused Approach*, New York: W. W. Norton.

Best, R. and Shuckworth, M. (2006) *Homes for Rural Communities: Report of the Joseph Rowntree Foundation Rural Housing Policy Forum*, York: Joseph Rowntree Foundation.

Bowlby, J. (1969) *Attachment and Loss*, London: Hogarth Press.

Brandon, D. and Brandon, T. (2001) *Advocacy in Social Work*, Birmingham: Venture Press.

Braye, S. (2000) 'Participation and involvement in social care', in H. Kemshall and R. Littlechild (eds) *User Involvement in Social Care: Research Informing Practice*, London: Jessica Kingsley.

Brown C. (1997) *Religion and Society in Scotland since 1701*, Edinburgh: Edinburgh University Press, p 95.

Butler-Sloss, Lord Justice E. (1988) *Report of the Inquiry into Child Abuse in Cleveland 1987*, London: HMSO.

Butt, T. (2004) *Understanding People*, Basingstoke: Palgrave.

Calasanti, T. (2003) 'Masculinities and care work in old age', in S. Arber, K. Davidson and J. Ginn (eds) *Gender and Ageing: Changing Roles and Relationships*, Maidenhead: Open University Press, pp 15-31.

Calder, M. and Hackett, S. (eds) (2003) *Assessment in Child Care. Using and Developing Frameworks for Practice*, Lyme Regis: Russell House.

Cann, J. (2006) 'Cognitive skills programmes: impact on reducing reconviction among a sample of female offenders', *Home Office Findings 276*, London: Home Office.

Cann, J., Falshaw, L., Nugent, F. and Friendship, C. (2003) 'Understanding what works: accredited cognitive skills programmes for adult men and young offenders', *Home Office Findings 226*, London: Home Office.

Caplan, G. (1964) *Principles of Preventative Psychiatry*, New York: Basic Books.

Carlen, P. (1988) *Women, Crime and Poverty*, Milton Keynes: Open University Press.

Carter, T. and Beresford, P. (2000) *Age and Change*, York: Joseph Rowntree Foundation.

Cavanagh, K. and Cree, V.E. (eds) (1996) *Working with Men: Feminism and Social Work*, London: Routledge.

Chadwick, E. (1842) *Report on the Sanitary Condition of the Labouring Population of Great Britain*, Edinburgh: Edinburgh University Press, c1965.

Clapton, G. (2008: forthcoming) '"Yesterday's men": the inspectors of the Royal Scottish Society for the Prevention of Cruelty to Children, 1888–1968', *British Journal of Social Work*.

Clare, A.W. (1989) *Psychiatry in Dissent: Controversial Issues in Thought and Practice* (2nd edition), London: Routledge.

Clark, C. L. (2000) *Social Work Ethics: Politics, Principles and Practice*, Basingstoke: Macmillan.

Clyde, Lord (1992) *Report of the Inquiry into the Removal of Children from Orkney in February 1991*, London: HMSO.

Cornes, M., Manthorpe, J., Huxley, P. and Evans, S. (2008: forthcoming) 'Developing wider workforce regulation in England: lessons from regulation in social work, social care and education: a review', *Journal of Interprofessional Care*.

Coulshed, V. and Orme, J. (2006) *Social Work Practice* (4th edition), Basingstoke: Palgrave Macmillan.

Cowen, H. (1999) *Community Care, Ideology and Social Policy*, London: Prentice Hall.

Craig, L.A. (2004) 'Limitations in actuarial risk assessment of sexual offenders: a methodological note', *British Journal of Forensic Practice*, vol 6, no 1, pp 16-32.

Crawford, K. and Walker, J. (2004) *Social Work with Older People*, Exeter: Learning Matters.

Cree, V.E. (1995) *From Public Streets to Private Lives: The Changing Task of Social Work*, Aldershot: Avebury.

Cree, V.E. (1996) *Social Work: A Christian or Secular Discourse?*, Waverley Paper, Edinburgh: University of Edinburgh.

Cree, V.E. (2000) *Sociology for Social Workers and Probation Officers*, London: Routledge.

Cree, V.E. (2002) 'Social work and society', in M. Davies (ed) *Blackwell Companion to Social Work* (2nd edition), Oxford, Blackwell, pp 275–87.

Cree, V.E. (ed) (2003) *Becoming a Social Worker*, London: Routledge.

Cree, V.E. (2007) 'Social work and society', in M. Davies (ed) *Blackwell Companion to Social Work* (3rd edition), Oxford: Blackwell, pp 289-302.

Cree, V.E. and Davidson, R.F. (2000) 'Enquiry and action learning: a model for transferring learning in practice', in V.E. Cree and C. Macaulay (eds) *Transfer of Learning in Professional and Vocational Education*, London: Routledge, pp 92-105.

Cree, V.E. and Davis, A. (2007) *Social Work: Voices from the Inside*, London: Routledge.

Cree, V.E. and Wallace, S.J. (2005) 'Risk and protection', in R. Adams, L. Dominelli and M. Payne (eds) *Social Work Futures*, Basingstoke: Palgrave Macmillan, pp 115-27.

Cross, N., Evans, J. and Minkes, J. (2003) 'Still children first? Developments in youth justice in Wales', *Youth Justice*, vol 2, no 3, pp 151-62.

Crow, L. (1996) 'Including all of our lives: renewing the social model of disability', in C. Barnes and G. Mercer (eds) *Exploring the Divide: Illness and Disability*, Leeds: The Disability Press.

CSCI (2005) *The state of social care in England, 2004-05*, London: CSCI (www.csci.gov.uk/publications/).

Currer, C. (2002) 'Dying and bereavement', in R. Adams, L. Dominelli and M. Payne (eds) *Critical Practice in Social Work*, Basingstoke: Palgrave Macmillan, pp 210-19.

Daniel, B., Wassell, S. and Gilligan, R. (1999) *Child Development for Child Care and Protection Workers*, London: Jessica Kingsley.

Davey, V., Fernandez, J.L., Knapp, M., Vick, N., Jolly, D., Swift, P., Tobin, R., Kendall, J., Ferrie, J., Pearson, C., Mercer, G. and Priestley, M. (2007) *Direct Payments, A National Survey of Direct Payments Policy and Practice*, London: LSE, Personal Social Services Research Unit.

Davidoff, L. and Hall, C. (1992) *Family Fortunes: Men and Women of the English Middle Class, 1780-1850*, London: Routledge.

Davis, K. and Woodward, J. (1981) 'DIAL UK; development of the National Association of Disablement Information and Advice Services', in A. Brechin, P. Liddiard and J. Swain (eds) *Handicap in a Social World*, London: Hodder and Stoughton.

DH (Department of Health) (1988) *A Guide for Social Workers Undertaking a Comprehensive Assessment*, London: HMSO.

DH (1995) *Child Protection: Messages from Research*, London: HMSO.

DH (1997) *The New NHS: Modern, Dependable*, Cm 3807, London: The Stationery Office.

DH (1998a) *Modernising Social Services: Promoting Independence, Improving Protection, Raising Standards*, Cm 4169, London: The Stationery Office.

DH (1998b) *Partnership in Action (New Opportunities for Joint Working between Health and Social Services), A Discussion Document*, London: The Stationery Office.

DH (1998c) *A Healthier Nation: Our Contract for Health*, Cm 3852, London: The Stationery Office.

DH (1998d) *They Look After Their Own, Don't They?*, London: The Stationery Office.

DH (1998e) *Independent Inquiry into Inequalities in Health: Report* (Acheson Report), London: The Stationery Office.

DH (1999) *Saving Lives: Our Healthier Nation*, White Paper, Cm 4386, London: The Stationery Office.

DH (2000a) *Framework for the Assessment of Children in Need and their Families*, London: The Stationery Office.

DH (2000b) *The NHS Plan: A Plan for Investment, A Plan for Reform*, Cm 4818, London: The Stationery Office.

DH (2001) *The National Service Framework for Older People*, London: The Stationery Office.

DH (2003) *Every Child Matters*, London: The Stationery Office.

DH (2004) *Every Child Matters: The Next Steps*, London: DH.

DH (2005) *Independence, Well-Being and Choice: Our Vision for the Future of Social Care for Adults in England*, London: The Stationery Office.

DH (2006) *A New Ambition for Old Age: Next Steps in Implementing the National Service Framework for Older People*, London: The Stationery Office.

DH, Cox, A. and Bentovim, A. (2000) *The Family Pack of Questionnaires and Scales*, London: The Stationery Office.

DHSS (Department of Health and Social Security) (1974) *Report of the Committee of Inquiry into the Care and Supervision Provided in Relation to Maria Colwell* (Colwell Report), London: HMSO.

DHSS (1980) *Inequalities in Health, Report of a Research Working Group* (Black Report), London: DHSS.

Doel, M. (2002) 'Task-centred work', in R. Adams, L. Dominelli and M. Payne (eds) *Social Work: Themes, Issues and Critical Debates* (2nd edition), Basingstoke: Palgrave.

Dominelli, L. (1996) 'De-professionalising social work: anti-oppressive practices, competencies and postmodernism, *British Journal of Social Work*, vol 26, no 2, pp 153–75.

Dominelli, L. (2002a) 'Anti-oppressive practice in context', in R. Adams, L. Dominelli and M. Payne (eds) *Social Work: Themes, Issues and Critical Debates* (2nd edition), Basingstoke: Palgrave, pp 3-19.

Dominelli, L. (2002b) *Feminist Social Work Theory and Practice*, Basingstoke: Palgrave Macmillan.

Dorling, D., Rigby, J., Wheeler, B., Ballas, D., Thomas, B., Fahmy, E., Gordon, D. and Lupton, R. (2007) *Poverty, Wealth and Place in Britain, 1968 to 2005*, York: Joseph Rowntree in association with The Policy Press.

Dwivedi, K.N. (2002) 'Culture and personality', in K.N. Dwivedi (ed) *Meeting the Needs of Ethnic Minority Children* (2nd edition), London: Jessica Kingsley, pp 42-65.

Engels, F. (1892) *The Condition of the Working Class in England*, London: Allen and Unwin.

Ennew, J. (1994) *The Sexual Exploitation of Children*, Oxford: Basil Blackwell.

Epstein, L. and Brown, L. (2002) *Brief Treatment and a New Look at the Task-Centered Approach*, Boston, MA: Allyn and Bacon.

Eraut, M. (1994) *Developing Professional Knowledge and Competence*, London: Falmer Press.

Erikson, E. (1959) *Identity and the Life Cycle*, New York: International Universities Press.

Erikson, E. (1995) *Childhood and Society*, London: Vintage.

Falshaw, L., Friendship, C., Travers, R. and Nugent, F. (2003) 'Searching for "What Works": an evaluation of the cognitive skills programmes', *Home Office Findings 206*, London: Home Office.

Farrall, S. and Bowling, B. (1999) 'Structuration, human development and desistance from crime', *British Journal of Criminology*, vol 39, no 20, pp 253-68.

Fawcett, H. (1975) *Brief description: Pauperism: Its Causes and Remedies*, Clifton, NJ: Augustus M. Kelley.

Fawcett, M. (1996) *Learning through Child Observation*, London: Jessica Kingsley.

Featherstone, B. (2003) 'Taking fathers seriously', *British Journal of Social Work*, vol 33, no 2, pp 239-54.

Featherstone, B. (2004) *Family Life and Family Support: A Feminist Analysis*, Basingstoke: Palgrave.

Featherstone, B. and Fawcett, B. (1995) 'Oh no! not more isms: feminism, post-modernism, post-structuralism and social work education', *Social Work Education*, vol 14, no 3, pp 25-43.

Featherstone, B., Rivett, M. and Scourfield, J. (2007) *Working with Men in Health and Social Care*, London: Sage Publications.

Feeley, M.M. and Simon, J. (1992) 'The new penology: notes on the emerging strategy of corrections and its implications', *Criminology*, vol 30, no 4, pp 449-74.

Ferguson, H. (2004) *Protecting Children in Time: Child Abuse, Child Protection, and the Consequences of Modernity*, Basingstoke: Palgrave Macmillan.

Finkelstein, V. (1980) *Attitudes and Disabled People: Issues for Discussion*, New York: World Rehabilitation Fund.

Finlay, L. (2003) 'The reflexive journey: mapping multiple routes', in L. Finlay and B. Gough (eds) *Reflexivity: A Practical Guide for Researchers in Health and Social Sciences*, Oxford: Blackwell, pp 3-20.

Fish, J. (2006) *Heterosexism in Health and Social Care*, Basingstoke: Palgrave Macmillan.

Fook, J. (1993) *Radical Casework*, Sydney: Allen & Unwin.

Fook, J. (2002) *Social Work: Critical Theory and Practice*, London: Sage Publications.

Foucault, M. (1977) *Discipline and Punish*, London: Allen Lane.

Foucault, M. (1980) *Michel Foucault: Power/Knowledge. Selected Interviews and Other Writings*, C. Gordon (ed), Brighton: Harvester.

Fraser, D. (2003) *The Evolution of the British Welfare State: A History of Social Policy since the Industrial Revolution* (3rd edition), Basingstoke: Palgrave Macmillan.

Fruin, D. (2000) *New Directions for Independent Living: Inspection of Independent Living Arrangements for Younger Disabled People*, London: Department of Health.

Furness, S. (2003) 'Religion, belief and culturally competent practice', *Journal of Practice Teaching in Health and Social Care*, vol 15, no 1, pp 61-74.

Garland, D. (1985) *Punishment and Welfare*, Aldershot: Gower.

Garrett, P.M. (2003) 'Swimming with dolphins: the Assessment Framework, New Labour and new tools for social work with children and families', *British Journal of Social Work*, vol 33, no 4, pp 441-63.

Gelsthorpe, L. and Morris, A. (1994) 'Juvenile justice 1945-1992', in M. Maguire, R. Morgan and R. Reiner (eds) *The Oxford Handbook of Criminology*, Oxford: Oxford University Press.

Gelsthorpe, L. and Morris, A. (2002) 'Restorative youth justice: the last vestiges of welfare?', in J. Muncie, G. Hughes and E. McLaughlin (eds) *Youth Justice: Critical Readings*, London: Sage Publications.

Ghate, D. and Hazel, N. (2002) *Parenting in Poor Environments: Stress, Support and Coping*, London: Jessica Kingsley.

Gillen, S. and Sale, A.U. (2007) 'Too close and personal', *Community Care*, 7 June, pp 16-18.

Gilligan, P. and Furness, S. (2005) 'The role of religion and spirituality in social work practice: views and experiences of social workers and students', *British Journal of Social Work*, vol 36, no 4, pp 617-37.

Gillis, J.R. (1975) 'The evolution of juvenile delinquency in England 1890-1914', *Past and Present*, vol 67, no 1, pp 96-126.

Goldson, B. (ed) (1999) *Youth Justice: Contemporary Policy and Practice*, Aldershot: Ashgate.

Goldson, B. and Muncie, J. (eds) (2006) *Youth Crime and Justice*, London: Sage Publications.

Gooding, C. (1996) *Blackstone's Guide to the Disability Discrimination Act 1995*, London: Blackstone Press.

Greene, G.J. and Kondrat, D.C. (2006) 'A solution-focused approach to case management and recovery with consumers who have a severe mental disability', *Families in Society: The Journal of Contemporary Human Services*, vol 87, no 3, pp 339-51.

Greenwood, P.W. and Abrahamse, A. (1982) *Selective Incapacitation*, Santa Monica, CA: RAND.

Gregson, B., Cartlidge, A. and Bond, J. (1992) 'Development of a measure of professional collaboration in primary health care', *Journal of Epidemiology and Community Health*, vol 46, no 1, pp 48-53.

Griffiths, R. (1988) *Community Care: Agenda for Action* (Griffiths Report), London: HMSO.

Hanson, R.K. and Thornton, D. (1999) *Static-99: Improving Actuarial Risk Assessments for Sex Offenders*, Ottawa: Department of the Solicitor General of Canada.

Hart, S.D., Michie, C. and Cooke, D.J. (2007) 'Precision of actuarial risk assessment instruments: evaluating the "margins of error" of group v. individual predictions of violence', *British Journal of Psychiatry*, vol 190, no 49, suppl s60-s65.

Hartley, L.P. (1953) *The go-between*, London: H. Hamilton.

Hasler, F. and Stewart, A. (2004) *Making Direct Payments Work: Identifying and Overcoming Barriers to Implementation*, Brighton: Pavilion/JRF.

Healthcare Commission (2006) *Living Well in Later Life: A Review of Progress against the National Service Framework for Older People*, London: Commission for Health Care Audit and Inspection.

Healy, K. (2005) *Social Work Theories in Context: Creating Frameworks for Practice*, Basingstoke: Palgrave Macmillan.

Hendrick, H. (2006) 'Histories of youth crime and justice', in B. Goldson and J. Muncie (eds) *Youth Crime and Justice*, London: Sage Publications.

Hirsch, D. (2006) *What Will it Take to End Child Poverty? Firing on All Cylinders*, York: Joseph Rowntree Foundation.

HMSO (1942) *Report on Social Insurance and Allied Services*, Cmd 6404, London: HMSO.

Hochschild, A. (1983) *The Managed Heart: Commercialization of Human Feeling*, Berkeley, CA: University of California Press.

Holland, S. (1999) 'Discourses of decision-making in child protection: conducting comprehensive assessments in Britain', *International Journal of Social Welfare*, vol 8, no 4, pp 277-87.

Home Office (1997) *No More Excuses*, Cm 3809, London: HMSO.

Home Office (2000) *National Standards for Youth Justice*, London: Home Office.

Home Office (2006) *A Guide to Anti-Social Behaviour Orders*, London: Home Office.

Horwath, J. (ed) (2001) *The Child's World: Assessing Children in Need*, London: Jessica Kingsley.

Howe, D. (1994) 'Modernity, postmodernity and social work', *British Journal of Social Work*, vol 24, no 5, pp 513-32.

Howe, D. (2003) 'Assessments using an attachment perspective', in M. Calder and S. Hackett (eds) *Assessment in Child Care: Using and Developing Frameworks for Practice*, Lyme Regis: Russell House, pp 375-87.

Hughes, G. and Follett, M. (2006) 'Community safety, youth, and the "anti-social"', in B. Goldson and J. Muncie (eds) *Youth Crime and Justice*, London: Sage Publications.

Hughes, B. and Mtezuka, E.M. (1992) 'Social work and older women', in M. Langan and L. Day (eds) *Women, Oppression and Social Work: Issues in Anti-discriminatory Practice*, London: Routledge.

Hughes, L. and Pengally, P. (1997) *Staff Supervision in a Turbulent Environment: Managing Process and Task in Front-line Services*, London: Jessica Kingsley.

Hurdman, R. (1995) 'Meeting social needs – the role of the social worker', in J. Robbins and J. Moscrop (eds) *Caring for the Dying Patient and the Family* (3rd edition), London: Chapman & Hall.

Husain, F. (2006) 'Cultural competence, cultural sensitivity and family support', in P. Dolan, J. Canavan and J. Pinkerton (eds) *Family Support as Reflective Practice*, London: Jessica Kingsley, pp 165-80.

Issett, M. (2000) 'Critical professionals and reflective practice', in J. Batsleer and B. Humphries (eds) *Welfare, Exclusion and Political Agency*, London: Routledge.

Jackson, S. (1999) 'Family group conferences and youth justice: the new panacea?', in B. Goldson (ed) *Youth Justice: Contemporary Policy and Practice*, Aldershot: Ashgate.

Jenkins, A. (1996) 'Moving towards respect: a quest for balance', in C. McClean, M. Carey and C. White (eds) *Men's Ways of Being*, Boulder, CO: Westview Press.

Jenks, C. (1996) *Childhood*, London: Routledge.

Jones, C. (2001) 'Voices from the front line: state social workers and New Labour', *British Journal of Social Work*, vol 31, no 4, pp 547-62.

Jones, C. (2002) 'Poverty and social exclusion', in M. Davies (ed) *Blackwell Companion to Social Work* (2nd edition), Oxford: Blackwell, pp 7-18.

Jones, R. (2006) 'Social work must brace itself', *Community Care*, 18-24 May, pp 32-3.

Jordan, B. (2006) *Social Policy for the Twenty-First Century*, Cambridge: Polity Press.

Justice Department (2001) *Criminal Justice Social Work Services: National Priorities for 2001–2002 and Onwards*, Edinburgh: The Scottish Executive.

Kadushin, A. and Harkness, D. (2002) *Supervision in Social Work* (4th edition), New York: Columbia University Press.

Kanel, K. (2003) *A Guide to Crisis Intervention*, Pacific Grove, CA: Brooks-Cole.

Katbamna, S., Ahmad, W., Bhakta, P. and Parker, G. (2004) 'Do they look after their own? Informal support for South Asian carers', *Health and Social Care in the Community*, vol 12, no 5, pp 398-406.

King's Fund (2006) *Securing Good Care for Older People: Taking a Long-term View*, London: King's Fund.

Kirschenbaum, H. and Henderson, V.L. (1989) *The Carl Rogers Reader*, London: Constable.

Klass, D., Silverman, P.R. and Nickman, S.L. (eds) (1996) *Continuing Bonds: New Understandings of Grief*, London: Taylor and Francis.

Knapp, M. and Prince, M. (2007) *Dementia UK*, London: Alzheimer's Society.

Knight, S.E. (1981) 'Introduction', in D.G. Bullard and S.E. Knight (eds) *Sexuality and Physical Disability: Personal Perspectives*, London: C.V. Mosby.

Kolb, D.A. (1984) *Experiential Learning*, New York: Prentice Hall.

Kubler-Ross, E. (1970) *On Death and Dying*, London: Tavistock.

Kushner, H.S. (1981) *When Bad Things Happen to Good People*, New York: Random House.

Laming, Lord (2003) *The Victoria Climbié Inquiry: Report of an Inquiry by Lord Laming*, London: HMSO.

Leathard, A. (2003) 'Models for interprofessional collaboration', in A. Leathard (ed) *Interprofessional Collaboration: From Policy to Practice in Health and Social Care*, Hove: Brunner-Routledge.

Lehfeldt, E.A. (ed) (2005) *The Black Death*, Boston, MA: Houghton Mifflin.

Lemert, E.M. (1951) *Social Pathology*, New York: McGraw-Hill.

Levitt, I. (1988) *Poverty and Welfare in Scotland 1890-1948*, Edinburgh: Edinburgh University Press.

Lindeman, E. (1965) 'Symptomatology and management of acute grief', in H. J. Parad (ed) *Crisis Intervention: Selected Readings*, New York: Family Service Association of America.

Lloyd, M. (2002) 'Care management', in R. Adams, L. Dominelli and M. Payne (eds) *Critical Practice in Social Work*, Basingstoke: Palgrave, pp 159-68.

McAra, L. and McVie, S. (2005) 'The usual suspects? Street-life, young offenders and the police', *Criminal Justice*, vol 5, no 1, pp 5-36.

McLeod, E. and Bywaters, P. (2000) *Social Work, Health and Equality*, London: Routledge.

McMullin, J. (1995) 'Theorizing age and gender relations', in S. Arber and J. Ginn (eds) *Gender and Later Life: A Sociological Analysis of Resources and Constraints*, London: Sage Publications.

McNeill, F. (2005) 'Remembering probation in Scotland', *Probation Journal*, vol 52, no 1, pp 23-38.

McNeill, F. (2007) 'Community supervision: context and relationships matter', in B. Goldson and J. Muncie (eds) *Youth Crime and Justice*, London: Sage Publications, pp 125-39.

McNeill, F. and Whyte, B. (2007) *Reducing Reoffending: Social Work and Community Justice in Scotland*, Cullompton: Willan Publishing.

McNeill, F., Batchelor, S., Burnett, R. and Knox, J. (2005) *21st Century Social Work: Reducing Re-offending: Key Practice Skills*, Edinburgh: The Scottish Executive.

McPeck, J.E. (1990) *Teaching Critical Thinking: Dialogue and Dialectic*, New York: Routledge, Chapman and Hall.

McWilliams, W. (1983) 'The mission to the English police courts 1876–1936', *Howard Journal*, vol 22, pp 129-47.

Malin, N. (ed) (2000) *Professionalism, Boundaries and the Workplace*, London: Routledge.

Malone, C., Forbat, L., Robb, M. and Seden, J. (eds) (2005) *Relating Experience: Stories from Health and Social Care*, London: Routledge.

Marsh, P. and Doel, M. (2005) *The Task-centred Book*, London: Routledge/Community Care.

Middleton, L. (1992) *Children First: Working with Children and Disability*, Birmingham: Venture Press.

Mill, J.S. ([1859] 1992) *On Liberty*, London: J.W. Parker.

Millar, M. and Corby, B. (2006) 'The framework for the assessment of children in need and their families – a basis for a "therapeutic" encounter?', *British Journal of Social Work*, vol 36, no 6, pp 887-99.

Miller, N. and Boud, D. (1996) *Working with Experience: Animating Learning*, London: Routledge.

Mills, C.W. (1959) *The Sociological Imagination*, Oxford: Oxford University Press.

Milner, J. and Myers, S. (2007) *Working with Violence: Policies and Practices in Risk Assessment and Management*, Basingstoke: Palgrave.

Milner, J. and O'Byrne, P. (2002) *Assessment in Social Work* (2nd edition), Basingstoke: Palgrave.

Milner, J. and O'Byrne, P. (2004) *Assessment in Counselling: Theory, Process and Decision Making*, Basingstoke: Palgrave Macmillan.

Mooney, G. (1998) '"Remoralizing" the poor?: gender, class and philanthropy in Victorian Britain', in G. Lewis (ed) *Forming Nation, Framing Welfare*, London: Routledge.

Moore, G. and Whyte, B. (1998) *Moore and Wood's Social Work and Criminal Law in Scotland* (3rd edition), Edinburgh: Mercat Press.

Moriarty, J. and Murray, J. (2007) 'Who wants to be a social worker?', *British Journal of Social Work*, vol 37, no 4, pp 715-33.

Morris, J. (1995) 'Creating a space for absent voices: disabled women's experience of receiving assistance with daily living activities', *Feminist Review*, vol 51, no 1, pp 68-93.

Morris, W. and Morris, M. ([1977] 1988) *Morris Dictionary of Word and Phrase Origins*, New York: HarperCollins.

Muncie, J. (2004) *Youth and Crime* (2nd edition), London: Sage Publications.

Muncie, J. and Goldson, B. (2006) 'States of transition: convergence and diversity in international youth justice', in J. Muncie and B. Goldson (eds) *Comparative Youth Justice*, London: Sage Publications, pp 196-218.

Munford, R. and Walsh-Tapiata, W. (2005) 'Community development: principles into practice', in M. Nash, R. Munford and K. O'Donoghue (eds) *Social Work Theories in Action*, London: Jessica Kingsley.

Munro, E. (2007) *Child Protection*, London: Sage Publications.

Myers, S. (2007) *Solution Focused Approaches*, Lyme Regis: Russell House Press.

Myers, S. and Milner, J. (2007) *Sexual Issues in Social Work*, Bristol: The Policy Press/BASW.

Neimeyer, R.A. and Anderson, A. (2002) 'Meaning reconstruction theory', in N. Thompson (ed) *Loss and Grief*, Basingstoke: Palgrave.

Newburn, T. (1996) 'Back to the future? Youth crime, youth justice and the rediscovery of "authoritarian populism"', in J. Pilcher and S. Wagg (eds) *Thatcher's Children*, London: Falmer.

Ng, S.M. and Chan, C.L.W. (2005) 'Intervention', in R. Adams, L. Dominelli and M. Payne (eds) *Social Work Futures: Crossing Boundaries, Transforming Practice*, Basingstoke: Palgrave Macmillan, pp 68-82.

Nichols, K. (2003) *Psychological Care of Ill People and Injured People: A Clinical Guide*, Maidenhead: Open University Press.

NISCC (Northern Ireland Social Care Council) (2006) 'Shaping the future: social care in Northern Ireland', Keynote speech by Paul Goggins, NI Social Services Minister, Fifth anniversary conference, 24 October.

Norman, A. (1985) *Triple Jeopardy: Growing Old in a Second Homeland*, London: Centre for Policy on Ageing.

O'Brien, M. and Penna, S. (1998) *Theorising Welfare: Enlightenment and Modern Society*, London: Sage Publications.

O'Connell, B. (2001) *Solution-focused Stress Counselling*, London and New York: Continuum.

O'Connor, I., Hughes, M., Turney, D., Wilson, J. and Setterlund, D. (2003) *Social Work and Social Care Practice*, London: Sage Publications.

O'Connor, J. (1995) *The Workhouses of Ireland: The Fate of Ireland's Poor*, Dublin: Anvil Books.

O'Hagan, K. (2001) *Cultural Competence in the Caring Professions*, London: Jessica Kingsley.

Oliver, M. and Sapey, B. (2006) *Social Work with Disabled People* (3rd edition), Basingstoke: BASW/Palgrave.

Orme, J. (2001) *Gender and Community Care: Social Work and Social Care Perspectives*, Basingstoke: Palgrave.

Osborn, H. (1996) 'One door – many mansions: 1974-1995', in J. Baraclough, G. Dedman, H. Osborn and P. Willmott, *100 Years of Health Related Social Work 1895–1995: Then–Now–Onwards*, Birmingham: BASW.

Parsons, T. (1951) *The Social System*, New York: Free Press.

Parton, N. (1994) '"Problematics of government", (post) modernity and social work', *British Journal of Social Work*, vol 24, no 1, pp 9-32.

Parton, N. and O'Byrne, P. (2000) *Constructive Social Work: Towards a New Practice*, Basingstoke: Macmillan.

Parton, N., Thorpe, D. and Wattam, C. (1997) *Child Protection: Risk and the Moral Order*, Basingstoke: Macmillan.

Payne, M. (2005a) *The Origins of Social Work: Continuity and Change*, Basingstoke: Palgrave Macmillan.

Payne, M. (2005b) *Modern Social Work Theory* (3rd edition), Basingstoke: Palgrave Macmillan.

Payne, M. (2006) *What is Professional Social Work?*, Bristol: The Policy Press/BASW.

Payne, M., Adams, R. and Dominelli, L. (2002) 'On being critical in social work', in R. Adams, L. Dominelli and M. Payne (eds) *Critical Practice in Social Work*, Basingstoke: Palgrave, pp 1-12.

Pearson, G. (1983) *Hooligan: A History of Respectable Fears*, London: Macmillan.

Pence, E. and Paymar, M. (1990) *Power and Control: The Tactics of Men Who Batter; An Educational Curriculum* (revised edition), Duluth, MN: Minnesota Programme Development.

Penna, S. (2005) 'The Children Act: child protection and social surveillance', *Journal of Social Welfare and Family Law*, vol 27, no 2, pp 143-57.

Perlman, H.H. (1979) *Relationship: The Heart of Helping People*, Chicago, IL: University of Chicago Press.

Perry, R. and Cree, V.E. (2003) 'The Changing Gender Profile of Applicants to Qualifying Social Work Training in the UK', *Social Work Education*, vol 22, no 4, pp 375–84.

Phillips, J., Ray, M. and Marshall, M. (2006) *Social Work with Older People* (4th edition), Basingstoke: Palgrave.

Phillipson, C., Bernard, M., Phillips, J. and Ogg, J. (2000) *The Family and Community Life of Older People*, London: Routledge.

Phillipson, C., Bernard, M., Phillips, J. and Ogg, J. (2001) 'The Family and Community Life of Older People: Social Networks and Social Support in Three Urban Areas', *Health & Social Care in the Community* vol 10, no 1, pp 60–1.

Piaget, J. (1952) *The Origin of Intelligence in the Child*, New York: Basic Books.

Pietroni, M. (1995) 'Nature and aims of professional education: a postmodern perspective', in M. Yelloly and M. Henkel (eds) *Learning and Teaching in Social Work: Towards Reflective Practice*, London: Jessica Kingsley.

Pitts, J. (2001) 'Korrectional karaoke: New Labour and the 'zombification' of youth justice', *Youth Justice*, vol 1, no 2, pp 3-12.

Priestly, M. (2000) 'Dropping "E"s: the missing link in quality assurance for disabled people', in A. Brechin, H. Brown and M. Eby (eds) *Critical Practice in Health and Social Care*, London: Sage Publications/Open University Press.

Priestly, M. (2004) 'Tragedy strikes again! why community care still poses a problem for integrated living', in J. Swain, S. French, C. Barnes and C. Thomas (eds) *Disabling Barriers – Enabling Environments* (2nd edition), London: Sage Publications.

Prins, H. (1999) *Will They Do It Again? Risk Assessment and Management in Criminal Justice and Psychiatry*, London, Routledge.

Prior, P. (1999) *Gender and Mental Health*, Basingstoke: Macmillan.

Prochaska, F.K. (1980) *Women and philanthropy in nineteenth-century England*, Oxford: Oxford University Press, p 11.

Prochaska, J.O. and DiClimente, C. (1984) *The Transtheoretical Approach: Crossing the Traditional Boundaries of Therapy*, Homewood, Ill: Dow Jones/Irwin.

Pullar, A. (2007) 'Violent and non-violent women offenders in Fife', PhD dissertation, University of Edinburgh.

Qureshi, H. and Walker, A. (1989) *The Caring Relationship*, Basingstoke: Macmillan.

Radley, A. (1994) *Making Sense of Illness: The Social Psychology of Health and Disease*, London: Sage Publications.

Rapoport, L. (1967) 'Crisis-oriented short-term casework', *Social Services Review*, vol 41, no 1, pp 31-44.

Reder, P. and Duncan, S. (2003) 'Understanding communication in child protection networks', *Child Abuse Review*, vol 12, no 2, pp 82-100.

Reeve, D. (2002) 'Negotiating psycho-emotional dimensions of disability and their influence on identity constructions', *Disability and Society*, vol 17, no 5, pp 493-508.

Reid, W.J. and Epstein, L. (1972) *Task-centred Casework*, New York: Columbia University Press.

Reid, W.J. and Shyne, A. (1969) *Brief and Extended Casework*, New York: Columbia University Press.

Rex, S. (1999) 'Desistance from offending: experiences of probation', *The Howard Journal of Criminal* Justice, vol 38, no 4, pp 366-83.

Robb, B. (1967) *Sans Everything*, London: Nelson.

Rogers, C.R. (1951) *Client-centred Therapy: Its Current Practice, Implications and Theory*, London: Constable.

Rogers, C.R. (1961) *On Being a Person*, Boston, MA: Houghton Mifflin.

Rogers, C.R. (1975) 'Empathic: an unappreciated way of being', *Counseling Psychologist*, vol 5, no 2, pp 2-10.

Rogers, C.R. (1980) *A Way of Being*, Boston, MA: Houghton Mifflin.

Rose, H. and Bruce, E. (1995) 'Mutual care but differential esteem: caring between older couples', in S. Arber and J. Ginn (eds) *Connecting Gender and Ageing*, Buckingham: Open University Press.

Rose, N. (1985) *The Psychological Complex: Psychology, Politics and Society in England 1869–1939*, London: Routledge and Kegan Paul.

Ross, R.R. and Fabiano, E. (1985) *Time to Think: A Cognitive Model of Delinquency Prevention and Offender Rehabilitation*, Johnson City, TN: Institute of Social Sciences and Arts, Inc.

Saleebey, D. (ed) (2002) *The Strengths Perspective in Social Work Practice* (3rd edition), Boston, MA: Allyn and Bacon.

Sawdon, C. and Sawdon, D. (1995) 'The supervision partnership', in J. Pritchard (ed) *Good Practice in Supervision: Statutory and Voluntary Organisations*, London: Jessica Kingsley.

Schneider, R. and Lester, L. (2001) *Social Work Advocacy: A New Framework for Action*, Belmont, CA, Brooks/Cole.

Schon, D.A. (1983) *The Reflective Practitioner: How Professionals Think in Action*, London: Temple Smith.

Schon, D.A. (1987) *Educating the Reflective Practitioner*, San Francisco, CA: Jossey-Bass.

Schrag, L. (2003) 'Restorative justice in Northern Ireland: an outsider's perspective', Paper presented to the Best Practices in Restorative Justice Conference, Simon Fraser University, 1-4 June.

Scottish Executive (1998) *Modernising Social Work Services: A Consultation Paper on Workforce Regulation and Education*, Edinburgh: The Scottish Executive.

Scottish Executive (1999) *Aiming for Excellence: Modernising Social Work Services in Scotland*, White Paper, Cm 4288, Edinburgh: The Scottish Executive.

Scottish Executive (2002) *'It's Everyone's Job to Make Sure I'm Alright'*, Report of the Child Protection Audit and Review, Edinburgh: Scottish Executive.

Scottish Executive (2004) *Getting It Right for Every Child*, Edinburgh: Scottish Executive.

Scottish Executive (2006) *Changing Lives: Report of the 21st Century Social Work Review*, Edinburgh: Scottish Executive (www.scotland.gov.uk/Publications/2006).

Scourfield, J. (2006) 'Placing gender in social work: the local and national dimensions of gender relations', *Social Work Education*, vol 25, no 7, pp 665-79.

Seebohm Committee (1968) *Report of the Committee on Local Authority and Allied Social Services*, London: HMSO.

Seed, P. (1973) *The Expansion of Social Work in Britain*, London: Routledge and Kegan Paul.

Shardlow, S. (1995) 'The boundaries of client–worker relationships', in R. Hugman and D. Smith (eds) *Ethical Issues in Social Work*, London: Routledge.

Sharkey, P. (2007) *The Essentials of Community Care* (2nd edition), Basingstoke: Palgrave.

Shaw, I. and Shaw, A. (1997) 'Keeping social work honest: evaluating as profession and practice', *British Journal of Social Work*, vol 27, no 6, pp 847-69.

Shaw, I., Greene, J. and Mark, M. (eds) (2006) *Sage Handbook of Evaluation*, London: Sage Publications.

Sheldon, B. (1995) *Cognitive-behavioural Therapy*, London: Routledge.

Shore, H. (1999) *Artful Dodgers: Youth and Crime in the Early Nineteenth Century*, London: Boydell Press.

Silver, E. and Miller, L.L. (2002) 'A cautionary note on the use of actuarial risk assessment tools for social control', *Crime and Delinquency*, vol 48, no 1, pp 138-61.

Smale, G. and Tuson, G. (1993) *Empowerment, Assessment, Care Management and the Skilled Worker*, London: National Institute for Social Work.

Smale, G., Tuson, G., Ahmad, B., Darvill, G., Homoney, L. and Sainsbury, E. (1994) *Negotiating Care in the Community*, London: HMSO, for National Institute for Social Work.

Smart, C. (1977) *Women, Crime and Criminology*, London: Routledge and Kegan Paul.

Smith, D.J. (2007) 'Crime and the life course', in M. Maguire, R. Morgan and R. Reiner (eds) *The Oxford Handbook of Criminology* (4th edition), Oxford: Oxford University Press.

Smith, R. (2007) *Youth Justice: Ideas, Policy, Practice* (2nd edition), Cullompton: Willan Publishing.

Social Work Services Group (1991) *National Objectives and Standards for Social Work Services in the Criminal Justice System*, Edinburgh: The Scottish Office.

Social Work Services Inspectorate (1998) *Women Offenders – A Safer Way: A Review of Community Disposals and the Use of Custody for Women Offenders in Scotland*, Edinburgh: SWSI.

Statham, J. (2000) *Outcomes and Effectiveness of Family Support Services*, London: Institute of Education.

Stephenson, M., Giller, H. and Brown, S. (2007) *Effective Practice in Youth Justice*, Cullompton: Willan Publishing.

Stroebe, M. and Schut, H. (1995) 'The dual process of coping with loss', Paper presented at the International Work Group on Death, Dying and Bereavement, St. Catherine's College, Oxford, UK (quoted in Thompson 2002b).

Swain, J., French, S. and Cameron, C. (2003) *Controversial Issues in a Disability Society*, Buckingham: Open University Press.

Taylor, C. (2004) 'Underpinning knowledge for child care practice: reconsidering child development theory', *Child and Family Social Work*, vol 9, no 3, pp 225-35.

Taylor, C. and White, S. (2000) *Practising Reflexivity in Health and Welfare*, Buckingham: Open University Press.

Taylor, P. and Vatcher, A. (2005) 'Social work', in G. Barrett, D. Sellman and J. Thomas (2005) (eds) *Interprofessional Working in Health and Social Care: Professional Perspectives*, Basingstoke: Palgrave Macmillan.

Thompson, N. (1997) *Anti-discriminatory Practice* (2nd edition), Basingstoke: Macmillan.

Thompson, N. (2002a) *Understanding Social Work: Preparing for Practice*, Basingstoke: Macmillan.

Thompson, N. (ed) (2002b) *Loss and Grief*, Basingstoke: Palgrave Macmillan.

Thorpe, D. and Bilson, A. (1998) 'From protection to concern: child protection careers without apologies', *Children and Society*, vol 12, no 5, pp 373-86.

Topliss, E. and Gould, B. (1981) *A Charter for the Disabled*, Oxford: Basil Blackwell.

Topss UK Partnership/Skills for Care (2002) *National Occupational Standards in Social Work and Statement of Expectations*, Leeds: Topss Training Organisation for Social Care England.

Townsend, P. (1962) *The Last Refuge*, London: Routledge and Kegan Paul.

Trevithick, P. (2005) *Social Work Skills: A Practice Handbook* (2nd edition), Maidenhead: Open University Press.

Trotter, C. (1999) *Working with Involuntary Clients*, London: Sage Publications.

Trotter, J. and Leech, N. (2003) 'Linking research, theory and practice in personal and professional development: gender and sexuality issues in social work education', *Social Work Education*, vol 22, no 2, pp 203-14.

Tsui, M.-S. (2005) *Social Work Supervision: Contexts and Concepts*, London: Sage Publications.

Tulloch, J. and Lupton, D. (2003) *Risk and Everyday Life*, London: Sage Publications.

Turnell, A. and Edwards, S. (1999) *Signs of Safety: A Solution and Safety Oriented Approach to Child Protection Casework*, New York: Norton.

UPIAS (Union of Physically Impaired Against Segregation) (1976) *Fundamental Principles of Disability*, London: UPIAS.

Walklate, S. (2001) *Gender, Crime and Criminal Justice*, Cullompton: Willan Publishing.

Watson, D. and West, J. (2006) *Social Work Process and Practice: Approaches, Knowledge and Skills*, Basingstoke: Palgrave Macmillan.

Webb, S.A. (2006) *Social Work in a Risk Society: Social and Political Perspectives*, Basingstoke: Palgrave Macmillan.

Webster, C. (2007) *Understanding Race and Crime*, Maidenhead: Open University Press.

Weir, A. (2002) 'A framework for assessing parents with mental health problems', in M. Calder and S. Hackett (eds) (2003) *Assessment in Child Care: Using and Developing Frameworks for Practice*, Lyme Regis: Russell House, pp 316-32.

White, V. (2006) *The State of Feminist Social Work*, London: Routledge.

Whitehead, P. and Statham, R. (2006) *The History of Probation: Politics, Power and Cultural Change, 1876-2005*, Crayford: Shaw & Sons.

Whyte, B. (2000) 'Youth justice in Scotland', in J. Pickford (ed) *Youth Justice: Theory and Practice*, London: Cavendish.

Wilding, P. (1982) *Professional Power and Social Welfare*, London: Routledge and Kegan Paul.

Willmott, P. (1996) '1895-1945: the first 50 years', in J. Baraclough, G. Dedman, H. Osborn and P. Willmott, *100 Years of Health-Related Social Work 1895–1995: Then–Now–Onwards*, Birmingham: BASW.

Wittgenstein, L. (1980) *Remarks on the Philosophy of Psychology*, Oxford: Blackwell.

Woods, M.E. and Hollis, F. (1990) *Casework: A Psychosocial Therapy*, New York: McGraw-Hill Higher Education.

Worrall, A. (1996) 'Gender, criminal justice and probation', in G. McIvor (ed) *Working with Offenders*, Research Highlights in Social Work 26, London: Jessica Kingsley.

Youth Justice Board (2004) *Strategy for the Secure Estate for Juveniles: Building on the Foundations*, London: Youth Justice Board for England and Wales.

Index

M

N

T

U

V

W

Y